1941:

TEXAS GOES TO WAR

1941:

TEXAS GOES TO WAR

Edited by:

James Ward Lee
Carolyn N. Barnes
Kent A. Bowman
Laura Crow

Foreword by Governor Ann Richards

A Center for Texas Studies Book
University of North Texas Press

Copyright © 1991 University of North Texas Press
All Rights Reserved
Printed in the United States of America

Requests for permission to reproduce material from this work should be sent to:
University of North Texas Press
P. O. Box 13856
Denton, Texas 76203-3856

10 9 8 7 6 5 4 3 2 1

Library of Congress Cataloging-in-Publication Data

1941 : Texas goes to war / edited by James Ward Lee, Carolyn N. Barnes, Kent A Bowman; foreword by Ann Richards.
  p. cm.
  ISBN 0-92939-829-7
  1. World War, 1939-1945—Texas. 2. Texas—History—1846-1950. I. Lee, James Ward. II. Barnes, Carolyn N. III. Bowman, Kent A. (Kent Adam), 1947— .
  D769.85.T4A14 1991
  940. 5.3'764—dc20
                                                          91-36090
                                                          CIP

The paper used in this book meets the minimum requirements of the American National Standard for Permanence of Paper for Printed Library materials, Z39.48.1984.

Logo and Cover Design: Mark Harris
Book Design: Laura Crow and Jane Tanner

Contents

FOREWORD i
   Governor Ann W. Richards

INTRODUCTION v
   James Ward Lee

ACKNOWLEDGMENTS ix

REMEMBER PEARL HARBOR 1
   Kent Bowman

GEARING UP FOR TOTAL WAR 23
   Clay Reynolds

TEXANS IN COMBAT 43
   Denise Kohn

USE IT UP—WEAR IT OUT 75
   John T. Smith

THE WORDS & PICTURES OF WAR 97
   Carolyn Barnes

TEXAS MINORITIES WAGE WAR 117
   David Zimmermann

WOMEN AT WAR 145
   Cynthia Guidici

LOVE, MARRIAGE, & THE FAMILY 173
   Sallie Strange

ENTERTAINMENT AT HOME & ABROAD 195
   Dawn Duncan

COMING HOME 217
   Mike Hobbs

INDEX 241

Foreword

GOVERNOR ANN W. RICHARDS

TEXAS GOES TO WAR takes me back to my own pre-war childhood in the Central Texas town of Lakeview, where I lived with my mama and daddy in a little two-bedroom frame house on an acre of land. Lakeview, on the Dallas highway a few miles north of Waco, is a country community. It has no city council, no government structure other than a school board. There were two stores and a filling station. And, as best I can tell, there was no lake to view.

Most Texans lived a rural or small-town life in the years before the war. We had no superhighways. Even our network of farm-to-market roads was yet to be built. If you wanted to go from Waco to Dallas, you could take the Texas Special—the Missouri-Kansas-Texas passenger train—or you could take the Interurban. Rush-hour traffic was unheard of, and flying was still exotic. We lived at a slower pace.

Before World War II, Dallas and Houston were big cities as far as we were concerned. They had less than 250,000 people. The state as a whole had 6.5 million people, less than a third of the population today. Texas was a different place in many ways, as Kent Bowman and Clay Reynolds point out in the opening chapters of *Texas Goes to War*.

The war changed our lives—mine and most every other Texan. Because of the war, the cotton and corn fields east of little Lakeview were paved over. Runways and hangars and barracks were built, and our little community had a sprawling new neighbor—Waco Army Air Base. The drone of B-25s and B-26s filled the skies above our house. Because of our proximity to a military base, I was convinced that my little hometown was the prime target of the Japanese.

Somehow, the Japanese spared us, but our lives were transformed, nonetheless. John T. Smith recalls how we who were schoolchildren bought war bonds and stamps, collected paper and aluminum foil, and made do when shoes, food, and gas were rationed.

For my family, the war meant expanded horizons. Daddy was drafted into the navy, and Mama and I followed him to San Diego. California was another country, as far as I was concerned. There were kids of different colors, with strange sounding names, and yet—to my pleasant surprise—they were just like me. And San Diego was a city, with so many things to see and do.

Because of the war, the world opened up for many families, as Sallie Strange points out in "Love, Marriage, and the Family." Even though my family moved back to Lakeview after the war, we were not the same.

Neither was Texas. The predominantly rural, agricultural state had turned into an industrial giant. After Pearl Harbor, the nation discovered our oil and gas reserves, our agreeable climate (with some exceptions, I have to admit), and our strategic location between America's two oceans.

One of the biggest changes the war made in Texas was the transformation of the state into a primary training facility for the military. Texans took FDR seriously when he boasted that America would become "an arsenal for democracy." By the end of the war, more than 100 military installations had been built in the state, as well as two naval hospitals, a number of arsenals and ordnance depots, and 21 POW camps and alien detention centers. (Had I known those figures as a youngster, I would not have been scanning the skies for *kamikaze* pilots buzzing on a beeline toward Waco Army Air Base.)

Texans helped win the war, as Denise Kohn reminds us in her story about Texans who fought and suffered and died in foreign fields. In addition to the thousands of pilots, bombardiers, navigators, and gunners trained in Texas, more than 20 combat divisions of infantrymen, artillerymen, and armored troops also trained at places like Fort Hood, Midland Army Air Field, Camp Wolters, and numerous other Texas sites. Most were from outside the state, but 750,000 soldiers, sailors, and airmen were Texans.

Audie Murphy, from a little North Texas town called Celeste, was America's most decorated soldier. Sam Dealey, from Dallas, was America's most decorated sailor. Doris Miller, a young navy mess steward from Waco, became the nation's first war hero because of his heroic efforts at Pearl Harbor.

Miller's wartime experience is a reminder that Texas was a fiercely segregated state before—and during—the war, as David Zimmermann points out in his chapter on Texas minorities. It took longer than the four war years for Texas and for America to shake off the shackles of segregation, but World War II sped up the process.

More than a few of the nation's war leaders came from Texas. The North Texas town of Denison claims General of the Army Dwight D. Eisenhower. Fleet Admiral Chester W. Nimitz came from Fredericksburg in the Texas Hill Country. General Claire Chennault of the famed Flying Tigers was a native of Commerce in northeast Texas, and Colonel Oveta Culp Hobby, organizer of the WACs, was—and is—a Houstonian.

Cynthia Guidici's "Women at War" reminds us that Texas sent some 12,000 women to war as WACs, WAVES, WAFs, WASPs and Women Marines. Women pilots were trained at Avenger Field near Sweetwater, the only all-female Army Air Force base in U.S. history.

Military service and defense work performed by women who had been housewives and mothers before the war changed American women as nothing before had. Women who had learned to fly a cargo plane or had riveted metal plates in shipyards on the Texas coast or had done electrical work on B-17s in Fort Worth would not settle back into prewar domesticity unless they wanted to. Nothing has been the same since, and all of us are the better for it.

In "Coming Home," Michael Hobbs describes the jubilation Texans felt when the war ended. He also tells of the trials that Texas men and women experienced when they came back to help build the state we know today. It took a while to grow accustomed to the changes—in themselves and in the state to which they returned.

On December 7, 1941, when America went to war, the nation was barely 150 years old. Texas had just celebrated its centennial. In the memory of some older Texans, the state was still a place where farmers plowed with mules, wore guns on the streets, and recalled Comanche raids as if they were yesterday. On December 7, 1941, all that changed.

Texas Goes to War is a wonderful exercise in nostalgia, but it is much more than that. I would call the collection "an indispensable form of human self-knowledge," to borrow a phrase from the historian Simon Schama. Writing in the *New York Times Sunday Magazine*, Schama paraphrases the Roman poet Horace who, in Schama's words, "wrote that a people without history remains locked in the mentality of an infant who knows neither whence he came nor whither he will go. To know our past is to grow up."

Texas Goes to War offers Texans young and old the opportunity to know from whence we came—and a sense of where we are going. We rediscover our not-so-distant past, and, as Horace would say, we grow up.

Introduction

James Ward Lee

For many of us, the modern world begins with World War II. "The War," as most of us still call it, changed our lives. Directly or indirectly, it brought us airline travel, super-highways, television, computers, microwaves, fast foods, Xerox, supermarkets, and air-conditioned malls.

World War II is responsible for instant international mass communication, miracle drugs, overpopulation, worldwide pollution, and gigantic cities. Before the war, there were 2 billion of us on the planet. Today we number nearly four times that. America had 130 million people when Pearl Harbor was bombed. Since then we have almost doubled our numbers.

Before the war there were no aluminum beer cans, no aerosol sprays, no permanent press. If you wanted a quart of milk, you either milked it from the cow, had it delivered by the milkman, or bought pints or quarts at the neighborhood grocery—in glass bottles. The plastic jug had not been invented. Nor had the waxed paper box to hold orange juice, soft drinks, or wine. And that land-fill abomination, the throwaway glass bottle, was still years away.

Eating out before the war almost always meant dining in a one-of-a-kind cafe or restaurant that cooked its food fresh. The era of frozen, dried, processed fast-food sold from the window of a franchised chain was in its infancy. The war brought us Spam, powdered eggs, and instant potatoes. Not to mention K- and C-rations that soldiers ate at the front. All these wartime "advances" in food technology, plus refinements in mass distribution of goods, helped pave the way for McDonald's and Jack in the Box.

The war taught us how to build housing almost overnight. The lessons learned led to the blessing of low-cost housing for the masses—and the curse of poorly built housing projects that now blight the landscape from Levittown to Yourtown. The work on quonset huts and command trailers for the military helped make the trailer park a feature of every city and town and the recreational vehicle a common sight on interstate highways—another outgrowth of the war.

During the Eisenhower administration, the federal government began building a vast network of controlled-access roads to make possible the rapid deployment of troops and transport of materiel. Interstate highways helped speed the decline of rail transportation and the rise of long-haul trucking, but it made possible civilian auto travel on a scale never seen before.

Before the war, most long-distance traveling was done by train or bus. It was possible to cross the country on fast trains, drinking cocktails in the club car, eating excellent food in the diners, and sleeping in Pullmans. Crack trains like "The Super Chief," "The Twentieth Century Limited," "The Broadway Limited," "The Empire Builder," "The Hummingbird," and "The Sunset Limited" had the cachet of fine hotels. Texans rode "The Texas Special" from San Antonio to Saint Louis or "The Sunshine Special" from St. Louis to El Paso along what is now Interstate 20. Movie stars rode the "Super Chief." And Hollywood made movies about it. There were even jokes—one has a warden telling a condemned man that he will die at 6:30 A.M. and adds, "You and 'The Super Chief' leave at the same time." These fabulous trains are no more, and flying on an airliner—even in the poshest first class section—is nothing like riding "The Sunset Limited" from New Orleans to L.A. (via Beaumont, Houston, San Antonio, Sanderson, Alpine, and El Paso) or "The Panama Limited" from Chicago to New Orleans.

The world before the war had 5¢ candy bars and Coca-Colas, 10¢ hamburgers, and nickel hot dogs. Cities and towns had downtown areas with movie houses, department stores, and real five-and-dimes—Kress and Woolworth and Newberry. There was no K-Mart, no Wal-mart, no scrimpy little mall theaters slightly larger than a living room. Blackboards in school were black, and the chalk came in wooden boxes with sawdust to cushion the contents. Most cities had streetcars. Some milkmen and icemen still drove horse-drawn carts—Schepps Dairy in Dallas used horses to pull milk wagons until after World War II.

The pre-war world was one of farms and ranches and small towns. The monster cities were still to come. Atlanta and Dallas and Miami and New Orleans and Houston all had populations of about 250,000. The nation's big cities were New York and Chicago. Before the war, national and state legislative bodies were still dominated by rural and small-town politicians. We were not a cosmopolitan people, but the war changed all that. It is impossible to put over 10 million men and women under arms and send them all over the nation and the world and still retain the small-town values of the pre-war days. Not only did we put nearly 10 percent of our national population in uniform, we put that many more in motion around the country—working in shipyards and arsenals, doing volunteer work with the Red Cross and the Salvation Army, following husbands from camp to camp. We learned from the war to become a nation on the move. Before the war, we tended to stay near where we were born; after the war, we began following the sun in search of opportunity.

The necessities of war caused advances in science and technology that revolutionized our lives. Penicillin and other antibiotics changed medicine, and frontline hospitals re-shaped surgical techniques and helped to develop the modern emergency room. The invention of radar led to refinements in television—purely experimental before the war—and other forms of microwave communication. And much later the microwave oven.

If it had not been for the war, minority citizens would have had to wait many more years to begin their painful quest for equality. We were a much more segregated society before the war—in some parts of Texas there were white, colored, and Mexican schools until well after the war. But the bravery and heroism of minority soldiers and sailors made it hard to deny them their civil rights, though the struggle to achieve them still continues. The Second World War also changed the roles that women play in our society. Rosie the Riveter was not always content to give up her hard-won equality and return to the role of housewife. Women who had earned a weekly paycheck in factories or served in the armed forces were reluctant to give up newfound careers and return to pre-war roles.

Old, Romantic Texas, with its ranches and cattle drives, lived after the war only in the popular imagination. Old-time Texans, who loved to brag about how much heat they could stand in summer, began driving air-conditioned pickups and sleeping in bedrooms that were a constant 72 degrees. Texas after the war became much like the rest of the nation. Texans installed televisions, quit building front porches on houses, and removed from the rear window of Fords the sign that said "Built in Texas by Texans." Dallas became a "northern" city and began building skyscrapers like those in Atlanta, Detroit, or San Francisco.

1941: Texas Goes to War tells the story of Texas during the war years. If Romantic Texas is indeed dead and gone, the writers of this book bring back to life those years that ended a time and a place and a dream. And they look forward to the new dream that is Texas today.

ACKNOWLEDGMENTS

The authors and editors offer thanks to all who lent pictures and provided information.

Special thanks are due the following:

>Jane Tanner
>Kathryn B. McGuire
>Elizabeth Wachendorfer,
>   M. D. Anderson Memorial Library, Houston
>Clarence Kingsley
>Ann Peeler, Ennis Public Library
>R. E. Montgomery, Denton
>Ron Marcello, Director, Oral History Project, UNT
>Richard Himmel, Director of Archives, UNT
>Charles R. Schultz,
>   University Archives, Texas A&M
>Institute of Texan Cultures
>Sarah Greene, *The Gilmer Mirror*
>Arnold Krammer, Texas A&M University

Thanks also to:

>Sylvia Moreno
>Tom Shelton and Diane Bruce of
>   the Institute of Texan Cultures
>Norval Jenkins
>Emalee Carruthers
>Ken Uchida
>Michael Wagner, Museum, Brooks AFB
>Theresa Spreutels, Fort Clark Springs Association
>Melvin Sikes
>Michael Cogswell, Music Librarian, UNT
>Jim Foster and the staff of
>   the Dallas Public Library, Archives Division
>Billy Hill
>Texas Woman's University Staff, Archives Division
>Dawn Letson, Georgia Bonatis,
>   Texas Woman's University Special Collections Archivists
>Meg Moring
>Clyde Shelton, Abilene
>Frank Ficklin, Granbury
>Albert Kennedy
>Mary Nell McGuire Froendhoff
>Mrs. Willie Benton
>Claude Rigsby, Chandler
>Lt. Col. Julian Phillips
>*The Denton Record-Chronicle*
>*The Dallas Morning News*
>Texas State Archives

REMEMBER
PEARL HARBOR

Hickham Field, Oahu, December 7, 1941 (National Archives)

by
KENT BOWMAN

In the autumn of 1939, a Houston dealer would sell you a new Hudson for less than $900. In Texarkana, a new Plymouth brought $700 (running boards optional). Dallasites could enjoy a movie matinee in cool comfort for 11¢, and in Wichita Falls the Orchid Shop would sell you a dressy dress for $10.

A young congressman named Lyndon Johnson drove the dusty roads of South Texas in his 1934 Ford, seeking to bring the benefits of the New Deal to his constituents. An older and more celebrated Texan, Vice-president Cactus Jack Garner, was mentioned as a possible presidential candidate after Franklin D. Roosevelt completed his two terms in 1940.

Like the rest of the nation, Texas was struggling to free itself from the Depression that had handcuffed its economy. Agriculture and oil, the two Texas mainstays, were beginning to recover. The war in Europe, though it had a tonic effect on the U.S. economy, seemed a world away. And the Asian conflict involving China and Japan was even more distant.

Except for the farmers, whose depression began in 1920, Texans shared America's boom of the 1920s and suffered with the rest of the nation when the crash came in the 1930s. Ma Ferguson found herself in an economic nightmare when she took office as governor of Texas in 1933. Even the deposed former governor Pa Ferguson, her loyal spokesman and helpmeet, did not have an answer to Texas's financial woes. The Depression had not reached Texas the year the Stock Market crashed in 1929, but by 1931, when cotton prices dropped to 5¢ a pound, Texans suffered along with Wall Street. The price of oil

Sophie Parker at a campaign rally for Congressman Lyndon B. Johnson, at the Municipal Auditorium, San Antonio, Texas, June 26, 1941
(Institute of Texan Cultures, *The San Antonio Light* Collection)

Gov. James V. Allred (left), and Sen. W. Lee O'Daniel (white suit)
(Institute of Texan Cultures, *The San Antonio Light* Collection)

followed cotton downward, even though Texas had fallen in love with the automobile in the "Roaring Twenties." It was the V8-Ford—the only car Clyde Barrow would steal—that enabled Depression-era outlaws to hit a bank in Cisco in the morning, one in Llano in the afternoon, and eat supper in San Antonio by dark.

The Fergusons couldn't end the Depression in Texas. In fact, they made its effect worse when they failed to raise revenues to help weakened county and local governments offer relief from the drop in farm prices. The Texas economy was also devastated by an ongoing drought, making a dust bowl of some areas of the state.

President Franklin D. Roosevelt
(Texas State Archives)

Vice-President elect Henry A. Wallace
on the tennis court at the
San Antonio Country Club, January 3, 1941
(Institute of Texan Cultures,
The San Antonio Light Collection)

By 1936, the New Deal had arrived in Texas. Roosevelt's plan brought some relief to agriculture and strengthened in most Texas voters an ironclad belief in the Democratic party. Texans enthusiastically supported Roosevelt's notion that if we all worked together and had faith, we could bring an end to the Great Depression—"all we have to fear is fear itself."

With Roosevelt's victory in 1932, Texans in Washington—Democrats all—became highly visible. John Nance Garner, who had been Speaker of the U.S. House of Representatives for a brief period, served as vice-president from 1932 to 1940, and Texans led six committees in the House, including the powerful Appropriations Committee. Sens. Morris Sheppard and Tom Connally gave Texas a

"180 families this week moved their possessions into Victoria Courts, the latest low-cost housing project to be completed in the city by the U.S. housing authority."
Published December 7, 1941
(Institute of Texan Cultures, *The San Antonio Light* Collection)

Fred Maizumi volunteering information about himself at the San Antonio police station, Monday morning
(Institute of Texan Cultures, *The San Antonio Light* Collection)

powerful voice in military expenditures and foreign affairs. In the House of Representatives such rising Texas stars as Sam Rayburn and Lyndon Johnson were making names for themselves.

With the help of these powerful politicians, the Texas economy began to improve by the mid-thirties. By late 1939, it had recovered because of large orders from a warring Europe and America's own growing armed forces. Still, the recovery was slow.

Although few Texans had taken much note, war clouds gathered on far horizons. The Kellogg-Briand Pact, an idealistic attempt to put an end to large-scale warfare, had done nothing to discourage Japan from invading Manchuria in 1931. Japan's success in Asia began a pattern of aggression that was to recur throughout the world. When the League of Nations failed to intervene, the Japanese overran Manchuria, completely dominating it by 1933. Roosevelt began to distance himself from the feckless League.

Portentous events were taking place in Europe, but the hard times of the early thirties kept Texans from paying too close attention to the bloody rise of Adolf Hitler in Germany and the consolidation of power in Italy by the chest-thumping Benito Mussolini.

When Mussolini invaded Ethiopia in 1935, those who did follow world events in the Lone Star State were reminded of World War I. A year later Hitler intervened in the 1936-39 Spanish Civil War to test his new and formidable weapons. Texans had no way of knowing that in little more than five years they would face the battle-tested German weapons.

In 1937, the first sailors killed in battle since World War I died in China on the gunboat *Panay,* provoking the first twinges of anti-Japanese feeling. Other deaths were to follow when the German Navy torpedoed the destroyers *Kearny* and *Reuben James,* leading Roosevelt to refer to German warships, in a phrase Texans could appreciate, as "the rattlesnakes of the Atlantic."

Even though they were angry at the loss of American lives, Texans believed strongly in isolationism or did not worry too much about the wars and rumors of wars taking place around the globe. Texans held Hitler and Mussolini in contempt, as may be noted in the various newspaper cartoons and feature items printed throughout the state. The combination of economic hardship and the belief that business and the arms merchants were to some degree responsible for U.S. entry into World War I hardened Texans' views against intervention in foreign conflicts—after all, weren't the isolationist sentiments of George Washington's farewell address sound foreign policy? Citizens of the Lone Star State clearly supported the neutrality acts passed by Congress after 1935 and lauded Garner's statement that the president planned to keep the United States out of war, even after fighting broke out in Europe.

And then there was the specter of Russian communism. Martin Dies of Texas was among those most concerned with its spread, and as chairman of the House Un-American Activities Committee, he watched the movements of those he feared would threaten the American way of life.

THE RANGE GOES TO WAR

My father was foreman on the McElroy Ranch near Crane in 1941, and we were in the midst of the winter roundup. Dad never was one to let the vagaries of weather get in the way of work, but a cold rain started during the night of December 6 and 7, and it continued pounding hard all day. For about the only time I can remember, he parked the chuckwagon in the barn, and everybody took the day off. It was Sunday anyway—December 7. The cowboys were all sitting in the bunkhouse playing dominoes, telling jokes, ribbing one another. I remember the cook, a Socialist by nature, taking a particularly hard drubbing for proclaiming that it was not fair for one person to have more than another, that all the money in the country should be put in one pot and divided equally.

The news of Pearl Harbor fell even colder than the rain. Within a short time, many of the cowboys who were there that day were off in the nation's service.

The ranching industry changed drastically during and after the war. The severe manpower shortage led to technological innovations that forever reduced the labor needs on ranches as well as on farms. Another was the ranches' much heavier dependence upon family men rather than on the bachelor cowboys of an earlier era. Family men as a group were more stable and less likely to drift over the hill to see what was on the other side.

The chuckwagon cook, by the way, changed his political stance after his family came into important oil money; he turned Republican. As Paul Patterson has said, there is no better cure for a Socialist than a good dose of capital.

—Elmer Kelton

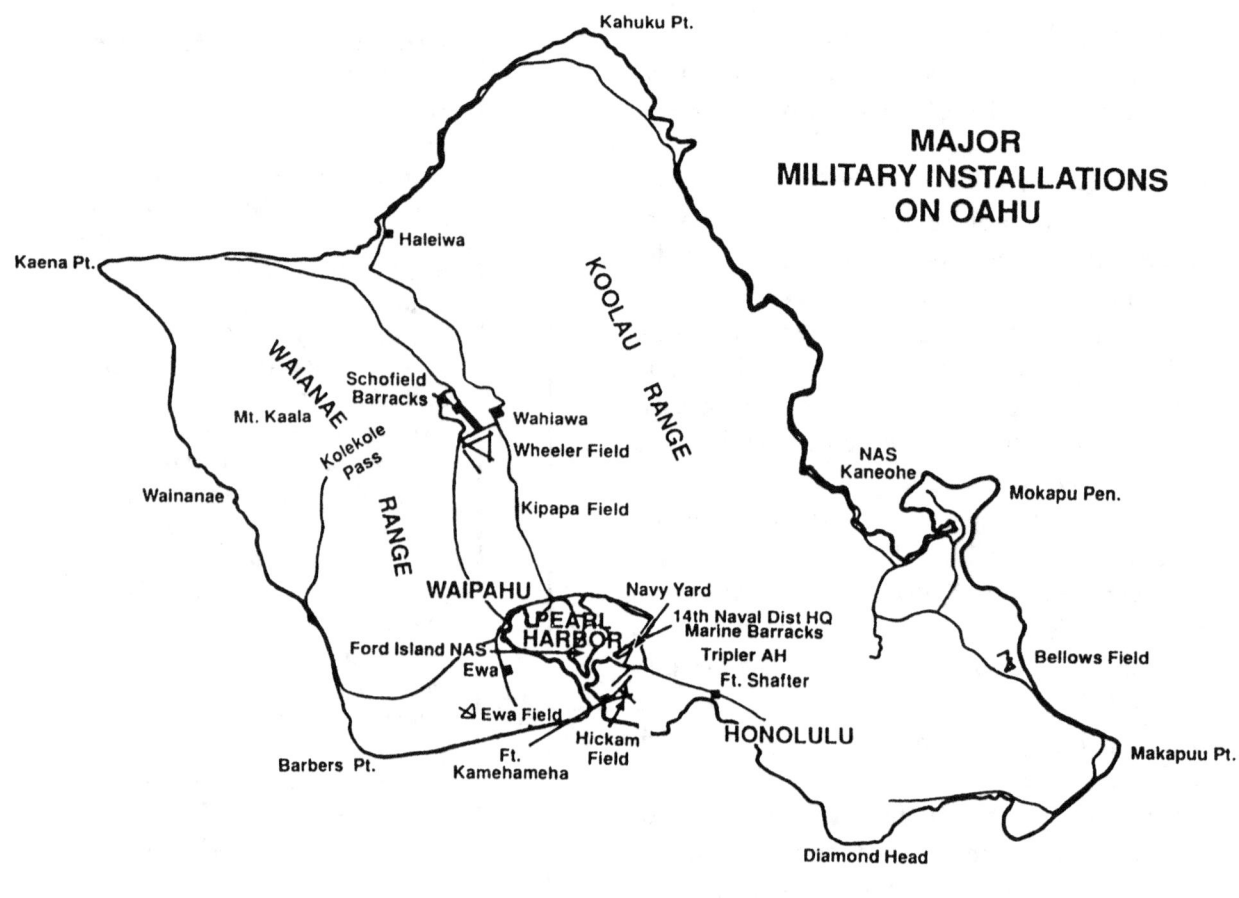

(National Archives)

During the 1930s, Army expenditures, as a result of an isolationist Congress, were cut to such a degree that between 1920 and 1939, Army strength dropped from 280,000 to 190,000. Artillery trainee Beverly Powell's experience in 1936 at Fort Sam Houston provides a classic example of the unpreparedness of the Army during the budget pinch. Ammunition was so scarce that less than one round per officer was available. The ammunition the Army had was old, and many of the rounds were duds. Even worse, any lost ammunition was charged directly to the officers.

As America drew closer to war, Roosevelt was elected to an unprecedented third term in 1940 and was backed by a strong Democratic Congress. "Pappy" Lee O'Daniel, a colorful flour salesman, became governor of Texas for a second time, mostly because of his popularity as a radio entertainer. Times were better than they had been, and prices remained low. Texans continued to buy gasoline for 12¢ a gallon, ice cream for a dime a pint, silk dresses for $1.00 at the Vanity Shop in Denton, and tires for $5.86 each at service stations from El Paso to Orange. Home mortgage interest stood at 4 1/2 percent.

Even though things had picked up a little, the Depression had not yet ended in Texas. Many of the 156,000 Texans who served in the Civilian Conservation Corps were still active—11,000 in the Lone

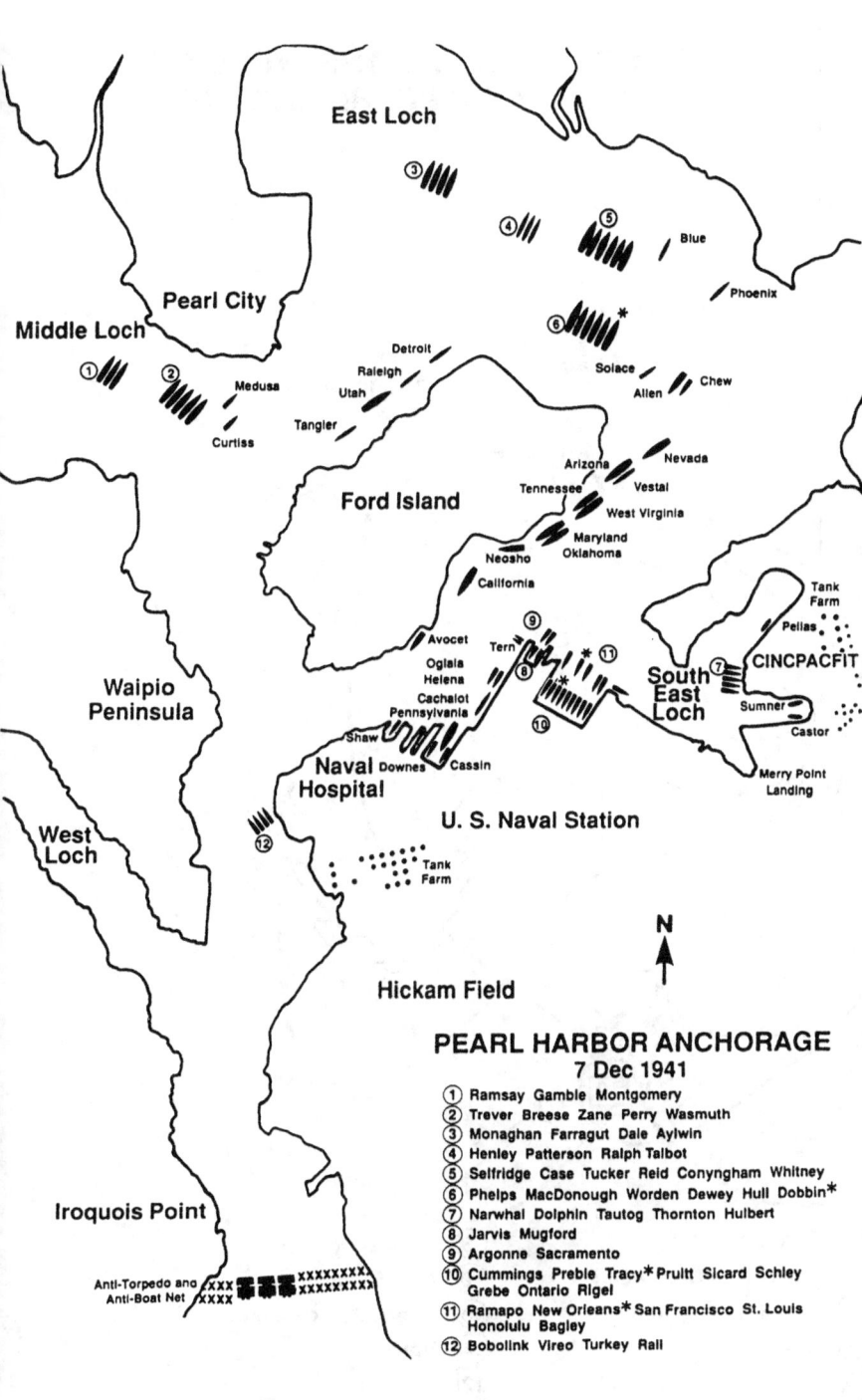

PEARL HARBOR ANCHORAGE
7 Dec 1941
1. Ramsay Gamble Montgomery
2. Trever Breese Zane Perry Wasmuth
3. Monaghan Farragut Dale Aylwin
4. Henley Patterson Ralph Talbot
5. Selfridge Case Tucker Reid Conyngham Whitney
6. Phelps MacDonough Worden Dewey Hull Dobbin*
7. Narwhal Dolphin Tautog Thornton Hulbert
8. Jarvis Mugford
9. Argonne Sacramento
10. Cummings Preble Tracy* Pruitt Sicard Schley Grebe Ontario Rigel
11. Ramapo New Orleans* San Francisco St. Louis Honolulu Bagley
12. Bobolink Vireo Turkey Rail

(National Archives)

Star State—and the WPA still provided employment for thousands of Texans building post offices, high school gymnasiums, and other public buildings.

By the time Roosevelt decided to seek a third term, the war in Europe and Asia began pushing local matters off the front pages of Texas newspapers.

The situation looked grim for France and Britain. Texans heard and read for the first time about *blitzkrieg*, the lightning-fast strike the Germans used to avoid French defenses and overwhelm France before it could prepare for the blow. They also heard and read about the miraculous "victory" at Dunkirk, where the heart of England's army was saved through the heroic efforts of British naval forces and amateur sailors who took small boats back and forth across the Channel.

By the latter part of 1940, Britain stood alone in western Europe against the combined might of the Axis powers. With the help of a new invention—radar—the English won the Battle of Britain in the night skies over London. Germany withdrew its invasion plans and decided not to send troops to attack the "Tight Little Island." Texans rallied around the "Mother Country" by sending packages for the besieged nation and by offering homes far from the war for English refugee children.

Although Britain had thwarted Hitler's invasion plans and broken the German secret code, the country needed more help in her battle to remain free from Nazism, so in a secret deal Roosevelt sent fifty outdated and mothballed destroyers across the Atlantic. It was becoming clear to Texans, as their newspapers and radios proclaimed, that we were drawing ever closer to joining Britain in the fight against the Nazi menace.

FDR requested a stronger American defense force. With the help of Texas congressmen, especially the influential Sen. Tom Connally, he was able to strengthen the armed forces after 1939.

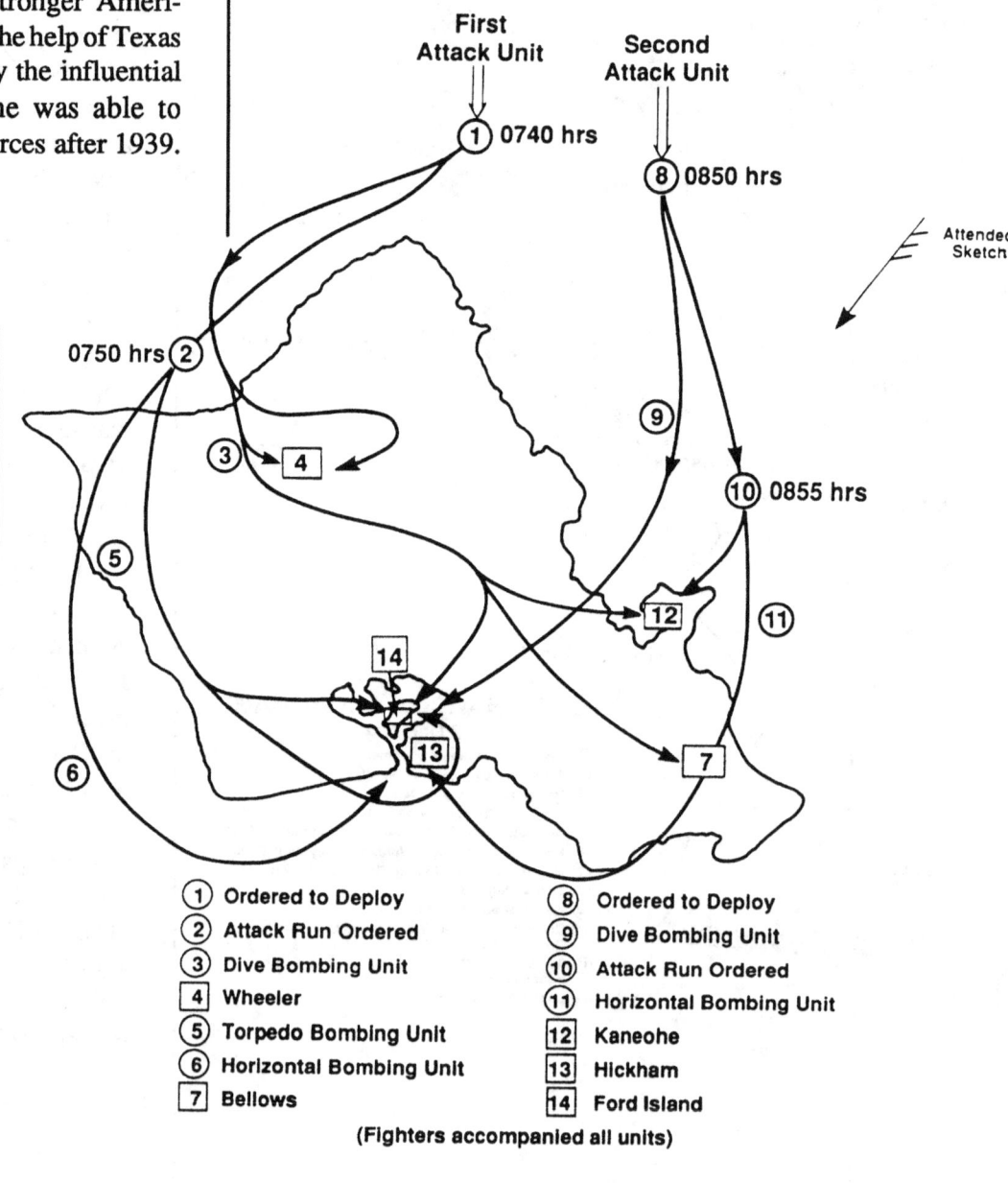

(National Archives)

The USS *Arizona* in the foreground, the *West Virginia* (far left) resting on the bottom, and the *Tennessee* (center), damaged but serviceable. Pearl Harbor, December 7, 1941

(U.S. Navy; Naval Institute Collection)

To begin the build-up, the U.S. instituted its first peacetime draft since 1917: after September 16, 1940, men between the ages of 21 and 35 were to register for the one-year draft. Congress tripled the military budget to $3 billion to boost Army strength to 375,000. Total manpower would reach 1 million by October, 1941, and 2 million by October, 1942.

Young Texans heard rumors that they would not be called up until 1941, but those holding the first draft number—158—realized that their civilian days were few.

Across the country, isolationists and interventionists squared off, but Texans backed FDR's determination to be prepared in case of war. One Texas cartoon shows a powerful and determined workman in a T-shirt with the words "An All-Out Armament" printed across the chest. The question "When Do We Call In The Big Boy" serves as a caption.

Texas newspaper editors voted the war the number-one news topic in the state—followed distantly, but predictably, by the weather.

In January 1941, the president proposed a lend-lease plan to provide materials for Great Britain without committing U.S. manpower. These materials would also aid in protecting American interests and lives. The Lend-Lease Act passed in March, 1941, with the approval of every Texas congressman and later was applauded by the Texas legislature. While the act did not send the country to war, the commerce secretary correctly noted, "We're preparing for it." Government spending in Texas confirmed the statement.

In the gearing-up process in 1941, $589 million was spent in Texas alone on military hardware and supplies. Texans developed synthetic rubber, manufactured petroleum products, and played a vital part in the steel and mineral refining industries.

It was in Texas that America's armor and anti-tank strategies were developed. Shortly after his appointment as Chief of Staff of the U.S. Army in 1939, Gen. George C. Marshall and his staff began developing a solution to the problems presented by the powerful German Panzer units, which had recently slashed through Europe's heralded defenses. The task of building a tank force to compete with the

USS *Arizona*, Pearl Harbor, December 7, 1941
(U.S. Navy; Naval Institute Collection)

Crew members rescued from the capsized USS *Oklahoma*
Pearl Harbor, December 7, 1941

(National Archives)

Nazi Panzers fell to Lt. Col. Andrew D. Bruce, a decorated World War I veteran and a graduate of Texas A&M University. With the help of transplanted Texas newspaperman Frank W. Mayborn and some Texas influence in Congress, Bruce was able to land Fort Hood as his base, deeming it an ideal location for training in armored warfare, a distinction it still holds.

As American preparedness grew more important, other military bases were built in the Lone Star State. There were 15 major army bases, 40 airfields, 2 naval hospitals, and a large navy training facility at Galveston. Later in the war, Axis prisoners were held in 21 locations.

After Pearl Harbor, Texas became the largest military training ground in the world with more than 100 installations, not counting ordnance depots, shipyards, recruitment and replacement centers, recreational facilities, POW camps, and alien detention centers. Twenty combat divisions representing more than 1.2 million troops would be trained in the Lone Star State, including the "Texas outfits"—the 112th Cavalry, the 2nd Infantry Division, the 103rd Infantry Division, the 1st Cavalry, the 90th Infantry Division, and the 36th Division and its famous "Lost Battalion."

Texans enlisted or were drafted in number far out of proportion to the state's population. By the end of the war, more than 750,000 Texans would see active duty, including more than 12,000 women in the armed forces.

Many of the men and women who served overseas had got their first experience in the Lone Star State. All this training was not without mishap, however. A pilot in the bombardier training base near Turkey, Texas, flew his plane so rambunctiously that the bombardier trainee was thrown about the cockpit and accidentally hit the bomb-release switch. Score: one bomb dropped into a field, one cow killed. The pilot steered clear of the town thereafter, but he later learned that he was not the only trainee ever to bomb Turkey, Texas.

By the middle of 1941, Hitler had invaded Russia and was moving rapidly toward Moscow; concentration camps were working to effect Hitler's "final solution"; Japan had control of much of China and was pressing British forces elsewhere in the Orient.

One Texan was already at war by this time: Commerce native Claire Chennault, founder of a squadron of mercenaries called the "Flying Tigers." Chennault, a former high school teacher, was the subject of books, stories, articles, and even a movie. His major accomplishments in China were the organization of an effective ground air-raid warning force and the recruitment of American pilots for the makeshift Chinese Air Force. (No doubt the $750 monthly salary and the $500 bonus for each confirmed "kill" greatly aided his cause.)

USS *West Virginia*, Pearl Harbor, December 7, 1941
(National Archives)

USS *California* crew forced to abandon ship because of burning oil, Pearl Harbor, December 7, 1941
(U.S. Navy; Naval Institute Collection)

At home Texans were filling the country's larder with exceptional wheat and barley crops. A bountiful cotton crop sold for 16¢ a pound, the highest price since 1930. Cotton, like all Texas products, was in great demand in Europe.

In July 1940, Texas newspapers pointed out that the first anti-aircraft gun had been delivered to the government and that serious glider training was underway in the state. Pro-defense rallies were held in more than 400 towns throughout the state.

Texans also were treated to some spectacular baseball history in 1941. The powerful 1941 New York Yankees, Series winners over the Dodgers in five games, featured a 56-game hitting streak by the "Yankee Clipper," Joe DiMaggio. (DiMaggio's famous teammate, Lou Gehrig, had died during the year.) Boston slugging great Ted Williams's average of .406 was the last .400-plus ever hit in the majors. Williams later became a G.I., serving as a Marine pilot in both World War II and Korea.

By late 1941, Texans, like most Americans, were apprehensive about the future. In December, it was clear that negotiations with Japan were on a tenuous footing, and Secretary of State Cordell Hull was suspicious of Japan's intentions toward the U.S. Just what Japan planned to do next was something

JAPANESE INVASION OF AMERICAN SOIL

On December 7th, a badly damaged Japanese plane crashed on Niihau, one of the outer Hawaiian Islands. Owned entirely by the Alymer Robinson family, Niihau was kept as nearly as possible in its original state: no phones, telegraph lines, or other modern means of communication. Hawila Kaleolano, an islander, found the stunned pilot and made off with his gun, his papers, and a map of Pearl Harbor. When it was clear to the native captors that the pilot could not speak English, they sent for Harada, a Hawaiian of Japanese ancestry, to question the pilot. The Japanese soldier and Harada then took control of the island with two guns stolen from the Robinson house. The two Japanese captured native Hawaiian Beni Kalahani, a sheepherder, and his wife. In a struggle, the pilot shot Beni Kalahani three times, once in the stomach. This so enraged Kalahani that he smashed the pilot's head into a stone wall and killed him. Fearing Beni Kalahani's blind rage, Harada shot himself. Thanks to Beni Kalahani, the Territory of Hawaii remained totally in American hands.

USS *Cassin*, *Downes*, and *Pennsylvania* at Pearl Harbor after December 7, 1941
(National Archives)

Japanese midget sub that tangled with the USS *Monaghan*
(U.S. Naval Historical Center)

of a mystery; its zig-zag patterns of the past four years provided few clues. The Japanese also remained vague regarding a pullout from China.

President Roosevelt's stand on Japanese aggression became tougher. He ordered an embargo that finally extended to oil, scrap metal, ammunition, and any other goods that might prove useful to the Nipponese war machine. FDR hoped to force Japan to reconsider its belligerent posture, but Japan was determined to pursue its chosen course, a path that would lead to war.

By the first week of December 1941, signs throughout the country pointed to the continued increase of America's defensive preparedness, yet everyone hoped for a peaceful Christmas. In most cases, life went as it always had. One newspaper feature speculated that a college education might make young women arrogant, and another described the rare Texana collection purchased by the University of Texas for the princely sum of $25,000.

Juxtaposed to these stories were the usual cartoons, including several of the patriotic variety, like "Dixie Dugan," "Tom Tyler's Flying Luck," "Yankee Doodle," and "Don Winslow of the Navy." The December 7th Winslow strip showed our aircraft carriers safely at sea—as they indeed were on Pearl

Aerial view of Hickham Field, Oahu, December 7, 1941 (National Archives)

Harbor Day! Had they been at Pearl Harbor, as the battleships were, our war in the Pacific might have been much harder to win.

Early December newspapers also featured patriotic ads sponsored by Plymouth automobiles and Lovera Cigars. And readers learned that Texas rail workers were ready to answer their country's call. Sen. Tom Connally warned America's would-be enemies (presumably Japan) that Americans could "shoot and shoot straight." Movie houses in North Texas underscored Connally's comments on American marksmanship when they showed Gary Cooper as Sergeant York. In the world of Texas football, Texas A&M defeated Washington State 7-0, while the University of Texas destroyed Oregon 71-7.

On Friday December 5, the stock market was mixed, labor troubles were reported, and the specter of new taxes added gloom to Wall Street. But the lead stories of the week were on U.S./Japanese relations.

Merchants in Texas, however, pressed on toward Christmas. Shaw's Jewelers in Denton had an eye-catching, full-page ad on the 7th. A furniture store in Beaumont offered eight-tube Zenith radios for $69.95. A San Angelo toy store had a wonderful electric train for $4.49. And a Fort Worth auto dealer announced that Buick had produced a car in the $1,000 range—ready for the Christmas market!

But then came the 7th of December. For those at home in Texas, it was, at least for a time, a Sunday much like any other. For Texans in Hawaii, the sunrise also brought the Rising Sun of Japan. An unprepared Pearl Harbor was smashed! America had broken the Japanese code, and Roosevelt and his top brass feared an attack on the U.S., but the time and place caught the army and navy completely off guard and startled the sleepy base into hasty defensive actions. America's major military failure at Pearl Harbor was the lack of any contingency plan in case of attack; the major failure of the Japanese was in not locating and destroying the American carrier fleet that would determine the fortunes of war in the Pacific and, secondarily, in not destroying the oil installations and storage tanks in Hawaii.

For those assigned to duty at Pearl Harbor, the day began as always—slowly. Only a few soldiers and sailors were on duty. They could not know that a Japanese fleet of 69 ships and 432 planes was preparing to change their lives utterly—or to end them. The Japanese High Command had planned an attack in two waves, hitting the big boats on Battleship Row, as well as the Army Air Corps installations at Hickham, Wheeler, and the other airfields. The first wave was to contain fighters and bombers of all varieties; the second would have bombers only. All accounts set the opening of the attack at about 8:00 A.M.—it ended about two hours later, leaving the navy's battlewagons and other ships, as well as nearly two hundred planes, tangled and burning in heaps of metal. More than 2,400 soldiers were killed. The Japanese lost 29 planes, five midget submarines, and one full-sized sub.

The *Arizona* was hit about fifteen minutes into the attack, and after a series of explosions, went to the bottom, taking with her more than 1,000 sailors. A Texas sailor, fifteen-year-old Martin Matthews,

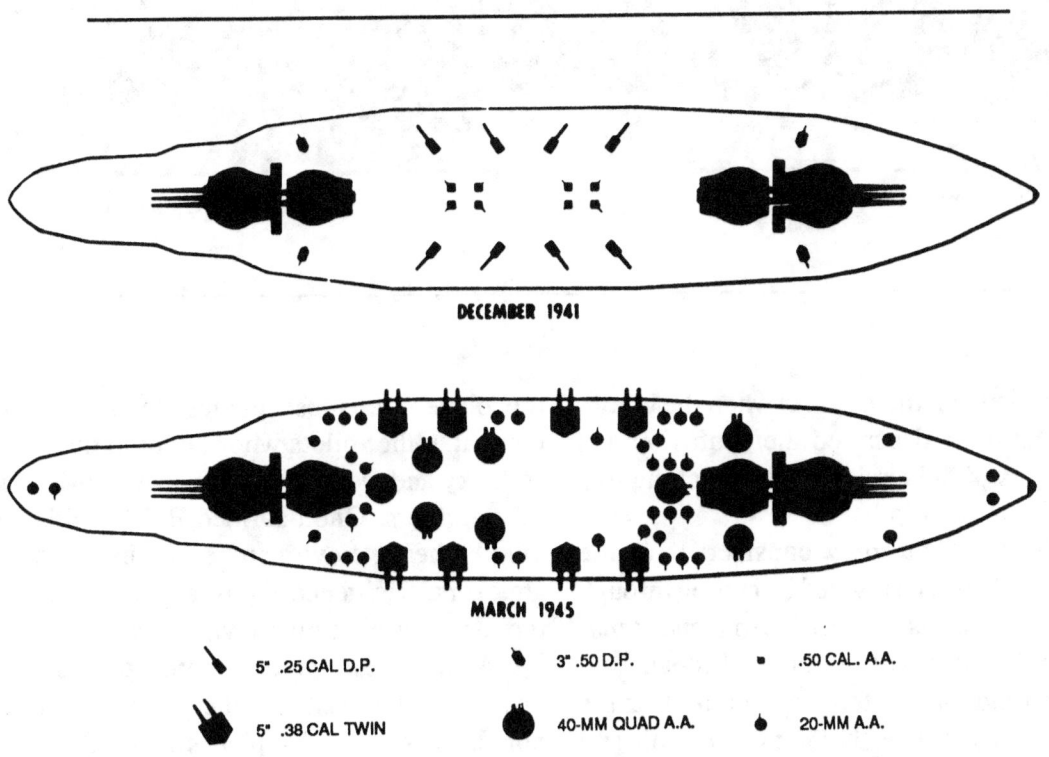

Diagram illustrating the lack of antiaircraft guns on the USS *Nevada* in December 1941 and the extensive additions to her AA battery by March 1945.
(Reprinted from *U.S. Navy Bureau of Ordnance in World War II*)

Pearl Harbor, December 1941 (U.S. Navy; Naval Institute Collection)

was visiting a friend on the *Arizona* when the bombing started. Matthews described the confusion and horrifying results of the explosions as he clung to a buoy not far from the ship.

The battleship *Oklahoma* capsized, and the trapped survivors had to be rescued by cutting through the hull to the air pockets. The *California* and *Pennsylvania* were damaged but not beyond repair, and the *Nevada* ran aground before she could clear the harbor. Smaller boats, like the *Shaw*, were hit and destroyed. Most of the out-of-date aircraft were destroyed on the ground, as were some unarmed incoming B-17s from California.

Two courageous Army pilots managed to take off in the heavy strafing and accounted for seven of the eleven Japanese planes downed in air-to-air combat. Other pilots who fought in the air were not so lucky and were shot down by the swarming Japanese fighters. One unarmed B-17 accidentally survived when a crew member, taking pictures of the attackers, frightened them, apparently giving them the idea that his camera was a machine gun.

A radarman spotted enemy planes headed for Pearl from the east, but the brass dismissed the report because friendly planes from California were expected. This and other controversial incidents led to investigations of American preparedness at Pearl Harbor that destroyed the careers of two high-ranking officers and remains a subject of controversy among military historians to this day.

Texans served throughout the Hawaiian Islands on December 7th—and most have tales to tell from that "day of infamy." Marvin Alexander found a downed Japanese pilot and saved the hand-drawn map of Pearl Harbor with the "X" marking the airman's target; Jack Brown helped to get sailors to safe cover under the blanket of Japanese machine-gun fire from the low-flying aircraft; Woodrow Board, a marine wounded on one of the ships, had paint chips driven into his skin from an explosion; Jose Perez vividly recalled firing his 1903 Springfield at Japanese pilots whose smiles were highlighted, he says, "by shining gold teeth." Perez also told of the fires in the sugar-cane fields caused by tracers fired by nervous sentries who kept imagining they saw Japanese invaders long after the enemy had returned to their carriers.

Waco sailor Doris Miller of the *West Virginia*, who was to win the Navy Cross for his bravery during the attack, recalled that one of his duties was to awaken a heavy-sleeping young Ensign, Edmund Jacoby. As an enlisted man, Miller was forbidden to touch the officer, so he simply bent near the ear of the sleeper and shouted loudly, "Hey, Jake," and then ran for his life. Texan James Power decided to treat the battle as another Alamo.

Hickham Field, Oahu, December 1941 (U.S. Navy; Naval Institute Collection)

The most curious Texas story about Pearl Harbor took place at "The Snake Ranch," an enlisted men's bar near Pearl. During the bombing, the club received a direct hit. The only undamaged object left in the club was one record on the juke box—Bob Wills's hit "San Antonio Rose." Later it became the only song the original patrons would play when they visited the rebuilt club.

As Texans remembered the attack, they recalled the confusion, shock, fear, and alarm that swept the islands on December 7th and for several days following.

President Roosevelt addressing Congress, December 8, 1941 (National Archives)

Rumors of a Japanese invasion spread, and it became the central topic of much scuttlebutt. Reports surfaced that the islands had been invaded by Japanese paratroopers, that Hawaii was honeycombed with spies, and that the attacking planes had actually been piloted by Japan's German allies.

Fear, especially the night of the 7th, led to panic, paranoia, and shooting incidents by military and civilians. The most tragic incident involved the shooting down of several American patrol planes, mistaken as the vanguard of a new attack. This incident cost more American lives. Mothers guarded their houses and children with guns. Some planned to kill themselves rather than be taken prisoner.

The President and Congress acted swiftly. Roosevelt's "Day of Infamy" speech before Congress on December 8th led to a declaration of war against Japan. Only one member of Congress, Congresswoman Jeannette Rankin from Wyoming, voted against the declaration, just as she had against Wilson's call for war in 1917. On December 11, the country also went to war with Germany and Italy. Texans served with distinction in both theaters of operations, contributing the most decorated members of both the army and the navy. After December 7, many Texans, destined to go to foreign shores for the first time, could say, as did Dwight D. Eisenhower to his wife at Fort Sam Houston, "I have no idea when I will return."

Gearing Up for Total War

Army Day Parade, San Antonio, Texas, April 7, 1941 (Institute of Texan Cultures, *The San Antonio Light* Collection)

by
Clay Reynolds

"We must become an Arsenal for Democracy"
—*Franklin D. Roosevelt*

Dawn on December 7, 1941, seemed to find Texas and Texans much as they had been for more than ten years. Although devastated by dustbowl drought, and the continuing ravages of the Great Depression, Texas chugged into the decade of the '40s under its own steam. The joke in the Panhandle at the time was that the "rich 'uns" had pulled up and gone to California to starve, while the "poor folks" just stayed hungry where they were.

What problems the state and its people had were to a great extent financial and to a greater extent home-grown. Following in a tradition forged out of a combination of southern determination and western pioneer spirit, most Texans believed that whatever solutions could be found would come from within the Lone Star State. Few anticipated international events would ever have much impact on the Southwest.

In 1941, Texas was essentially still a rural state. Most farming was done by hand and animal labor; in some areas even the mail was delivered on horseback. Local grocers and druggists knew everyone in town, extended credit on a person's word, and often bartered goods and services. Ready money was

Soldiers help out at Maude Booth Settlement house, located at the corner of Van Ness and North New Braunfels Streets in San Antonio, Texas. July 27, 1941 (Institute of Texan Cultures, *The San Antonio Light* Collection)

Rural Texas, 1930s (Institute of Texan Cultures, *The San Antonio Light* Collection)

scarce, and, as one woman from Crowell remembered, "Nobody had nothin', not even then. Ever'body was as poor as Job's goat, but since we were all in the same boat, nobody paid it any mind."

Urban life was little better. The dusty metropolitan centers of Dallas and Houston were hardly more than sleepy villages in comparison to the industrial cities of the North. Fort Worth and San Antonio were best known for their meatpacking plants and railheads; Austin, the seat of Texas's government, was chiefly characterized by the state university, which sprawled across 40 acres north of the capitol. Apart from an occasional movie house and one or two churches, few buildings were cooled even by the newly invented "swamp coolers." Dust storms blew in from the prairie, turning on street lights at noon, and everyone complained about the new automatic traffic signals that didn't work right most of the time.

Texas's population had shown a steady growth since the '20s and stood at about 6.5 million in 1941. Some already were migrating to the cities in a trickle of response to quietly growing industrial development. The birth rate was low by Eastern standards, doctors still made house calls, many people were still born at home, and the greatest causes of death were pneumonia, tuberculosis, small pox, scarlet fever, whooping cough, and mumps.

No one could buy a legal drink at an open saloon in Texas. In many counties, even beer was illegal, as was horse racing for money. High school football was already the crown prince of Texas sports, but in the spring, Texas League baseball dominated the state's sports pages. And everyone was still talking about the fantastic seasons that Ted Williams and Joe DiMaggio had had in 1941.

At the beginning of the war, most townspeople in Texas lived in tiny gatherings of stores and shops centrally located to serve farmers and ranchers. In a majority of counties, more people lived outside than inside city limits. Towns with fewer than 2,000 souls pockmarked rail lines, and the train was the most common mode of long-distance transportation.

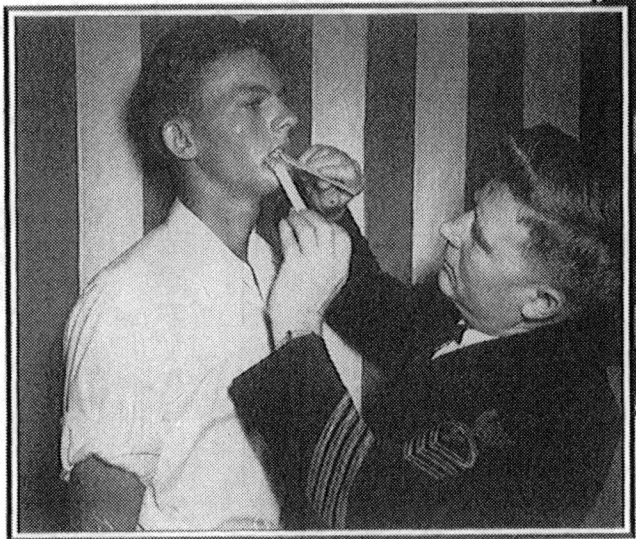
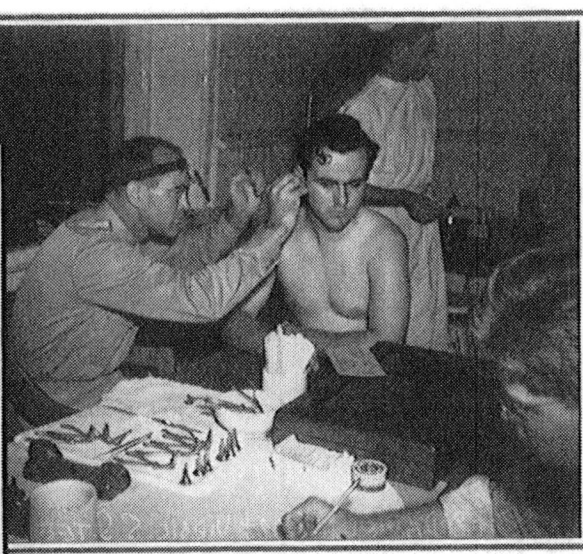

(Institute of Texan Cultures)

GREETINGS:
The Draft Board called me up so fast that somebody else had to finish my 18th birthday cake.
—Elmer Kelton

"Blitz Buggy" Jeep in Salado Creek, 1941
(Institute of Texan Cultures,
The San Antonio Light Collection)

Cattle raising had finally begun to rebound after two wet seasons in a row rejuvenated dust-choked grasslands. Growing sheep for mutton and wool was still an experiment regarded with suspicion by ranchers.

There were few soup kitchens in Texas, but hobos rode the state's rails seeking work of any kind, and a surplus of black, Hispanic, and poor white unskilled laborers continued to migrate across the state's orchards and fields. Aside from a handful of new heavy industrial plants on the outskirts of a few cities, little in the way of major production could be observed anywhere. For the most part, Texas was a dusty, sleepy province best known to most Americans as the setting for Grade-B western movies—most actually filmed in Southern California.

Marine volunteers depart for boot camp, 1942
(Institute of Texan Cultures, *San Antonio Light* Collection)

Along the Gulf Coast from Port Arthur to Port Isabel, maritime trade prospered and was beginning to be rivaled by a small but thriving fishing and canning industry. But neither the former Gulf Coast boom town of Beaumont nor the traditional seaport of Galveston was serious competition for the big eastern ports or even California's Barbary Coast. Manufacturers had sharply decreased Atlantic shipping from the Gulf Coast because of the threat of German U-boat attacks in the Florida Straits. Insurance rates were high, and business was depressed.

> There were 37 million automobiles in the U.S. at the outbreak of World War II. Texas provided more than half the gasoline burned in these cars.

On December 7, 1941, Texas was far from a modern state by general American standards. Several counties were still ten years away from total electrification; running water and city sewer services were luxuries in hundreds of communities. Only a few small towns had organized police forces or full-time firefighters. Numerous communities had no central telephone exchanges, and dial phones were still 20 years away for some towns. There were few dams, lakes, and reservoirs. The WPA was responsible for most of the state's public parks, courthouses, libraries, and post offices, especially in smaller towns. The CCC had planted saplings for shelter breaks across the treeless prairies, while old-timers scoffed and watched mesquite creeping into their pastures. Many communities continued to rely on one-building—if not one-room—school houses from which classes were routinely dismissed for cotton picking in the fall. The lumber industry was strike-prone, and there were only a handful of pulp or paper mills in the Piney Woods. In spite of government-sponsored conservation measures, farming methods were slow to change. Merchant and military ship building along the coast had fallen off during the depression, and only now was the industry beginning to feel the benefits of national defense production orders. The oil industry, though steady, was heavily regulated and far from being as prosperous as it had been when boom towns sprang up from Texarkana to El Paso after the big strikes at Spindletop, Burkburnett, and Electra.

Texas National Guard, Camp Bowie, Texas
(Institute of Texan Cultures, *San Antonio Light* Collection)

TEXAS GOES TO WAR   27

ROYAL IRISH REGIMENT OF REFUGIO

As the war in Europe spread in the spring of 1940, the men of the American Legion Post of Refugio were sure the United States would be drawn into the war. They decided to ready themselves and defend the state by organizing the Refugio County All-Purpose Defense Unit. With much patriotic fanfare they recruited over 900 men and renamed the unit The Royal Irish Regiment to honor the county's early Irish colonizers. Colonel Allen Driscoll Rooke was appointed commander of the regiment. Members provided their own khaki uniforms, food, equipment, and weapons.

The National Defense Act of 1916 did not allow states to maintain troops other than the National Guard. Congress amended the act in October 1940 to allow organized militia if the National Guard became federalized. The Texas National Guard was federalized in November 1940, allowing for the organization of the Texas Defense Guard, which would be used for internal state security. The TDG allotted three companies to the Refugio County area. These were filled by members of the Royal Irish Regiment and became the 21st Battalion. The TDG guarded sensitive public installations and provided mobile patrols in Southeast Texas in the event of enemy activity in the Gulf.

In 1946 the State Adjutant General directed that a green service ribbon, to be called the Emergency Defense Ribbon, could be worn by men who joined these early Home Guard units. In special recognition of the Royal Irish Regiment for their early entry and prominent role in the development of a state force, a silver shamrock would be attached to the ribbon by ex-members. These men can be very proud of themselves and their early contribution to the development of what is now the Texas State Guard.

—Bill Block

Some historians estimate that in 1941 as many as a third of all Texans had never seen a modern airplane or an electric refrigerator; some had never witnessed a talking motion picture or heard a record player. For many Texans, manufactured ice was a luxury, central heat and cooling a dream, and a tractor or combine beyond reach.

Even so, when December 7, 1941, dawned, Texas already produced more than half the nation's oil and natural gas and possessed or provided a goodly portion of other materials, particularly food, cotton, and minerals. The state exported more goods than any six other states combined and was almost completely self-sufficient.

Texas school children studied Latin and Shakespeare, civics and botany. Few schools had programs for technical skills development—even typing and shorthand. Some rural schools continued to use maps that showed the empires of Nippon, Austro-Hungary, and Tsarist Russia. Hawaii, as a U.S. territory, appeared only on the most modern atlases. Some schoolbooks didn't carry Pacific history beyond the Russo-Japanese War, European history past the Franco-Prussian War, or American history beyond the Wilson administration. For many Texans, World War I, the "Roaring Twenties," and the Great Depression were still current events.

Yet Texans were aware of what was happening abroad. Radios and daily newspapers were full of war news, and no movie started without newsreel footage of Nazis and Italian Fascists. Texans hated Communism, the U.S.S.R., and the unions that caused debilitating strikes. There was little toleration of any ideology that disrupted the business of business. Texans deplored the persecution of the Jews in Europe, but at home, racism against blacks was strong, against Hispanics growing.

Polls taken in the late '30s indicated that most Texans thought Adolf Hitler was at the least a nuisance and at most an evil force in the world. Many voiced the opinion that he ought to be stopped, although no one suggested that the United States should be the one to do it. Giving Bundles to Britain was one thing; shouldering up next to her for a fight was something else. No one seemed to want to do business with Nazi Germany, but no one was particularly happy about sacrificing European markets over issues that seemed, in the main, trivial. Few if any pollsters put questions to Texans about Japan's expanding aggression. Given the importance of oil and gas to the state, many might have thought that Japan's cutting off Asian oil fields could have a positive impact on the petroleum in Texas.

Brig. Gen. Hubert R. Harmon pins wings on President Roosevelt's son. Elliott Roosevelt "asked no favors and received none." (Institute of Texan Cultures)

Since its admission to the Union, Texas had been a center of military importance to the United States. Generals from Robert E. Lee to William Tecumseh Sherman served in the state; John J. "Blackjack" Pershing made his headquarters at Fort Bliss in El Paso when he was chasing Pancho Villa. In the 19th century, hunting Indians and outlaws also provided practical training for the U.S. Cavalry. After World War I, the military discovered that Texas's unique combination of wide-open spaces, consistently clear skies, and centrally located transportation centers made it an ideal place to train pilots for army air corps and navy service.

Randolph Field in San Antonio, the leading air base in the U.S., was dubbed by the military press "The West Point of the Air" in 1943.

San Antonio had always been a center of military activities; Spanish Imperial and later Mexican troops were headquartered in Bexar; Texas Rangers rode out of the city to do battle with Comanches, Comancheros, and Mexican regulars near the Halls of Montezuma. The first military action of the Civil War took place at the corner of St. Mary's and Houston streets, when the United States monetary exchange office was seized; the final battle of the war was fought by RIP Ford along Boca Chica Peninsula near Brownsville. Troops from San Antonio were sent to garrison the Indian Line, a series of forts stretching from the Rio Grande to the Red River. Theodore Roosevelt recruited his Rough Riders in the saloon of the Menger Hotel. Soldiers marched off to France in 1918 from Fort Sam Houston, and, by 1940, "Fort Sam" and Fort Bliss, near El Paso, were regarded as premier training bases for cavalry

Seven Beech AT-7s in flight
(Institute of Texan Cultures, *The San Antonio Light* Collection)

and infantry units. Several American warships called Texas home, and since 1836, Galveston had been a center of naval activity.

The military presence in Texas was regarded as both an economic boon and a civic inconvenience in 1941. Fewer than 23 army posts and air fields existed in the state, and some of these were not garrisoned. About a half-dozen naval facilities, including a shipyard at Orange and a few naval hospitals, were scattered around the state. The military's social domination of such cities as El Paso and San Antonio caused problems with police and other civic organizations. Generally speaking, the military, severely downscaled in the post-World War I years, contributed little to the state's prosperity.

Predictably, the army air corps would see more Texans than recruits from other states, but Texans were also disproportionately enrolled in the marine corps and navy. Per capita, more flatlanders from the Panhandle and alkali ranches of West Texas enlisted in combat maritime services than men from all the seaboard states put together.

> The combined bases of the Naval Air Station in Corpus Christi covered over 20,000 acres in 3 counties and was thought to be the largest facility of its kind in the world.

L-R: Maj. Gen. G. C. Brant (commander of the Gulf Coast Training Center at Randolph Field), R. A. Lovett (Assistant Secretary of War for Air), and Maj. Gen. Henry H. Arnold (Chief of the Army Air Force) in San Antonio to view flying fields. August, 1941 (Institute of Texan Cultures, *The San Antonio Light* Collection)

Training tank drivers

Chow line, Camp Bowie, Texas
(Institute of Texan Cultures,
The San Antonio Light Collection)

(Institute of Texan Cultures,
The San Antonio Light Collection)

Along with the new military facilities, aircraft and naval manufacturing centers, munitions plants, and assembly factories were also built across the state; with them new towns grew, and tiny rural hamlets prospered into important urban and even industrial centers. In some cases, over 10,000 recruits would invade almost overnight; along with them came often half again as many civilians, whose job it was to build and maintain the installations. Palacios, for example, expanded its fewer than 2,000 population in 1940 to more than 20,000 by 1943; Orange, a sleepy shipping village on the upper coast, jumped from fewer than 7,000 to more than 33,000 with the installation of a military shipyard. Port Neches, Texas City, Kileen, Freeport, Grand Prairie, Vernon, Childress, Midland, San Angelo, and dozens of other small towns found their populations trebled, even quadrupled. By 1943, the state's population grew by nearly a million, a 5.8 percent increase that would continue to grow through the postwar years.

At dawn on December 7, 1941, the United States was about to enter "total war," allying with the Empire of Great Britain, the Soviet Union, and the Republics of China and Free France. These allies came to be known as "The Big Five," but the Lone Star State almost qualifies as a "sixth" major power in the alliance against the Axis.

COLLEGE DAYS

When I first came to Denton, Texas, on or about Washington's birthday, 1943, riding the Katy (with a steam locomotive) out of Dallas, I paid very close attention to my surroundings. It was my first trip east and south from Salt Lake City. I had recently been commissioned a second lieutenant in the field artillery, and more recently still my application for training as a liaison pilot had been accepted. I was sent to my flight school in Denton, full of hope and wonder, age 21.

I met a few of my fellow cadets-to-be on the train, and we set forth together from the depot to reconnoiter, after first depositing our bags in the command vehicle sent from headquarters. We ourselves elected to walk, fortified with directions, after looking at our bags piled high. Even the driver was lucky to have a seat.

We went west from the depot, across the square, and west on Hickory, pausing at a small stone-and-mortar grocery for a bottled drink, which we each selected from a metal container full of water, with a huge chunk of floating ice.

We continued walking west to Avenue A, the eastern boundary of North Texas State Teachers College toward Chilton Hall, a recently constructed dormitory. This was to be our new home. It was not lavish, but it nevertheless communicated a certain graciousness seldom found in later architecture. The structure was U-shaped, open to the west, providing an esplanade with a view, where we held our formations for roll call before piling into trucks for the ride to Hartlee Field. Everything I knew about the countryside en route I gleaned out the back of our truck.

In the middle of the open side of the esplanade, there was an interesting statue—"The Student"—which I visited frequently. (I even had a friend take my picture there.) The subject was a young man, larger than life, seated on the ground, naked to the waist, his legs folded to one side. Deep in thought, he was looking down upon an open book laid flat before him. He was evidently intended to apotheosize the spirit of education. And it worked—even in wartime.

—James Davidson

Texas has always been a land of superlatives. The biggest, best, and most find their natural homes here. If anyone had asked, the average Texan would have claimed in December of 1941 that Texas was the "most ready" of any state to gear up for total war. Possessing the second-longest coastline in the country—protected by the longest barrier island in the world—Texas boasted more serviceable and safe deep water ports than any other state. Texas also opened to the warm waters of the Gulf of Mexico. Although Texas also faced more miles of foreign frontier than any other state, its topography and military posture made the state's border more defensible than the coast of any state of either seaboard.

Additionally, Texas had direct access by rail and water to both coasts, and because of its size and open geography, it was an ideal center for supply, distribution, training, and secret experimentation. In 1941, Texas also held the greatest potential of any state for development of raw material, vegetable and mineral resources, manpower, and agri-

James Davidson, with "The Student"
(University of North Texas Archives)

cultural and livestock production; it was an ideal "Big Sixth" to the Allied strategy for total war.

In 1941, Texas had at its disposal greater reserves of oil and natural gas than any single nation (other than the 47 United States) on either side of the conflict; coal was also plentiful, and the pine and hardwood forests of East Texas seemed inexhaustible. The state's mineral deposits were also largely unmined, and agricultural potential was poised on the verge of record-setting production years, even without the stimulation of the war.

In spite of internal problems and union disruption, Texas railroads possessed over 22,000 miles of track, more than any other state; the eight systems which ran trains in Texas carried more than 91 tons of freight and 5 million passengers in 1941, figures that doubled during the war.

Possibly the most highly publicized if not the most important industry in Texas was oil. Although refineries and chemical plants existed and were prospering prior to the war, the demands of the U.S. military and the Allies after 1941 applied pressure to an underdeveloped industry. Sinkings of U.S. tankers by German U-boats at the outset of the war harmed the market and created supply problems in early 1942; this was exacerbated in the summer of that year when "wildcatting" was discouraged in order to preserve metals.

Guarding the ammunition dump, Camp Bowie, Texas, 1941
(Institute of Texan Cultures, *The San Antonio Light* Collection)

COLLEGE DAYS

In the summer of 1942, I attended North Texas State Teachers College and lived in Chilton Hall, which was then what it had been built as—a boys' dorm. It was a terrible place: the rooms were huge, sleeping about four boys— maybe six, I forget—with no furniture but the basics, no covering on the concrete floors, plaster walls and ceilings. All of the inside suites had windows opening on the central court, where "The Student" sat surrounded by an expanse of grass on each side. The din was unbelievable! With no air-conditioning, in August, with every window open, the racket made by several hundred boys reverberated around in that courtyard, re-entered through the windows, bounced around off those reflective floors, walls, and ceilings, and made a hellish cacophony which lasted from early morning until all too late at night.

All of this came to a temporary halt for me on May 8, 1943, when I was called into active duty in the army. I was not to return until the beginning of the fall semester, 1946. I found that the campus hadn't changed very much on my return: the global war which remade so much of the face of the earth left little mark on our campus, or on the small town which surrounded it.

—Hugh Kirkpatrick

Almost immediately following Pearl Harbor, a butadiene (synthetic rubber) plant at Port Neches and a toluene plant at Texas City were opened. These were only two of the dozens of chemical plants, sulphur plants, and cracking units that began to spring up across the state. Baytown, Houston, Freeport, Borger, Dallas, Corpus Christi, Monahans, Deer Park, Wichita Falls, Fort Worth, Odessa, and Longview, along with many other communities, saw new construction of petro-chemical plants and high octane refineries. In terms of "giving it the gas," Texas petroleum quickly geared up for total war, and by mid-1943 production was at maximum levels. Wildcatting was now encouraged; employment and investments flowed in.

By contrast, mineral smelting and production was never a high priority in Texas before the war. While mining did go on, most of the ore was shipped out of state for smelting and processing. Only eight major metal plants existed in Texas prior to 1941, and many of these were outmoded. By 1945, ten new plants had been constructed from Dumas to Laredo, from El Paso to Texas City. The steel industry also began immediately to modernize, particularly along the Texas coast where shipyard demands were highest. But even as far inland as Daingerfield, where a blast furnace was constructed on the site of an old Confederate cannonball plant, the sky was blackened with the gearing up of heavy industry in the state.

The most important industrial gearing up in Texas came from industries directly related to the war effort. From the TNT plant at Karnack on Caddo Lake to the shell and bomb-loading plants at Amarillo, McGregor, and Texarkana, to the B-17 plant in Fort Worth, Texas cities and small towns became centers for the production, assembly, and shipment of every conceivable type of military hardware. From airplane plants in Fort Worth, Garland, Grand Prairie, and Dallas to the manufacture of vehicle engine parts and

Liberty ships under construction at Irish Bend Island Shipyard, Houston, Texas. (Texas State Archives, The Cyril Adams Collection)

DRAFTEES

Syphilis patients were not only drafted but were also given treatment. At the time I served at Fort Sill, known carriers were given a series of shots containing arsenic. A former semipro baseball player who was assigned the bunk over mine always became so nauseated after his shots that he vomited.

In the early years of the war, being unable to read excluded a person out of hand. To close this loophole, the army created special training units and assigned illiterates to a 12-week program to teach them to read simple instructions. Many men trained in these units were grateful. One who had been owner of a small trucking company in Fort Worth would no longer have to hide his incapacity from his literate employees. The most curious case I learned about was a college graduate who was by mistake assigned to this elementary program. He came to us in the classification section after several weeks of instruction to complain that he knew army methods were deliberate and repetitive, but he thought perhaps he was wasting his time. He was sent the next day to a training center which started at a slightly higher level.

We had two draftees whose service so was impaired that they disappeared. "Smoky Joe" started for the mess hall at least an hour before each meal. After shuffling along for about fifty yards, he became so worn out that he sat on a curb for a while before going on. Doctors who examined him insisted that he had no physical disability. Our captain talked to him each day before lunch when he rested outside our building, always asking about the weather, which Smoky invariably predicted accurately. After a few months he disappeared, probably to return home. He was always cheerful and not opposed outwardly to soldiering; he simply refused to move far or fast.

Another was an American Indian who had been considered draftable at an induction center, but when he arrived at Fort Sill, he could not be persuaded to speak any language or to give any evidence that he understood a word said to him. Our captain was so bemused by this selectee that he attempted several ruses to surprise him into oral response. Placing the young man in a chair, the captain sat across from him and talked calmly about a number of matters. The captain would place either a candy bar or an opened package of cigarettes at his own elbow. Then in the midst of his monologue, he would ask, without gesturing toward or looking at the bait, whether the speechless one wanted a smoke or a bar of candy. Perhaps this person really could not understand; he never responded. Like Smoky Joe, this visitor disappeared, to what destination I have no notion. There are degrees of ignorance and of obstinacy which disqualify a man for service in any conflict.

—William F. Belcher

---

tents and uniforms in small-town factories all over the state, war industries took priority in almost every regulated category from transportation to manpower.

By far the largest single defense industry during the first months of the war in Texas was the ship building plant in Orange. Other plants in Brownsville, Beaumont, Houston, and Galveston also geared up, responding to a combined $300 million investment in providing—and replacing—American military and merchant shipping needs. Texas deep water ports from the Sabine-Neches confluence down to Brownsville also made the Texas Coast an ideal location for refitting and repairs for both military and commercial ships.

By the beginning of 1943, Texas industries had geared up for total war. In the month of February of that year, for example, 80 separate projects ranging from the construction of army camps, to ordnance plants, to military schools, to refineries, to smelters, to aviation construction factories, to the building of dams and reservoirs, hospitals, and iron and steel plants were underway or nearing completion. Skilled labor was at a premium, and the dusty days of economic depression in Texas were left far behind as the state marshalled its industrial might behind the war effort.

During the war, more than 500,000 Texans would relocate from rural communities to the cities; most would never return. After the lean years of the

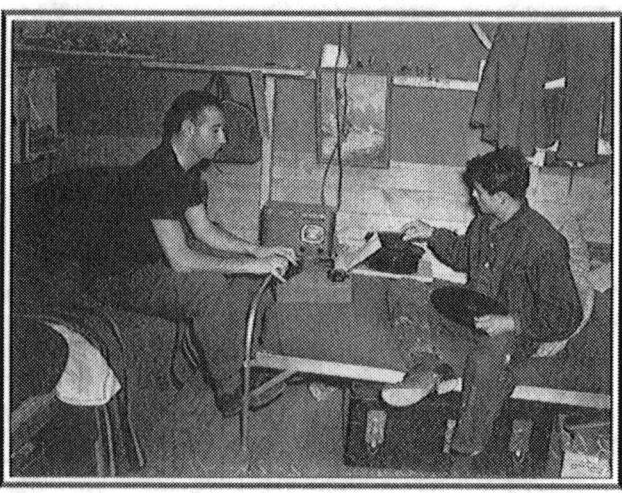

Relaxing at Camp Bowie, Texas
(Institute of Texan Cultures,
The San Antonio Light Collection)

"Fort Worth's Trading Area of nearly 400,000 families (1,466,224 population) is an integral part of the Allied Arsenal of Democracy. In addition, it is the training ground for tens of thousands of American troops intent on giving the Axis an old fashioned 'country licking.'"
—*Advertisement for the* Fort Worth Star Telegram *in the Texas Almanac*

The "Scouts of the Solomons" training at Freeport, Texas
September, 1942

'30s, it seemed that modern, urban prosperity was never-ending. The face of Texas had changed forever.

Possibly no area of Texas's potential was touched by the war as extensively as agriculture. Good rains in 1940 coupled with good economic forecasts to stimulate what was probably the most devastated part of Texas economy in the '30s. By 1943, over 38 million acres were under cultivation in the state, and for the first time in most farmers' memories, there was a hungry and almost limitless market for their produce; but in December 1941, from the blacklands to the sandylands to the redlands, "produce" in Texas meant "cotton."

In 1940, cotton averaged just under a dime a pound, only a marginal improvement over any price seen for nearly a decade, and even farmers who could afford to irrigate were barely breaking even. But cotton is vital to war, particularly total war. Its uses range from uniforms and tents to insulation and packing, to high explosives and even food preservation. By 1945, the price was over 21¢ a pound. At the same time, the number of active gins decreased from about 3,000 in 1940 to around 2,000 in 1945. The decline in numbers of gins reflects the centralization of this all-important wartime agricultural industry. In addition, there was a massive farm labor shortage—including the virtual disappearance of small tenant farmers—which sped up the application of mechanized farming techniques. Growing cotton in Texas, something that had once been associated with 40 acres of bottom land and a good mule, now geared up during the war to become big business. Waste was eliminated and a better and more useful product (medium and long staple cotton) was cultivated. Cottonseed oil and other by-products of the crop pushed Texas cotton farmers to the forefront of the war effort. And because the soil, climate, and topography of West Texas made the state ideal for producing massive amounts of cotton, it regained its place as king of Texas crops.

Cotton represented 75 percent of all Texas farm crops in 1941; that figure dropped to less than 50 percent by 1945, largely because of the utilization of Texas farm land for food crops and stock raising. Of particular importance, for example, was the military and civilian demand for grains, vegetables, cane sugar, and citrus, all of which could be grown in abundance in the state. Flour, sugar, and rice mills sprang up all along the coast and near rail centers, and feed grains and grasses were planted throughout the state. In terms of stem crops, however, the restrictions on metal use for the construction of mechanized farm implements restricted a boom in wheat, barley, and feed grain production.

Texas was always known for meat, especially beef, production. Aside from the increased demand for horses and mules by foreign governments, the war in Europe had little impact on Texas stockmen before 1942. In that year, however, Fort Worth and its famous stockyards, which sat alongside the Swift and Armour packing houses, once more became a national market for meat production. Because of the suddenness of

Lone Star Defence
CORPORATION
NEEDS
LABORERS
To Meet Production Schedules

Steam-heated sleeping quarters, $1 per week.
Sleep and eat where you work.
A U. S. Employment Service representative and a representative of Lone Star Defense Corp. will be at the

GILMER COURTHOUSE
AT 4 P.M.
MONDAY
FEBRUARY 12

Bring your luggage and be prepared to leave for Texarkana.
Free Transportation.

W. M. C. Regulations must be complied with.

The Gilmer Weekly Mirror, February 8, 1945.

In 1942, the Fort Worth Exposition and Fat Stock Show was suspended for the first time since 1896.

Center photo: Command and Reconnaissance cars, Army Day Parade, Alamo Plaza, San Antonio, Texas, April 7, 1941
Smaller photos picture visitors' day at Camp Bowie, Texas
(Institute of Texan Cultures, *The San Antonio Light* Collection).

Bombardier training at Goodfellow Air Force base at San Angelo: two men running to a Beech AT-7 airplane, at night in the rain
(Institute of Texan Cultures)

the United States' entry into the war, however, Texas ranchers came up short. A massive slaughtering of "light" cattle was the response not only to military needs, but also to the increased civilian demand for beef as a result of the new buying power of war industry workers in Texas. This forced an increase in prices, and the Stockyards themselves—devastated by a horrible flood in April of 1942—were almost overwhelmed. The situation was not helped any by a labor shortage caused by both military enlistments and by the more attractive salaries offered by war industries in the Dallas-Fort Worth area.

Poultry also was vital to the war effort. A pamphlet prepared by the Texas State Education Agency encouraged school children to inspect every farm in their counties and to make sure that every hen house was "filled to capacity." Eggs, butter, and even salt were premium farm products not to be either wasted or neglected in the gearing up for total war.

Over 4,500,000 head of livestock were slaughtered in Fort Worth in 1943, an increase of 1 million over 1942, and the count would rise as the war continued. Throughout the war, over 2 million sheep were slaughtered, and over 1 million hogs and cattle per year went to market. The best year for cattle—1944—saw 5,250,000 animals sold for slaughter in Fort Worth, and half of these were processed by Armour, Swift, and five smaller packers in the Fort Worth area; the rest were shipped to the Midwest.

Manpower problems were not unique to the livestock business. Farmers, particularly in the cotton fields of West Texas and in the citrus groves and cane and vegetable fields in the Valley, noted an immediate labor shortage. This was a result of new opportunities opening up around war plants and related industrial centers. The labor shortage was partly a result of the enthusiastic response to military manpower needs, and partly from the Mexican government's restriction on temporary work visas for migrant farm laborers. American migrant workers, the former mainstays of the cotton and livestock industry, abandoned Texas for the beet fields of Colorado and Wyoming, the citrus groves and vegetable farms of California, and the industrial centers of the North and East. Wages were higher there, and workers used to being paid less than a dollar a day for back-breaking labor in Texas fields found lucrative employment as far away as Detroit and San Francisco and as near home as Houston and Dallas.

As prices and wages rose, though, labor returned. And as the restrictions on metal use relaxed, farmers, ranchers, oil men, and small industries discovered the modern wonders of mechanization and production on scales larger than they ever imagined. It was all part of the total war effort, all part of gearing up to join the United States and its allies in achieving a total victory.

Pfc. Leonard Koller, Mission, Texas, places a mine at the open end of a barbed wire entanglement
(Texas State Archives,
165th Signal Photographic Company)

40   Gearing up for Total War

Captured Japanese submarine in Alamo Plaza, San Antonio, Texas, ca. 1943 (Institute of Texan Cultures, *The San Antonio Light* Collection)

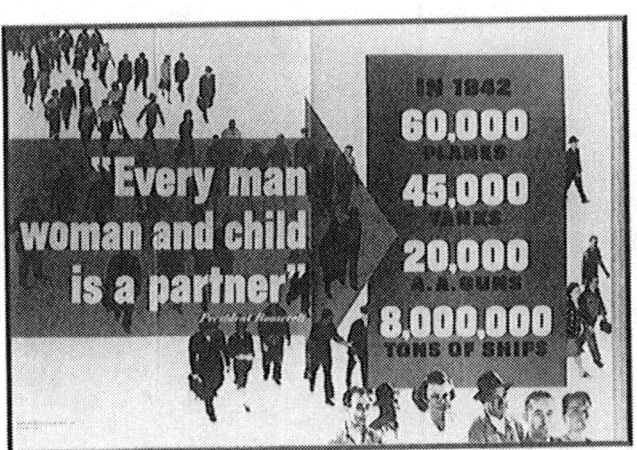

At dawn on December 7, 1941, probably few Texans could easily have located Pearl Harbor on a globe. Some might not have been able to locate the Hawaiian archipelago, formerly the Sandwich Islands.

But Texans were raised with the memory of the Alamo and San Jacinto, and to them, Pearl Harbor became another Alamo, another Goliad; and once more, Texans believed they would have to teach some foreign enemies a lesson about frontier spirit and the love of freedom.

TEXANS IN COMBAT

by
DENISE KOHN

The young captain from Celeste, Texas, saw six German tanks and 250 soldiers bearing down on him. Ordering his men to "Get the hell out of here," he grabbed a carbine and started shooting at the German infantrymen only 200 yards away. When his ammunition gave out, he seized his field telephone and ran to a burning American tank destroyer. The body of an American lieutenant, whose throat had been cut, covered the hatch. The young Texan rolled the lieutenant's body onto the snow-covered ground. His telephone rang, and a voice asked, "How close are they?" The captain replied, "Just hold the phone and I'll let you talk to one."

Then he lay down behind the tank's machine gun and started firing. He only stopped his barrage to direct the artillery to fire—at his own position. The devastated German forces retreated, and an exhausted Audie Murphy climbed down from the tank and walked back into the forest.

In becoming America's most decorated soldier, Audie Murphy went to hell and back. And then to Hollywood. His story became a symbol of the heroism of American troops—especially those from Texas.

More than 90 Texans received the Navy Cross. More than 30 Texans received the Medal of Honor, including Sam Dealey of Dallas, who was the Navy's most decorated sailor. At least 155 generals, including Dwight D. Eisenhower, were from Texas. Twelve admirals, Chester Nimitz among them, were Texans. Their true stories are taller than any Texas tale.

But these famous men are not the only Texans with stories to tell. More than 750,000 Texans served in the armed forces. And Texans and their families back home paid the awful price of war: 15,764 Texans in the army and 7,258 Texans in the navy and marines were killed. Although the state made up only 5 percent of the nation's population, it provided 7 percent of the total armed forces. At the end of 1942, Texas had contributed more of its male population to the armed forces than any other state. When these Texans left their farms and towns to fight for their country, many of them were still teenagers. When they came home, they were heroes.

Texans in the Pacific

Adm. Chester Nimitz of Fredericksburg, Commander-in-Chief of the Pacific Fleet (Nimitz Museum)

USS *Arizona* sinking after attack on December 7, 1941 (U.S. Navy photo)

"The sea, like life itself, is a stern taskmaster," believed Fleet Adm. Chester Nimitz, the most famous of all Texans to serve in the Pacific. Even though Nimitz grew up in landlocked Fredericksburg, the sea and its lessons were an important part of his life. He lived with his family at the Nimitz "Steamboat" Hotel, built and run by his grandfather, Capt. Charles Nimitz. The captain shipped out as a merchant seaman in Germany, rode with the Texas Rangers, and in the 1850s built his hotel, well known for its crow's nest and ship-like profile. The young Nimitz worked as the hotel handyman and crawled out of bed at three o'clock every morning to do his chores and study before school.

The hard-working Nimitz rose rapidly through the navy ranks, even though he was court-martialed in 1908 for grounding a destroyer on a mud bank in Manila Bay. In 1941, ten days after the attack on Pearl Harbor, he was appointed Commander-in-Chief of the Pacific Fleet.

As soon as he could organize enough men and ships, Admiral Nimitz took the offensive in the Pacific. His strategic skill was vital to victories in the Coral Sea, Midway, and the Solomon Islands. The Coral Sea battle in May 1942 was the world's first naval battle fought entirely from the air—not a shot was fired between surface vessels. The battle was also an important morale booster, coming only six months after Pearl Harbor and two days after the fall of Corregidor in the Philippines. Throughout the Pacific War, Nimitz plotted the amphibious conquest of island after island as the navy drove toward Japan.

The Battle of the Philippine Sea during the attack on Saipan in the Marianas chain became known as the "The Marianas Turkey Shoot." Nimitz's navy pilots shot down hundreds of Japanese carrier planes and effectively destroyed Japanese naval air power. Nimitz later decisively defeated the Japanese fleet in the Battle of Leyte Gulf in October 1944. President Roosevelt was so pleased with Nimitz that in 1944 he nominated and appointed him to the navy's highest grade—fleet admiral—the day after Congress approved the new position.

The next year the admiral's long-range strategy paid off at Iwo Jima and Okinawa and helped bring the war to a close. Victory, though, came at a high price. Nearly 7,000 marines and sailors died on Iwo Jima, and more than 12,000 Americans lost their lives at Okinawa.

Among the many Texans who fought in these battles was William Harrell of Rio Grande City, a marine sergeant who faced enemy troops alone on Iwo Jima and kept fighting even after losing his hand to a missile. Harrell won the Medal of Honor at Iwo Jima, as did Jack Lummus of Ennis, whose valor cost him his life but inspired his marines to continue their relentless drive over enemy ground. At Iwo Jima, said Nimitz, "Uncommon valor was a common virtue."

Nimitz, the great naval leader who grew up in the Texas Hill Country, was one of the U.S. dignitaries who signed the Japanese surrender aboard the *Missouri* in Tokyo Bay. After the war Nimitz became a peacemaker, cutting down the size of the navy he had built. He worked as a good-will ambassador for the United Nations and helped to rebuild relations with Japan by raising funds to restore the battleship *Mikasa*, Admiral Togo's flagship during the 1905 Russo-Japanese War.

> Ensign Earl Donnell of Temple, a naval aviator, was awarded the Air Medal after he "gallantly gave up his life" during an attack on the Marshall Islands. To honor the Texan, the Navy in 1943 named a 1,300-ton destroyer the USS *Donnell*.

SAMUEL DAVID DEALEY

Samuel David Dealey, born in Dallas on September 13, 1906, was the most decorated man in the navy during World War II. Along with the Medal of Honor, his other awards include the Navy Cross with three Gold Stars and the Silver Star. He received the Medal of Honor for "conspicuous gallantry and intrepidity at the risk of his life above and beyond the call of duty" serving as the commander of the submarine USS *Harder*.

Dealey sank five vital Japanese destroyers in five short-range torpedo attacks. On a night with a bright moon in Japanese-controlled waters, the *Harder* was spotted by an enemy destroyer escort. As the Japanese approached to attack, Dealey dived and then opened fire, sending his target down in flames. He plunged deep to avoid depth charges and then surfaced. He sighted another destroyer and nine minutes later sent it down tail first. He then moved into the confined waters of Tawi Tawi with the Japanese Fleet base only six miles away and torpedoed and sank two more destroyers. The next day, he made another "down-the-throat" shot at the lead destroyer and crash-dived beneath the exploding ship.

After the war, the U.S. sub base in New London, Connecticut, named its recreation center after Dealey and American Legion Post 581 in Dallas was named in his honor. For young men at the Naval Academy, it became an honor to stay in Dealey's former room, which was named after him.

Crew of USS *Houston*
(USS Houston Memorial Collection, M.D. Anderson Library, University of Houston)

Before the United States entered World War II, President Roosevelt sailed on a number of vacation cruises aboard the USS *Houston*. This drawing was made to commemorate one of Roosevelt's cruises aboard the Houston, which was often called the "president's yacht." Wealthy Texans donated a baby grand piano and an immense set of silver decorated with Texas themes to make life aboard the ship comfortable, but the ship was stripped of such luxuries after Pearl Harbor.
(USS *Houston* Memorial Collection, M. D. Anderson Library, University of Houston)

The navy and Texas were hit hard at the end of February 1942 by the sinking of the cruiser USS *Houston* in the Sundra Strait. The battle-scarred *Houston* steamed into a strong Japanese force and destroyed two loaded transport ships before it sank. The day before, the *Houston* had been one of only two Allied ships to survive the Battle of the Java Sea, called "that forlorn battle" by Winston Churchill. And only a few weeks before, on February 4, 1942, the *Houston* had lost 48 men and a turret when it ran into 54 enemy planes. The *Houston* had a crew of more than 1,000 men, but only 370 survived the battles and the sinking.

Houstonians were shocked when they learned their ship and men had been lost. On Memorial Day 1942, 150,000 people gathered in downtown Houston to pay their respects to the lost sailors. In a twilight ceremony that evening, 1,000 young volunteers were sworn into the navy to replace the lost force, and a new navy recruiting poster urged men to "Avenge the *Houston*! Join the Navy with the Houston Volunteers." Texans already had purchased enough war bonds to pay for the construction of a new USS *Houston*, a light cruiser.

One of the many Texans who served aboard the *Houston* in the Pacific was Albert Kennedy of Edna. As he started up the ladder after the order to abandon ship, a shell exploded at the top, knocking him back down. Wearing his life jacket, he jumped overboard cannonball-style into the water which was churning with exploding shells. Kennedy made it to a raft, but it was full, so he hung on to one of the side ropes. On the raft he saw an old friend from Marshall and tried to joke with him, asking if he wished he had his sharkskin suit with him. His friend didn't laugh.

Families across Texas were outraged when they learned of the sinking of the USS *Houston*. More than 1,000 Texans lined up outside the Music Hall in Houston to volunteer for the navy.
(USS *Houston* Memorial Collection, M. D. Anderson Library, University of Houston)

Later that night, Kennedy swam toward the Java shore, finding refuge aboard another raft at daybreak. The sailors from both rafts floated into a fleet of Japanese merchant ships and were taken to shore by an armed landing craft. Once ashore the sailors were lined up on the beach by a Japanese officer, who, to Kennedy's surprise, spoke perfect English and was a graduate of U.C.L.A. The sailors from the other raft were never seen again, and Kennedy believes they were machine-gunned to death. "I think we're alive probably because of that Japanese officer," he said.

Albert Kennedy (left) and J. O. Burge (right) on liberty in Manila before the start of war. Both survived the sinking of the *Houston*, and both were POWs.

The survivors of the *Houston* were sent to prison camps across the Pacific with the Texans of the 2nd Battalion, 131st Field Artillery, a part of the 36th "Texas" Division. This combined group of 903 sailors and soldiers was dubbed "the Lost Battalion" because no one at home knew for more than a year what had happened to them. Some of the first news of the unit was received when a U.S. short-wave operator picked up a Radio Tokyo broadcast that included a statement from Pvt. Robert Cook of Abilene.

The men of the Lost Battalion spent the rest of the war fighting for their lives against starvation, torture, beatings, and disease. One hundred and sixty-three died in camps across Java, Burma, and Japan. Many were used as slave labor to build the infamous "Death Railway" through the jungles of Burma. This railway had several river bridges, including two over the Kwae-Noy made famous by the novel and movie *Bridge on the River Kwai*.

Clyde Shelton of the 131st, like many Texan youths, lied about his age and enlisted when he was only 16. Before the Mexia native was captured, he loaded bombs on B-17Ds at Java. His first air raid was chaotic: GIs were grabbing helmets off each other and trying to dig holes to hide in. Shelton ran across a small field and tried to hide from a Japanese Zero pilot in some tall weeds that reminded him of West Texas milkweeds. "I thought he couldn't see me," Shelton said, "but I happened to look up, and I could see the grin on his face." The Zero pilot missed Shelton, and the air raids became routine until the battalion was captured. Shelton became a POW before he turned 18.

Frank Ficklin of Wichita Falls remembers that the men crisscrossed Java in broad daylight in long truck convoys. Along with Dutch, British, and Australians who did the same, they hoped to convince the Japanese that a large force would be needed to take the island, which would buy the Allies time to strengthen the defense of Australia. The Japanese took the bait and captured the 131st in March 1942.

Frank Ficklin of the Lost Battalion

At first the prisoners were treated fairly well; guards insisted that Ficklin and several others sing American songs and teach them how to dance the boogie-woogie. As the war dragged on, their treatment worsened. Prisoners were forced to bow to all Japanese; those who did not were beaten. And whether they bowed or not, most endured beatings—usually administered with a rifle butt—as a routine part of life as a POW. Some prisoners were tortured. "You could hear this Dutchman screaming," said Clyde Shelton, who later found out that guards put out their cigarettes on the Dutchman's face.

Although he suffered at the hands of Japanese soldiers, Shelton credits Japanese civilians with twice saving his life. Once, when he was caught smoking on a work detail, he was brutally beaten with a sledgehammer handle on his back and legs until the handle broke. When the blows finally ceased, an interpreter brought Shelton *sake* and made sure he was not returned to work for three months until he regained some strength. Later, in a mining camp in Arao, Japan, the Texan was near death from malnutrition and dysentery. A Japanese civilian shared his rice and fish with Shelton and persuaded the guards to put him in a hospital. When captured, the 5-foot, 8-inch Shelton weighed 155 pounds. At the end of the war, he weighed 89 pounds.

A PRISONER OF THE JAPANESE

On February 8, 1942, I was wounded by a fragmentation bomb on Bataan just before it fell to the Japanese. Being in the hospital probably saved my life, for I was not able to march in the Bataan Death March. I spent 29 months in four POW camps in the Philippines before being loaded on a ship to be sent to Formosa.

The hold of the ship I was put in had a foot of coal on the floor. Men were sitting on the floor of the hold with their feet drawn up to their haunches and fellow prisoners seated between their legs.

The suffering of the American POWs was intense. Men died daily. The doctor who operated on me in the hospital died before we were well at sea. Men went insane. One soldier knifed another and tried to suck his blood. One sailor had wet beri-beri. He was swollen all over, and his testicles were the size of a small wash tub.

All across the Pacific we were attacked by American planes and ships, but the coal barge we were on made it safely to Hong Kong and then to Formosa, where I remained until January 1945, and then I was transferred to Japan.

—Tom Chandler

The men in the Lost Battalion who worked on the Burma railway also suffered from illness and starvation. They subsisted on small servings of rice full of worms and weevils. At first the Texans picked out the bugs. As conditions worsened, they ate them. On rare occasions they received meat—but it was always green. Working 16 hours a day, the weakened men used picks, axes, and shovels to carve a railway through the hills of the jungle. During the monsoon season, they worked during steady downpours in knee-deep mud. Some grew so weak they could no longer stand.

Malnutrition caused many of the 163 deaths in the Lost Battalion. Others suffered from beri-beri, dysentery, and ulcers. The smallest sore could become life-threatening in the jungle with no medicine to stop infection. Texan Willie Jordan of Newport tripped and skinned his leg, and the small scrape developed into a severe ulcer. "I could just see myself losing my leg," he said, so he agreed to be "put under the spoon." Several men held Jordan down while another used a sharpened spoon to dig out the infected flesh. As terrible as the conditions were for the captured Texans, Jordan and many others maintained their will to live. Jordan's childhood on a Texas farm had prepared him for a life of hard work, and he knew how to conserve his energy during long days in the heat. "You just wanted a steady gait, and you were used to not having everything you wanted," he said.

Starving POWs could not help but fantasize about the food they could not eat. Says one Texas POW: "At night you'd remember how Grandmother used to make them big ol' biscuits, and you'd poke a hole in that biscuit and pour syrup in there, and then you'd eat that biscuit. I remember I've ate many a biscuit at night in my sleep with syrup in it."

HOW THE LOST BATTALION WAS "FOUND"

Robert Cook of Abilene, a member of the Lost Battalion, was ordered to make a recording for Radio Tokyo. His comments were controlled by the Japanese and did not reflect the true difficulties faced by the prisoners. On February 11, 1943, the broadcast was picked up by a short-wave operator in California and was the first news the folks back home heard about the Lost Battalion. The text of the broadcast follows:

"This is Robert G. Cook, 1526 North 6th Street, Abilene, Texas, U.S.A. This is Pvt. Robert Gould Cook speaking from Java.

"Dearest Mom: You can't keep a good man down. I am well and OK. Our battery was captured by Nippon, and we have had no casualties. We are fed well-cooked food every day and have a good building to live in and have plenty of clothes. The Nippons treat us all right, and we are out of danger. Let all the family and friends know that I am well and happy and that there is nothing to worry about. I hope and pray that all of you are in good health and that I will be back with you soon. The Nippon authorities are very good to us, so we have nothing to worry about. But we are homesick. We are in good spirits, and we have very good medical care. I hope you have not been worrying about me. I will see you soon.

"My buddies from Abilene are all well and in good health. Virginia, I am OK, and I hope you are still waiting for me. This is not half as bad as I thought it would be. I pray that I will be home soon and be with you again."

TEXAS BATS OVER TOKYO

Along with the A-bomb, the military was busy secretly testing another bombing brainstorm: bats. Navy strategists believed the 30 million bats in Ney Cave, 30 miles northwest of Hondo, could destory Tokyo. Under Project X-Ray, miniature incendiary bombs would be strapped to each bat, and then the bats would be dropped over Tokyo. The plan did have a certain type of logic; after all, these bats could fly by night or day aided by their own state-of-the-art sonar systems. Project X-Ray, however, was not a success. A load of bats was dropped over an unsuspecting Tokyo, but not a single building was damaged.

A dog helps Texas troops find their way through the jungle
(Dallas Historical Society)

Gathering intelligence from a prisoner of war
(Dallas Historical Society)

TEXAS GOES TO WAR   51

Along with the soldiers and sailors, Texas cavalrymen played an important role in the Pacific. The cavalry has a long history in the Lone Star State, dating back to the Texas Revolution. The 112th Cavalry, stationed at Fort Bliss in El Paso and Fort Clark in Brackettville, left Texas in 1942 and became the last unit to serve on horseback during the war. The regiment of 1,500 men was made up mostly of Texans. Billy Burden of Dallas, which was still a small city in the 1930s, had neighbors who kept horses. He learned to ride bareback without even a bridle before he joined the cavalry. "When I got to sit in those big leather saddles," he said, "it was just like sitting in a rocking chair."

Before they went overseas, the 112th joined maneuvers between the 2nd and 3rd Armies in Louisiana. The Texas cavalry was inspected by two famous generals from Texas—Walter Krueger and Dwight Eisenhower, who at the time was only a lieutenant colonel. The day after Pearl Harbor, the cavalrymen began patrolling the roads along the Mexican border and manned an outpost at the Pecos River Bridge where they stopped and searched trains for German and Japanese agents.

> When the Texas cavalry was sent overseas, its guidons were old and tattered. Herb Campbell and his wife bought red, white, and yellow silk, and his wife made new guidons for all the men of the 112th before they left Texas. When the horsemen staged a review for Admiral Nimitz, it was a great source of pride for Campbell to see his wife's beautiful handwork flying over the troops.

Texas soldier fires a .50-caliber machine gun at the enemy, New Britain
(U.S. Army photograph, Courtesy Dallas Historical Society)

The cavalry was first sent to New Caledonia, where it guarded an air base and set up outposts. They received horses by ship from Australia and spent three months breaking the untamed horses for an approaching review by Nimitz. "The horses were always cared for as well as humanly possible," said Burden. After a long day on horseback, the Texans always watered, fed, and combed their horses before they found chow and water for themselves. One shipload of 300 horses was sunk by a Janpanese submarine.

When MacArthur wanted troops to build an airstrip on Woodlark Island in the Solomon Sea, the cavalrymen traded their horses for jungle gear. On their way to Woodlark, the men were astonished to hear Tokyo Rose report that they all had been killed by a Japanese sub attack. Six months later, the cavalry suffered heavy losses when it led the U.S. attack on Aarwe, New Britain. About 80,000 Japanese soldiers were on the island when the 1,500 men of the 112th landed. Marines did not arrive to support the cavalry until 11 days later.

In the jungle, the Texans battled snipers nested in coconut trees and assassins who lurked in caves. On Christmas Day 1943, the Japanese launched a large counterattack, and the men once again heard Tokyo Rose erroneously report their demise. After six months on the island, the 112th left to fight with the 1st Cavalry in the Philippine jungle as part of the Leyte and Luzon campaigns.

TARAWA

In 1943, my enlisted buddies and I used to stand and watch the marine flyboys wearing Waikiki-flowered shirts climb out of their F-4F Grummans.

We didn't know what they were doing—looking for the Japanese who had bombed us, killing one of our best sergeants, we supposed.

Soon the big boys came, and B-24 engines filled the daytime hours for a week or so. By the end of November it was over. The bombers moved on, and an army fighter squadron relieved the marines.

It was then that we heard about Tarawa. All these missions had been pre-landing preparations. To wipe out Japanese beach fortification. Take out their big guns. Destroy machine-gun emplacements.

But the 2nd Marine Division still suffered over 1,000 dead in the 76 hours it took to take an island you could walk over in a day.

Five thousand Japanese dead. Hardly any prisoners.

—Warren Ferguson

Two members of 112th Cavalry come in from the outpost line for noon chow
(U.S. Army photograph)

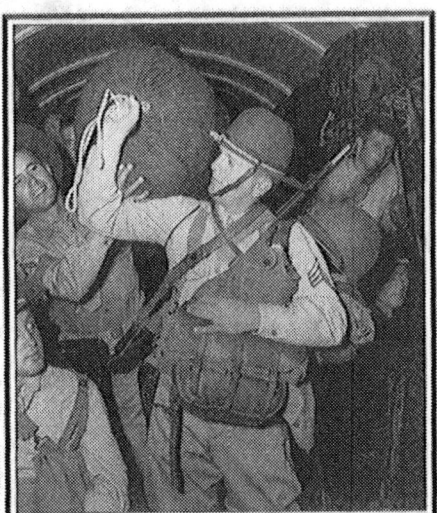
Sgt. S. W. Campbell of Dallas gets a hand with his gear. Campbell was loaded down with a 75-pound A-bag, saddle bags, helmet, M-1 rifle, pistol, cartridge belt, gas mask, field glasses, and dispatch case.
(U.S. Army photograph)

Marine alligator tank, New Britain
(U.S. Army photograph, Dallas Historical Society)

The 1st Cavalry Division, which had also been stationed at Fort Bliss and Fort Clark, included many men from the Texas plains among its ranks. In addition to the fighting at Leyte and Luzon, the division is famous for its attack on Los Negros Island in February 1944. Under MacArthur's command, the dismounted Texans launched a surprise invasion on the Japanese-held island, the key position in the Admiralty group. Thirsty Texans were pleased to find that the enemy had left behind 1,000 cases of lemon-flavored soda. They were shocked, though, to find 100 Japanese who had killed themselves with their own grenades rather than be captured.

The 1st Cavalry also fought in what must be one of the strangest counterattacks of the war. After the cavalry had taken the Los Negros Island, a suicide squad of Japanese charged the island airfield—to the tune of "Deep in the Heart of Texas." Though they were surprised by the background music, the Texans didn't stop firing until the airfield was safe. The next day they found a phonograph in the jungle not far from the cavalry's position.

THE LANDING CRAFT WAR IN THE PACIFIC

One of the familiar newsreel sights during World War II was of soldiers and marines being discharged from landing crafts into the surf of Pacific atolls as the U.S. island-hopped toward Japan. The boats that carried the infantrymen ashore were called LCIs (Landing Craft Infantry), but the one I served on for a year in the Pacific—LCI G-439—had a "gunboat" designation. My boat carried 600 rockets instead of the 100 troops that the early models had carried.

For 30 seconds, an LCI had the firepower of a cruiser. We could fire 40mm and 20mm guns and launch 600 five-inch rockets, giving the soldiers going ashore an extra half-minute of breathing room as they hit the enemy beach.

G-439 first used rockets in the Marshalls. In the landing at Guam, while attempting to smoke out a 5-inch Japanese gun, the G-439 had three killed and 20 wounded.

My first invasion on the G-439 was at Leyte Gulf. I thought the "softening up" by battleships, cruisers, and destroyers, followed by our run to within 100 yards of the beach while firing our lethal dose was the most spectacular event I had ever witnessed.

But the two months of day-and-night attacks by Japanese kamikazes off Okinawa was the most exhausting and terrifying experience of my life.

When "The Bomb" was dropped on Hiroshima, we already had landing maps for our assault on Honshu, one of Japan's main islands. Few of us who served during the landings and the kamikaze attacks can find fault with Harry Truman for dropping the A-bomb on Japan.

—Bill Mercer

Gen. Claire Chennault
(U.S. Army photograph)

In China, the most famous Texan was Brigadier General Claire Chennault, born in Commerce. Chennault commanded the legendary Flying Tigers before Pearl Harbor, and later led young army air force pilots. Although Chennault was short on supplies and the Japanese had a larger air force, the former Texas schoolteacher managed to drive back the Japanese only a few months after he was appointed Commander-in-Chief of the China Task Force in 1942.

Chennault also taught the Chinese how to set up a large radio system to warn the Allies of Japanese attacks, a network that saved many lives throughout the war. The "Old Man" was particularly well known for his unorthodox tactics and dislike of red tape. Instead of fighting to form, he simply set a general plan and allowed his pilots to fill in the details as they saw best. There was no rank among the Flying Tigers, and Chennault once said he'd be a second lieutenant if he thought it would help him win the war.

"Chennault was a fine commander," remembered James Jones of Crawford, who served two years as a communications officer in China. Jones infiltrated Japanese territory to help the Chinese set up the radio bases, work that was extremely dangerous because the stations usually were within one to four miles of a Japanese air base. Of the 120 men in his combat group, Jones said, only 14 survived the war.

Jones was once shot down in a bombing attack and walked 250 miles through the jungle in ten days. On missions, he was heavily armed and

---

Gen. Walter Krueger of San Antonio was one of the many generals from the Lone Star State. Krueger, who was born in Germany, commanded the Third Army, which was headquartered in Texas and trained soldiers from across the country. Many of the men from the Third were shipped overseas to serve in France under Patton. In 1943, at the request of MacArthur, Krueger began commanding the Sixth Army in the Philippines. His many battles include the invasion of Leyte, the largest island in the Philippines.

wore an "escape belt," which contained a scarf with a map of China printed on it, gold coins, a compass, and chocolate bars. American soldiers could hide safely in the abbeys run by Catholic nuns, Jones said. The abbeys were guarded by people deformed by leprosy, and the Japanese were frightened to pass by the lepers.

Before he was a marine captain, Ed Singletary served as captain of the Rice Owls football team. Singletary was in the first assault groups at Guadalcanal.

Chennault and his Tigers weren't the only Texans in China before the war began. Willie Benton of Waxahachie took great pride in being a North China marine in 1939. Benton and the other men in his unit were guards at the American embassy in Peking. Although he had lived through the Depression in Texas, the 21-year-old Benton was unprepared for the extreme poverty he saw in China. People were starving to death, and it wasn't uncommon to see the body of a dead person lying across the sidewalk. A haircut cost 4¢, and a T-bone dinner with French fries, coffee, and salad could be had for 17¢ in pre-war Peking. Chinese women were sold as slaves, he said.

After Pearl Harbor, the 60 marines in Benton's barracks were forced to surrender when thousands of Japanese arrived. Although he suffered from malnutrition and hunger, Benton considered himself lucky because he was only beaten once during his 44 months as a prisoner. At a camp in Shanghai, the embassy marines shared their cigarettes and clothes with the starving survivors of Wake Island, who only had torn khakis to wear in the below-freezing weather. At another camp, the men subsisted on "tojo water," a thin soup with greens. At the end of the war, Benton had lost 50 pounds and weighed only 125.

Throughout the war, many prisoners sabotaged enemy projects to get revenge. When Benton and other marines were ordered to bury large drums of alcohol for the Japanese, they poked holes in the drums so the alcohol would run out. When he worked in a Japanese garage, Benton would "accidentally" break wrenches and damage truck motors. At a foundry, Benton and his buddies put rocks into the molds. Like the folks back home, Texans overseas learned that there were many different ways to fight the war.

Dallasite Edward Charles McGuire, an army air force captain, flew the first American plane to land in China after peace had been declared. He was the flight commander of the aircraft that flew the Chinese generals from China to Manila, where they proceeded by military ship to Tokyo to witness the Japanese surrender to MacArthur on the battleship *Missouri*. The Texan then flew the generals back to Chungking. To show his appreciation, Gen. Hsu Yung-Chang gave McGuire a porcelain vase, which was later identified as belonging to the Chi'en Lung Dynasty circa 1735. The exquisite blue and white vase has a custom-carved teakwood case and an ebony stand. Captain McGuire received the Distinguished Service Cross with oakleaf cluster and the Air Medal for his outstanding service in World War II.

Japanese soldier searches for approaching American troops. This photo is from a roll of film taken by a Japanese soldier and later developed by men of the 112th Cavalry
(Dallas Historical Society)

Soldiers display war souvenirs captured on the island of New Britain
(Dallas Historical Society)

NOTES FROM A TEXAS MARINE'S DIARY

Getting Ready to Hit the Beach

After two weeks of practice landings on Guadalcanal, the 1st Marine Division set sail to join the main task force in the Caroline Islands for an attack on Okinawa. I couldn't believe the size of that task force! From the highest point on the ship, you could look in all directions and see ships all the way to the horizon.

Then followed 30 days of apprehension. We had not been told our destination until our final briefing. My unit was to make a landing on Yellow Beach, which had a 12-foot wall that we had to scale to get ashore. We were given a scaling ladder to take with us, but when we got there, we found the wall destroyed by naval gunfire and air strikes.

Some Shit Birds Never Get the Word

The day following briefing, we were issued ammo but were told not to load our weapons. We were to fill cartridge belts and our BAR (Browning Automatic Rifle) magazines. Each man was given two fragmentation grenades.

As the marines say, "Some shit birds never get the word." One man loaded his BAR with the safety off and laid it on his bunk with the trigger up. A second shit bird came by and pulled the trigger, firing off four rounds. I was standing there with two grenades in my hand, and I thought they had gone off. Our bunks were stacked six high, and there were 265 men in a space the size of a large living room. I thought we were all dead, but, miraculously, no one was hurt.

Going Ashore

We were called to reveille at midnight on Easter Sunday 1944 and fed a breakfast of steak and eggs—the meal the navy and marines always feed you when they think it might be your last. About 3 A.M. we went over the side using a cargo net for a ladder. Every man had a full field pack. We got aboard our landing craft and began circling the ship slowly until it became light.

When dawn broke, I could see our aircraft in the distance, firing rockets, dropping bombs, and making strafing runs. Overhead, large naval shells passed over on their way in. You could see them and hear a sound like boxcars rumbling as the 16-inch shells from battleships came over. Smaller shells whistled and screamed. Anyone who isn't scared in a situation like this is a fool.

We started making our run to the beach, landing craft at half throttle. About 1,000 yards from shore, the boats lined up abreast and hit full throttle. When the boats hit the beach, the front gates fell, and we ran ashore opposite Kadena Air Field. Surprisingly, we picked up only a few rounds of mortar fire and very little machine-gun fire going in. This was my first and only combat landing. It was a piece of cake, especially for the South Pacific. The reason our landing on the south part of Okinawa was so easy was that we had tricked the Japs into thinking we were going to land on the north part of the island near Naha, the capital city.

Condition Red

About dark on Easter Sunday, all hell broke loose. About 300 *kamikaze* planes attacked us and the ships that had landed us. The sky was lit up like day when the ships began firing anti-aircraft shells and tracers at the incoming planes. My buddy and I had a foxhole, but I wasn't in it when the shooting started. I was out by a stone fence about 30 inches high when the shrapnel started raining like hail. I was afraid to run for the foxhole, so I hunkered down by the fence, waiting for the Japs that weren't shot down to turn tail and run. While I was behind the fence, a Jap *kamikaze* plane came in for a perfect three-point landing on our airstrip. The plane didn't seem to be in trouble, and the pilot climbed out and stood on the wing. You can imagine what happened to him then!

Friendly Fire

Our objective was to set up a defensive position in case of a Jap counterattack. We secured our position early and set up a command post in an open field with tents, jeeps, ambulances, tanks, and amtracks well marked. As we were eating our C-rations, we saw three marine Corsairs overhead. We stood around and admired them as they made circles above us. Then they came streaking toward us launching rockets and firing machine guns at us. Our CP was destroyed and 30 marines were killed.

Naha

After we had been on the island about 16 days, we were sent to cross the river near Naha where fierce fighting was going on. Several attempts to cross a bridge there had failed, but our outfit succeeded. When we got to Naha, we found nothing but rubble. We also found hundreds of Jap soldiers dead along the road as we moved to the north shore of the island. When we got to the cliff on the north shore, we heard that many soldiers and civilians had jumped to their deaths from the high cliffs.

First Casualty

Our first casualty was our company commander, Capt. Ed Tiscornia. He had survived three major landings in the South Pacific. Rumor had it that he had been an all-American football player at either USC or UCLA. Capt. Ed could out-run, out-walk, out-jump any man in the company.

He had been called to a meeting to plan an attack on a village in front of us. On the way back, he was shot by a sniper about 30 feet from our CP. We brought him back in, and the corpsman tried to administer plasma. But his veins had collapsed. The only words he uttered were, "My God, the pain."

Three men and I put him on a stretcher and took him down a wet, muddy, shell-torn hill, across a ravine, through a deep creek, and back up the hill to the pick-up point. Going downhill with the stretcher, we had to sit down and slowly slide. About half-way down, we were caught by a Jap mortar barrage. None of us got hit, but the C.O. arrived D.O.A.

V-E Day in the Pacific

At 11 A.M. on the day following VE Day, we were ordered to fire all weapons—from small arms to big guns—at the Japs.

Ernie Pyle

All enlisted men in World War II knew Ernie Pyle, truly an enlisted man's reporter. The day before he was killed, he visited our unit, talked to us, and ate C-rations. He was loved by all.

Counterattack

A friend of mine from Pampa, Ben Moore, was on outpost duty on the beach one beautiful moonlit night when he looked out in the surf and saw movement. He used his sound-powered phone to call for flares. He saw Japs wading ashore and immediately opened fire with his BAR. He said it was like a war scene in the movies. He was awarded either the Bronze or Silver Star.

The next day I was carrying an arm load of bazooka shells down the hill when I looked up and saw a Jap at the mouth of a cave on my left. I had no gun with me, and when he fired at me, I dropped the bazooka shells and pulled out one of my grenades. I thought I would never be able to pull the pin. (Don't believe those movies about troops pulling pins with their teeth!) When I got it pulled, I dropped the grenade down the cave. Later I retrieved his rifle and brought it home as a souvenir for my son.

The Girls We Left Behind Us

When I went into service, my 19-year-old wife was left behind to raise our young son. Times were hard and everyday necessities were scarce. Everything was rationed—sugar, shoes, coffee, meat. My wife Lucy had a $75-a-month allotment from my pay. Our apartment rent was $30, which left her $45 to pay for food, medicine, clothes, and other necessities. When I left home, my son was 13 months old. When I saw him again, he was almost 4 years old, and I was a stranger to him. I have the greatest admiration for my wife and the great job she did while I was away. All the young wives and mothers had as great a part in winning the war as we did. There has never been enough credit given them for a job well done!

—*Elmer Houston Monk*

Texans in Europe

Gen. Dwight D. Eisenhower
(U.S. Army photograph)

Thirty-sixth Infantry Division landing at Salerno, Italy, D-Day
(Texas State Archives)

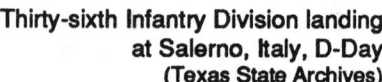

"Nothing is easy in war," said one of the most famous Texans in World War II, Dwight D. Eisenhower. Although he was raised in Kansas, Eisenhower was born in Denison and later returned to his home state in 1915 when he joined the 19th Infantry at Fort Sam Houston. Like Nimitz, Eisenhower rose rapidly through the military ranks. Five days after Pearl Harbor, Eisenhower left Texas for Washington to become chief of the War Plans Division. In June 1942, he was appointed commanding general of the European theater. He directed the invasions of Sicily and Italy and was made a full general in 1943. On Christmas Eve 1943, Texans listening to war news and Christmas carols on the radio heard President Roosevelt announce that Eisenhower had been appointed supreme commander of the Allied forces.

The five-star general from the Lone Star State was the principal architect of the invasion of Normandy. He directed one of the greatest military forces in history, leading the Allies to victory in Germany. Although he possessed an explosive temper, Eisenhower also was famous for his geniality and genius in getting people of diverse backgrounds and opinions to work together. During his D-Day broadcast in Western Europe, he called upon "all who love freedom to stand with us now. Together we shall achieve freedom." After the war, Texans and the rest of the nation continued to "like Ike."

Texans were among the first Americans to invade Europe. The 36th "Texas" Division, perhaps the most famous of all Texas troops in World War II, stormed the beaches of Salerno, Italy, on September 9, 1943. Texans from more than 75 towns throughout the Lone Star State had traveled to Camp Bowie in Brownwood to sign up with the 36th Division, which was part of the National Guard and traces its history back to the Republic of Texas. The T-Patchers, so called because of the large "T" on their insignia, began overseas service in early 1943 in North Africa. After success at Salerno, the 36th suffered horrifying casualties at the Rapido River near Cassino, Italy, a mission that many rightly feared was doomed to fail and that their commander opposed. But the T-Patchers rallied, taking Rome on June 4, 1944, and invading Southern France in August 1944.

"I am confident of success," Gen. Fred Walker, commander of the 36th, recorded in his journal several days before the invasion of Salerno. During the first few moments, the Texans were relieved when they encountered no German gunfire on the beach. But their happiness was short-lived. Only a few hundred yards up Yellow Beach, men began to be hit by the enemy, whose tanks were hidden in haystacks close to the beach. The waves of landing forces faced relentless fire as German shells rained on them from the hills above the beachhead. Flares of different colors lit up the sky, and machine-gun tracers zigzagged over the beaches. Some soldiers had to swim to shore as their boats began sinking after taking enemy hits.

Maj. Gen. Fred L. Walker
(U.S. Army photograph)

McNeil native James Logan of the 36th landed with the first assault wave and killed three Germans with three shots. Machine-gun fire hit the ground, splattering him with rock fragments from the impact of the bullets. He charged another 200 yards and captured an enemy machine gun. Running ahead once more to reach a sniper hidden in a house, Logan shot the lock off the front door and killed the sniper.

The T-Patchers suffered heavy casualties but fulfilled their commander's prediction of success as they made their way inland. Brought ashore in the landing was a Texas flag presented to Walker by Gov. Coke Stevenson. The flag was unfurled as the Texans fought their way through Europe, including at a customhouse on the German border. When Walker retired from the army after the war, he became commander of the Texas National Guard and published his wartime journal, *From Texas to Rome*.

THE STORY OF TWO TEXAS INSIGNIAS

The 36th Division first began using the T-patch during the First World War. The division was made up of men from the Texas and Oklahoma National Guards. Texans were in the majority though—at the time Oklahoma had only been a state for about a decade. One design under consideration was the Lone Star of Texas with an Indian head in the center to represent Oklahoma. This insignia, however, was adopted by the 2nd Division, another unit with many Texas members. The 36th then created a patch with a big "T" to signify Texas in the center of an arrowhead background to represent Oklahoma. Ever since, the soldiers of the 36th have been called T-Patchers.

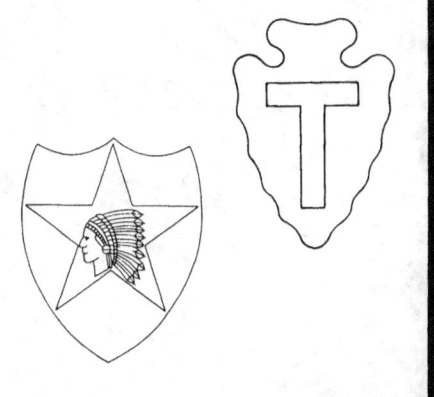

TEXAS GOES TO WAR

> Lt. James Mahoney, a Texas artist who painted murals at the Hall of State in Fair Park, taught the art of camouflage during the war. Mahoney, an officer in the 8th Air Force, traveled to U.S. Air Force stations throughout England to teach Americans how to hide their men and equipment.

One of the many other Texans at Salerno was Lt. Col. Samuel Graham of Huntsville. When Graham hit the beach, he quickly organized a group of 70 men and led them inland to clear out the enemy machine-gun and mortar positions. Graham, who taught agriculture at Sam Houston State, received more than 20 medals for valor and distinguished service. He became Texas's second most decorated soldier.

The 36th Division fought in a total of seven campaigns: Naples-Foggia, Anzio, Rome, Arno, Southern France, Rhineland, Ardennes-Alsace, and Central Europe. The division's casualty figures are among the highest in the war: 19,466 total casualties, 3,717 killed in action, 12,685 wounded in action, and 3,064 missing in action. As the war raged on, men from across the nation joined the 36th, but the division was always known as a Texas unit. No matter what state incoming soldiers called home, when they joined the 36th they became honorary Texans.

The 45th Infantry Division also counted many Texans among its ranks. Stationed at Camp Barkeley near Abilene, the unit fought in many of the same campaigns as the T-Patchers, including the invasion of Southern France and the landing at Salerno.

> **from the poem *"Foot Reflexologist, Farmers and Christmas"***
>
> *...on December 24, 1943, an angel*
> *stepped into a foxhole outside Taranto, Italy,*
> *where a farm boy fresh from the States*
> *prayed softly, bleeding, counting stars*
> *through broken limbs of winter trees.*
> *And the angel laid his hands upon the wound*
> *and prophesied good news:*
> *Peace. A slight limp.*
> *A hundred-acre farm in Oklahoma.*
>
> —Bob Fink

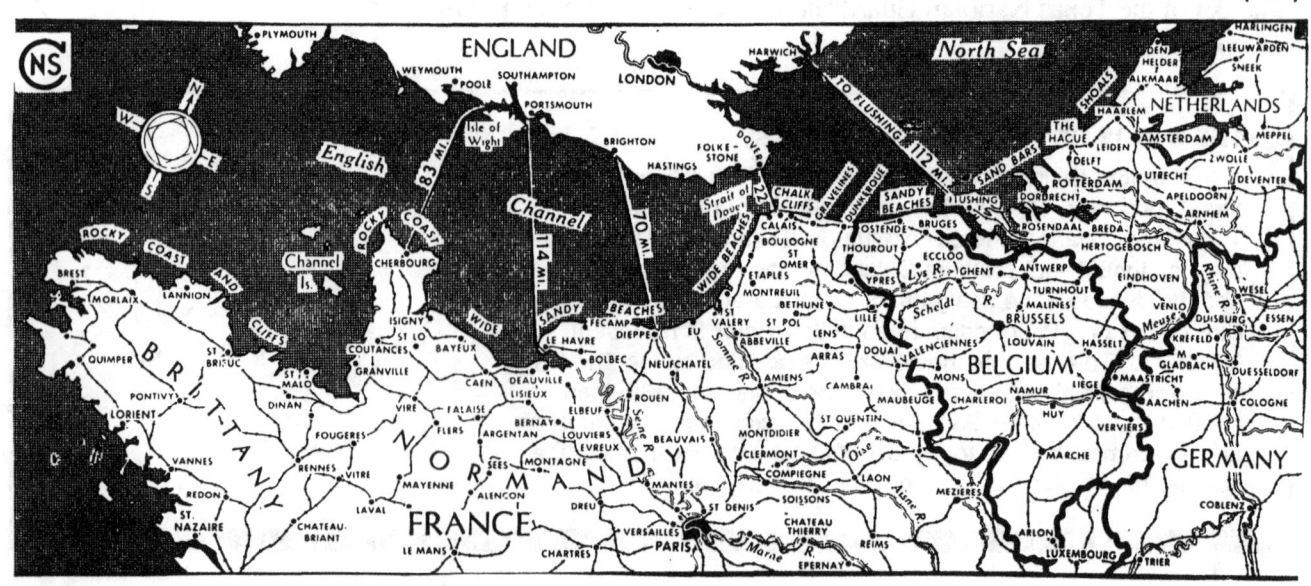
(Brief)

64 TEXANS IN COMBAT

Another distinguished Texan in Italy was General Hamilton Howze, a member of another family of Texas soldiers. His father, Major General Robert Lee Howze, was a Medal of Honor winner who fought in the last Sioux campaign. Camp Howze in Gainesville, named after the elder Howze, was the training site for the 84th, 86th, and 103rd infantries during World War II.

Hamilton Howze went overseas in 1942 as a captain in the 1st Armored Division. He fought first in North Africa after several months in various Allied ports in Europe. "It was a tough campaign," he said, because the men couldn't train properly when traveling. "It was like sending a football team to the Super Bowl without any practice for a year."

Howze and the 1st Armored Division then went to Italy, where they fought during the rest of the war. At Anzio, he commanded a group called Task Force Howze. They hit a "soft spot" where there was little German resistance and were able to march miles straight through the German line. Howze suggested that the American troops follow his path on their way to Rome, but Gen. Mark Clark rejected the idea, choosing a shorter route and consequently meeting heavy fighting, Howze said.

Howze and his men later encountered the Hermann Goering Division. The German infantrymen didn't realize American tanks were in their territory and advanced through a wheat field in full view of the Americans. "It was a bad show for the Germans," Howze said. In 1945, the Texas soldier was stationed in Lake Como when he received a report stating that Mussolini had been captured nearby. Italian partisans shot the dictator and his mistress, then took their bodies to Milan where they were hung by their heels in the city square.

NOTHING NEW UNDER THE SUN

While many Texas soldiers relied upon new, advanced weaponry during the war, the 74 Dallas men of Company D, 51st Battalion, added weapons that were almost 100 years old to their arsenal: Civil War bayonets. The long, thin bayonets were discovered in an old warehouse in Virginia, and the Texas State Guard company in Dallas later attached the bayonets to the muzzles of their shotguns. Every Thursday night from 7:30 to 10:00 the men met at their armory, an old building in Oak Cliff, to practice their drills.

A PRISONER OF THE GERMANS

On July 19, 1944, I bailed out of a P-51 fighter over German-occupied France, and spent two or three weeks being interrogated by Chief Interrogator Hanns Scharff before being taken to a POW camp in Germany.

Scharff showed me pictures of men in American uniforms being crushed by vices and pulled apart by machines. He said, "That is what happens to those who do not cooperate." He said if I answered his questions, he would send me to a camp that had "Saturday night dances, German girls, and good food." (What a joke! When I was captured, I weighed 190 pounds. When I was freed, I weighed only 80.)

During my weeks in the Interrogation Center, I gave only name, rank, and serial number, but I made the mistake of writing my name instead of printing it. I was surprised when Scharff showed me a statement signed by me giving pertinent information about the plane I was flying. They had lifted my signature.

After the war, I learned that Hanns Scharff came to America and cooperated with Raymond F. Toliver on a book entitled The Interrogator. *Scharff remained in America and became a well-known mosaic designer. His mosaics can be seen at Cinderella's Castle at Disney World in Florida, where five of them—each 15 by 10 feet—form a series of arches.*

In 1977, Hanns Scharff was living in California and celebrated his 77th birthday.

—William D. Wilson

Troops land on "Omaha" Beach during the initial landings, June 6, 1944. They were brought ashore by a coast guard LCVP.
(National Archives)

Texans in Europe listened quietly on June 5, 1944, as they heard Eisenhower announce: "Soldiers, sailors, and airmen of the Allied Expeditionary Force! You are about to embark on the Great Crusade!" Twenty-four hours later, many Texans landed on the beach at Normandy as part of Operation Overlord, the largest seaborne invasion in history. Texans were among many different U.S. units that landed on D-Day, including the 2nd Infantry Division, which had been stationed at Fort Sam Houston, and the 90th Infantry Division, which had been stationed at Camp Barkeley near Abilene. Like the 36th, these divisions fought their way across the continent after they landed.

After graduating from the pilot training program at Kelly Field, Lt. C. W. Biggs of Denton became the private pilot of Gen. Mark Clark. This gave him the opportunity to meet such notables as Gen. George Patton and President Roosevelt. Not satisfied with his secure job, Lt. Biggs volunteered for combat. Biggs flew a number of missions, including some during the fierce fighting following D-Day. Lt. Biggs and his crew were reported lost September 21, 1944, over Holland.

—*Cathy Biggs*

USS *Texas*

Another famous Lone Star representative, the USS *Texas*, also fought during the longest day. The battleship, a veteran of World War I, began firing its big guns 12,000 yards offshore early in the morning. By noon the ship and its men came within 3,000 yards of the coast to hit enemy snipers, and at the end of the day the ship took out a German anti-aircraft battery. Later that month, the *Texas* was engaged in heavy fighting off Cherbourg. Surrounded by exploding shells, the ship kept firing on enemy fortifications even after a shell destroyed the fire control tower, killing the helmsman and nearly everyone on the navigation deck. An armor-piercing shell then crashed through the port bow but failed to explode. During the three-hour battle, Germans near-missed the *Texas* more than 65 times.

Also fighting near Cherbourg was Lt. Col. Robert Cole of San Antonio, a member of the 101st Airborne. After Cole and his battalion took four bridges, they were pinned to the ground by heavy machine-gun and mortar fire. After an hour of being trapped under a downpour of fire, Cole stood up with his bayonet and pistol and charged forward. He inspired his men to move forward and establish a vital bridgehead at the Douve River and inspired Congress to award him the Medal of Honor.

More than 30 Texans received this most prestigious of war medals—but often they were killed in the actions that made them famous. In Germany, Herman Wallace of Lubbock stepped on a concealed mine. He knew that if he stepped aside the mine would be thrown upward, explode above ground, and kill the two men behind him. So Wallace sacrificed his own life by putting his other foot on the mine a few seconds before it exploded. Truman Kimbro of Madisonville led a squadron assigned to mine a vital road in Belgium. On their way, they met an enemy tank and 20 infantrymen. Kimbro crawled ahead alone and laid his mines before he was killed by gunfire. Jack Mathis of San Angelo was the lead bombardier of a squadron over Vegesack, Germany. At the start of the mission he was hit in the side and abdomen, and his right arm was shattered. He dragged himself to his bombsight, released his bombs, and died at his post.

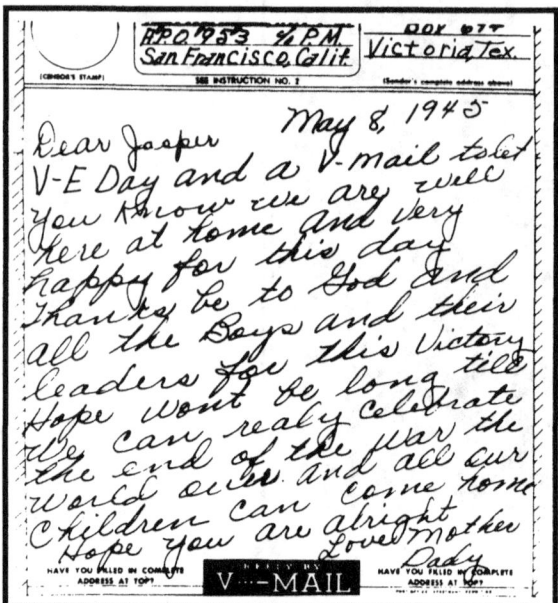

Texas soldiers and sailors overseas eagerly awaited mail call to receive the latest news from the folks back home. Letters to and from the armed forces were often sent as V-mail: letters would be reduced to microfilm to conserve shipping space and then enlarged and printed for delivery. To send packages overseas in time for Christmas, families had to finish their holiday shopping early. In August 1944, the War Department told GIs to remind their folks that October 15 was the latest date that packages could be mailed from the states for delivery to the battlefields by Christmas.

After censors were finished with a letter, there often wasn't much news left for a soldier or the folks back home to read. When Sterling Edwards of Dallas wrote "Many ships were sunk" in a letter home about Pearl Harbor, censors blacked out the line.

For POWs, the censors and mail service was much worse. "Censors were pretty happy," said one Texan. "You might get a letter that'd have two or three words in it. Everything else was cut out." Willie Benton of Waxahachie, a POW in China, was allowed to write his mother a postcard on New Year's Day in 1945. He got home in October, and his mother received the card in November.

THE CENSOR

The Office of Censorship in San Antonio had been organized by the army, and officers instructed civilian employees in censoring mail. Civilians in the office read international—never domestic—mail, both incoming and outgoing. For a month or so I read chiefly personal mail, mostly letters to Mexico from farm laborers sending cash to their families at home. Wartime rules of the U.S. government prohibited the exportation of any currency except two-dollar bills. There were so few of them that I was not aware that I had ever been given one in change. But the Mexican laborers found them; almost every letter home contained one or two. Their letters were always on cheap tablet paper written in pencil without any capitalization or punctuation, and they all followed a conventional formula.

There were many Spanish translators in the San Antonio office, but there were also a few readers in nearly all of the other modern languages. One Chinese translator was a former missionary who, after 30 or 40 years in China, could read perhaps one short letter a day. But a Chinese laundryman in San Antonio took an hour or so off his job in the mornings as his contribution to the war effort to read all the rest of the Chinese mail.

—William F. Belcher

AUDIE MURPHY IN ACTION

Immediately before and after January 26, 1945, the day Audie Murphy stood on the burning tank destroyer and repulsed two German companies, killing 50 men in an action that would win him the Medal of Honor and inscribe his name in the legends of American military history, Murph, as his men called him, performed with extraordinary heroism. The Medal of Honor was no accident, it was just the italicized climax of a long series of impressive combat actions that stretched over a 2-1/2 year period. I knew this, but never so vividly as when, after my biography of Murphy appeared in 1989, William M. Weinberg, a scout in B Company, wrote me a long letter offering corrections to some of my errors of fact and more importantly detailing his own account of Audie Murphy in action. I cite two instances. Each adds a dimension to the Murphy story.

Just outside of Maison Rouge, a hamlet in Alsace near the Riedwihr woods where the action on the 26th occurred, Murphy's company was pinned down by heavy German machine-gun fire. The whole attack had bogged down. Men lay in the snow in an open field without cover. Then Murphy got up and started walking straight toward the Germans manning the machine gun. He held his carbine waist high and kept walking toward them as they fired. Shooting from the hip, he killed them all, then led the company forward. Says Weinberg, "It was an act of bravery, but a greater act of responsibility." According to Weinberg, Murphy always did what had to be done to protect his company. This previously unrecorded and undecorated act of bravery took place on the 25th.

Weinberg also gives a fascinating glimpse of Murphy's combat aggressiveness in another episode that took place several days later. B Company was ordered to cross the Rhine-Rhone Canal. One frozen dawn Weinberg heard tanks rumbling nearby. He thought they were Germans and woke up Murphy, asleep in a foxhole. Murphy was irritated and said they were our tanks. Weinberg was right; suddenly 50 or so Germans appeared in the woods, relaxed and confident because they were miles behind their own lines. In the rush to form a perimeter to counterattack, Weinberg grabbed Murphy's carbine, which was immaculate, while his own was glazed with ice and dirt. Murphy was furious because when he got behind a tree and pulled the trigger the gun didn't fire. Then Weinberg told him how to de-ice a frozen carbine: "Piss on it." Murphy did not think this was funny. But Murphy had failed to see how many Germans there were, and had he fired on them, he and the 15 or so men left in B Company might well have been wiped out. Weinberg liked to remind Murphy how he had saved his life by switching carbines. But Murphy never seemed to appreciate the humor of it.

The history of a combat soldier can never be completely told. But every fact, anecdote, and episode about Audie Murphy's war with the Germans confirm his absolute heroism, his remarkable accomplishments on the battlefield.

—*Don Graham*

Audie Murphy

Born: June 20, 1924, in Hunt County, son of a sharecropper.

Died: May 28, 1971, in a plane wreck north of Roanoke, Virginia.

Buried: Arlington National Cemetery. His gravesite is one of the most visited in the cemetery, second only to JFK's.

Andy Brown

Andy Brown of Anson was another of the many Texas aviators who lost their lives during the war. Before he joined the service at age 35, Brown made sodas and filled prescriptions at the corner drugstore. As a technical sergeant in the 8th Army Air Force in England, he flew 26 bombing missions, including several over Berlin. During his final mission, Brown's plane burst into flames over England. With the fire in the cockpit growing closer to the bomber's gas lines, Brown encouraged the nine other crewmen to parachute to safety while he fought the fire alone. His own parachute was destroyed in the fire, and the plane exploded before Brown could bring the bomber down for a crash landing.

Texas led the nation in training aviators for the war. From 1942 to 1944 more than 44,000 pilots got their wings in the Lone Star State. With the large number of airfields and training centers in the state, it was no wonder that so many Texans became pilots during World War II. In the Whitson family of Denton, all the boys became pilots. Bill and Warren flew B-17s in Europe and their brother John flew B-24s. "I couldn't swim," said Bill Whitson, "so there was no use in going into the navy." And the brothers agreed that they'd rather fly in the air force than walk with the infantry.

Bill Whitson, a member of the 305th Bomb Group, still has part of the nose section of his plane, "Old Bill," that was shot up over Germany in 1943. In a raid on Bremen, his squadron met a group of Focke-Wulf 190s. Although his navigator was killed and he was shot in the leg and the back, Whitson made it back to his base in England. He flew a total of 25 missions, dropping armor-piercing bombs on sub and air bases throughout France and Germany. Never

The North American Aviation plant at Grand Prairie produced thousands of these aircraft, which were powered by Packard-built engines. The Mustangs gave U.S. bombers the protection they needed to penetrate the Nazi heartland. Even Goering knew the air war was lost when the first Mustangs appeared over Berlin.

Young Capt. Chuck Yeager flew Mustangs against Goering's *Luftwaffe*. Although he was shot down and missed months of combat, Yeager came home a decorated ace. He finished the war as an instructor, teaching the right stuff to young pilots at Perrin Field near Sherman. For fun, Yeager and his wingman staged terrifying mock dog fights over the unfilled bed of Lake Texoma. Today the old field is the peaceful home of Grayson County Junior College.

—R. E. Montgomery

once during the war did Whitson think that anything would happen to him. "You just get up in the morning and do what you're supposed to do," he said. The same day he returned to the states, his bomb group lost 17 out of 18 planes during a raid over Germany.

Warren Whitson flew 19 missions from his station in Ipswich, England. On one mission, he lost an engine and crash-landed about a mile behind the Russian lines. On his way back to England, he flew with opera star Lily Pons and her husband, conductor Andre Kostelanetz, who were both performing in USO shows. Warren Whitson didn't see any ground fighting—until his last mission during the final month of the war. On a raid into Berlin, he and his crew had to bail out after their plane was hit. He and two others spent 26 days as POWs until they were liberated by a British tank force. For a while they were kept at an air-base guardhouse, although Whitson tried to persuade the Germans to move them because he knew the base was one of his bomber group's targets. Later they were kept in a barn.

As the Allies advanced, the German guards tried to surrender to Whitson and his fellow captives. But Whitson and his crew told the Germans to keep their guns because they didn't want to risk an attack by any retreating German forces. When Whitson and his crew were liberated, they found thousands of Red Cross packages that the Germans never delivered.

> Red Cross packages were important morale-boosters for Texans during the war. Red Cross packages would contain tinned roast beef, coffee, cigarettes, chewing gum, Spam, Klim, tea bags and chocolate bars. One Texas soldier said that he felt just like a kid with a new bicycle when he received his first Red Cross package.

Fred Vaughan was hangar chief at Kelly Air Force Base in San Antonio when he heard the news on December 7, 1941, that forever changed his plans. He had enlisted in 1939 as a "poor old country boy" to learn a trade as a mechanic and get a job at Delta Airlines. Instead, he became an aviation cadet and flew more than 75 missions.

Stationed on the island of Corsica in the Mediterranean, Vaughan bombed bridges and railroads in Italy. On one bombing run amidst heavy flak, Vaughan was hit in the head but couldn't stop to check the severity of the wound. "If you don't start bleeding soon you aren't going to get a Purple Heart," his pilot said. "If we don't get out of this flak soon, I won't need a Purple Heart," Vaughan replied. Later, his crew was assigned to fight in the Battle of the Bulge, but bad weather prevented their takeoff. "The man who wasn't scared was crazy," said Vaughan, "and we had a few of those who never showed any fear."

> Sgt. Orbin Rutledge was wounded on one of his 62 missions over Germany. He also served in the Korean War and after his retirement from service became a teacher and counselor. He is the president of his local DAV.

Sgt. Orbin Rutledge

TEXAS GOES TO WAR 71

German prisoners of war disembark from a British LCT following their capture at Normandy
(National Archives, Coast Guard photograph)

SPECIAL ORDERS FOR GERMAN-AMERICAN RELATIONS

1. **To remember always that Germany, though conquered, is still a dangerous enemy nation.**

   a. It is known that an underground organization for the continuation of the Nazi program for world domination is already in existence. This group will take advantage of every relaxation of vigilance on our part to carry on undercover war against us.

   b. The occupational forces are not on a good-will mission.

2. **Never to trust Germans, collectively or individually.**

   a. For most of the past century, Germany has sought to attain world domination by conquest. This has been the third major attempt in the memory of men still living. To many Germans, this defeat will only be an interlude—a time to prepare for the next war.

   b. Except for such losses of life and property suffered by them, the Germans have no regrets for the havoc they have wrought in the world.

   c. The German has been taught that the national goal of domination must be attained regardless of the depths of treachery, murder and destruction necessary. He has been taught to sacrifice everything—ideals, honor, and even his wife and children for the State. Defeat will not erase that idea.

3. **To defeat German efforts to poison my thoughts or influence my attitude.**

   a. The Nazis have found that the most powerful propaganda weapon is distortion of the truth. They have made skilful use of it and will re-double their efforts in the event of an occupation in order to influence the thinking of the occupational forces. There will probably be deliberate, studied and continuous efforts to influence our sympathies and to minimize the consequences of defeat.

   b. You may expect all manner of approach—conversations to be overheard, underground publications to be found; there will be appeals to generosity and fair play; to pity for victims of devastation; to racial and cultural similarities; and to sympathy for an allegedly oppressed people.

   c. There will be attempts at sowing discord among Allied nations; at undermining Allied determination to enforce the surrender; at inducing a reduction in occupational forces; at lowering morale and efficiency of the occupying forces; at proving that Nazism was never wanted by the "gentle and cultured" German people.

4. **To avoid acts of violence, except when required by military necessity.**

   For you are an American soldier, not a Nazi.

5. **To conduct myself at all times so as to command the respect of the German people for myself, for the United States, and for the Allied Cause.**

   a. The Germans hold all things military in deep respect. That respect must be maintained at all times or the Allied Cause is lost and the first steps are taken toward World War III. Each soldier must watch every action of himself and of his comrades. The German will be watching constantly, even though you may not see him. Let him see a good American soldier.

Texas soldiers were told "never to trust Germans" in a booklet from the U.S. Army

Texas soldiers display spoils of war

No matter whether they were fighting in the steamy jungles of the Pacific or on the frozen ground of Europe, most Texans never doubted that the United States would win the war. The only question was when. At first, most believed the war would be won quickly. As the battles continued, Texans in combat, like their families back home, did not lose faith. One Texas soldier summed up the thoughts of many when he said faith was the key to survival: "Faith in the good Lord, faith in our country, and faith in myself. I never lost confidence in my country. I never lost confidence in myself. I never lost confidence in the buddies that were with me."

The war forever changed these men. Both Texans and Texas were forced to grow up fast. "The war was the biggest, most overwhelming experience of my life," said James Davidson of Denton, who served as a spotter pilot in the Pacific. "It was such an upheaval in my personal life as well as the life of the country that I'm still trying to pick up some of the pieces and put them together. I learned, I hope, a lot from it."

USE IT UP— WEAR IT OUT

by
JOHN T. SMITH

Use it up, wear it out,
Make it do, or do without.
—*Wartime Slogan*

There were no floodlights shining on the Capitol building in Austin, and Pegasus had to fly in the dark atop Dallas's Magnolia Building. Schools were dismissed for two days because the buildings were used to sign up Texans for rationing. There was endless talk about "shortages," "hoarding," and "the black market." There were shortages of food, clothing (especially shoes and silk and the new nylon stockings), gasoline, tires, washtubs, rubber bands—all the stuff of daily life that everybody took for granted.

The speed limit was reduced to 35 mph, and Texans, who lived in a state with more than 20,000 miles of public highways, were faced with the prospect of not getting around so easily as they had.

Kids, like grownups, couldn't understand at first what had happened to chewing gum and candy bars.

Within a month of Pearl Harbor, Texans were daily confronted with the ways the war would hit them personally. But no matter what might come, Texans felt that they could make it through—after all, they had the Alamo and San Jacinto to live up to

"Standard Time" was changed to "War Time" on February 9, 1942; thus, CST became CWT.

Texans practice air raid drills in San Antonio, November 20, 1942
(Institute of Texan Cultures, *The San Antonio Light* Collection)

as examples of what fighting a war was all about.

By early 1942, Texans began to learn how quickly and how widespread the changes in their lives would be. They knew that vital goods would go first to the military, and they did not complain. Often it was hard to keep up with the agencies, bureaus, boards, and associations that seemed to have control over everything. Texas newspapers became guidebooks to the maze of new bureaucracies that were reshaping life to meet the new and frightening experience of war.

There were real fears about attacks by air or sea, especially along the coast where the shipyards and so much of the booming petrochemical industry were located. In January 1942, Galveston, San Antonio, and Dallas prepared for the first blackout and air raid drills. Citizens suddenly found themselves in an eerie world of total darkness. Block wardens were selected or appointed to patrol neighborhoods. Schoolchildren were introduced to first aid and told what to do if the sirens sounded.

Most cities reported great success following the first practice drills. As the war lengthened, the fear of enemy attack decreased, but submarines and long-range modern bombers made Texans feel more vulnerable, less protected by the great distances separating the United States from the war zone.

Texans learned fast how to cope with what became one of the common features of family life—shortages caused by war and the inevitable rationing of goods. Almost daily announcements came from Washington about what might be rationed and how rationing would be implemented. Rationing meant organization and procedures, and Texas communities began to set up the necessary rationing boards required by the national program. Sugar was one of the first items on the list. By late January 1942, Texans learned that the ration might be as little as one pound per week.

Military personnel on duty at 3rd Army HQ draw a total of 27 sugar rationing books for themselves and their families.
(Texas State Archives)

> **RATIONING**
> During harvest Dad was taking a load of wheat to the mill when he blew out a tire on the truck. Harvesting stopped until he could replace the tire. Dad took me with him to the ration board where he asked for a coupon. The official said he had to turn in a tire suitable for retreading before he could get another tire. My father was not a patient man, especially when the harvest was threatened by wind and rain. He pointed at me and said, "If this boy was as stupid as you I would knock him in the head." I was convinced Dad was going to knock the official in the head, but the man made a strategic withdrawal. Dad went to the tire store where he was known, placed money on the counter and said, "I'm taking that tire and if you want to stop me you'll have to call the sheriff." No one stopped him. Later he was given a coupon for the tire which he gave to the store.
> —*Robert Flynn*

Tires and gasoline came next. Both were vital to the military, and rubber was imported. Texans hoped, at first, to escape some of the consequences of gasoline rationing, which initially was confined largely to the East Coast.

Texas was oil-rich and had refineries, so the pinch was not felt much for most of 1942. Many Texans thought that the state's favorable location and vast distances might persuade the federal government to be generous. Texas politicians, including Gov. Coke Stevenson, argued the case repeatedly. But by late fall the national needs were obvious, and the state patriotically accepted the inevitable.

Restrictions on the sale of new automobile tires also were announced in February 1942. A total ban followed quickly, leaving the average Texan with what rubber he had for the duration. Other than in cases of exceptional need (such as for doctors), there would be no new tires until the end of the war.

A Texan who wore out his tires on hot Texas highways had little choice but to put the family car in the garage and find other ways to get about. The numbers in the *Texas Almanac* tell the story: in 1942, the first full year of the war, automobile registration dropped by more than 200,000, and the picture did not change until after the war.

Sugar, tires, and gasoline were only the beginning. Texans always thought of their state as abundantly blessed by nature and good location, but since the "war effort required all and then some," Texans watched while much of what the state produced went elsewhere.

> Mr. and Mrs. Curtis Roach of Ochiltree County had a "victory pig" from a litter born just before Christmas 1942. The pig was too weak to live without special attention, so they took it to Colorado for the holidays with kinfolks.

Texans could deal with the rationing of gas and tires. The summer vacation could be postponed, the unnecessary trip shelved. But everybody had to eat. As the war intensified and with no one certain how long it would last (Sen. Tom Connally predicted three years), food—especially staples like meat, butter, and canned goods—disappeared from the local grocery shelves. Rationing again was required to give everybody a fair share.

For food rationing to be effective, shoppers had to be educated. It was relatively easy to determine a gas ration for each motorist—so many gallons allocated for a given period of time. But food supplies vary from place to place and season to season, and the rationing process had to be adjusted to meet these changes. An elaborate system of rationing "points" was established for each commodity, and the newspaper became a source of information for the often bewildered consumer.

Before making a trip to the market, Texans had to consult complicated tables and charts to plan their meals. Alongside the tables of required points might be a diagram of a cow with the cuts of meat carefully labeled—not every Texan had grown up on a ranch! In short order, the average Texan got a quick education in shopping for food in a world of limitations, with almost every week bringing new changes as unexpected shortages or interruptions in supply occurred.

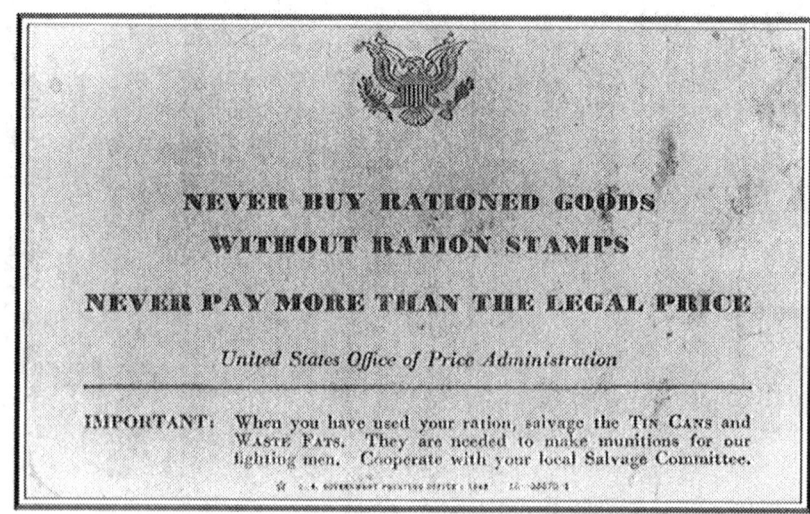

The trip to the grocery store always required rationing stamps and coupons. But there was no guarantee that once shoppers got to the grocery store, they would find what they wanted. Shelves were often half empty, there was no meat, and sugar supplies had run out. Texans quickly learned the art of substitution. Since mutton and turkey were never rationed, new tastes were acquired. In addition to meat shortages, there were often problems finding fresh fruit and vegetables, butter, and, since sugar was rationed, such sweeteners as corn syrup and molasses. Homemakers learned to "make do." They used meat substitutes, they experimented with new recipes, they used what vegetables were available, such as eggplant or squash, which they had never used before. In order to keep families nourished, housewives began using more store-bought breads and cereals that were enriched with vitamins A and D. Iron, thiamine, riboflavin, and niacin were added to white flour. Oleomargarine—at first that horrible, white, lard-looking stuff that had to be kneaded so that yellow dye would veil its real nature—became a favorite. It was soft and spreadable—and it kept. And, of course, though homemakers were not aware of it then, it was free of cholesterol.

This woman dug up her flower beds to plant a victory garden.
(Texas A&M University Archives)

Soap was scarce and the laundries were overcrowded. The best they could do was to promise a load of laundry back in two weeks—or three. Women got out their washboards.

If Texans could not buy the food they wanted or needed, they could follow the advice of the federal government and grow it. The "victory garden" became as much a part of home life as listening to the news. Flower beds were converted to vegetable gardens, and many a backyard was plowed and planted.

The victory garden provided fresh produce at modest cost. If one family produced more than it could use, they could share or preserve the surplus. One Richardson housewife canned between 15,000 and 20,000 jars and cans of fruit and vegetables after a summer of intensive agriculture.

TEXAS GOES TO WAR 79

What families couldn't buy or grow, they learned to do without—"Meatless Tuesdays" and no desserts became commonplace. And nobody complained; it was, after all, a modest contribution to the war effort. Patriotism worked.

Those who tried to hoard or buy food on the black market—like choice beef cuts from a dishonest butcher—were quickly reported. It wasn't "squealing." It was simply doing your part to make sure the system worked.

Clothing, too, was a universal need. What Texans wore or could find to wear became at times as much of a challenge as setting the table. The military had enormous needs for both the raw products and the skills for producing clothing.

Style show focusing on updating garments to get maximum wear
(Texas Woman's University Archives, *College Bulletin*, 1944)

Raw materials, like silk, disappeared. Cotton was sometimes in short supply, but cotton was a Texas product, and Texans were urged to use it. It was economical and durable, and, with careful management, it was the best clothing choice. One solution to the limited supply of clothing was the imaginative recycling of used clothes. Worn dresses or shirts could be mended, or two garments combined, to last another season. Newspapers and magazines ran endless articles and tips on how to make over or repair clothing or how to make new clothing last longer.

NEIMAN MARCUS GOES TO WAR

The America of 1941 had no experience in the preparation for the war that Pearl Harbor thrust upon it. The Great Depression that had paralyzed the country by its severe deflation and resultant unemployment began to recede as armament plants went to three-shift production. Cash money began to flow as the war threat mounted.

At Neiman Marcus, we became aware, very quickly, of the new customers who were employed at North American Aviation in Grand Prairie, officers from the 8th Army Service Command in the Santa Fe Terminal Building, and the thousands of soldiers who flooded into Dallas on weekends.

Simultaneously, we encountered longer delivery dates from our suppliers and growing unavailability of many staple products that were in great demand—men's white broadcloth shirts, the newly introduced nylons, and gabardine fabric for women's and men's clothing.

The only way to meet the demands of the new customers and serve the needs of our old clientele was to purchase in greatly increased quantities. Some of our senior executives questioned whether we should expose ourselves to the risks of speculative buying, particularly in view of the new high tax rates. "The extra profits will be eaten up by taxes. It's not worth the gamble," they contended.

We decided, and I think wisely, that as long as we maintained an open-door policy that permitted anyone to enter N-M, we had to have enough goods to take care of both old and new customers. As a result, we made thousands of new customers, as well as holding on to the old faithfuls.

Nylon yarn went to war early in the game. Silk, imported from Japan, was totally unavailable. Suddenly rayon was the only yarn available for us—and it too became in short supply.

We foresaw a serious distribution problem of the hose we could get—and we didn't fancy the idea of long lines—so we devised a "Neiman Marcus Hosiery of the Month Club" and mailed two pair of stockings, in the most fashionable shades, to everyone who signed up. There was no membership fee.

Soon 100,000 members had signed up—society leaders, debutantes, war workers, wives of tank captains from Fort Hood, and naval officers at Grand Prairie NAS all received their two pair of stockings and were forever grateful to Neiman Marcus.

We brought different activities to the store, ranging from bond sales to providing officer uniforms, from bartering stockings for supplies of gabardines and cosmetics. It was an exciting period that increased our list of customers a hundredfold.

We recognized the challenge of maintaining good service and not yielding to the temptation to blame our problems on shortages of staff or supplies. Our organization responded magnificently and helped us to win the respect and appreciation of a public that was forced, in too many instances, to put up with the rudeness of a seller's market.

We won.

—Stanley Marcus

Ads for clothing stores, laundries, and dry cleaners echoed the same theme. It was a vital part of the war effort to buy long lasting, well-made goods and to care for them at a reliable cleaning establishment. Fewer civilian demands for clothes meant more for the fighting men—no one was ever allowed to forget the serviceman and woman.

Slipper Bin
(Institute of Texan Cultures,
The San Antonio Light Collection)

(*Denton Record-Chronicle,* April 16, 1942)

(*The Gilmer Weekly Mirror,* February 15, 1945)

Unlike tires and sugar, clothing was in short supply but was not rationed. The one exception was shoes. A shortage of leather finally forced the federal government to ration footwear—usually two pairs per person a year. And often the quality was poor. Shoes frequently were made of various unsatisfactory synthetics, even paper, and they did not last. Children, always hard on shoes, were reminded by their parents to take care of their shoes so they would last.

Shoe repair was likewise affected. Half soles and new heels also meant a substitute for leather and rubber, and the repairs never lasted. For the children, at least, the scarcity of good shoes made a wonderful excuse to go barefooted in the long, hot Texas summers.

Probably one of the most memorable effects of the clothing shortage was the advent of "liquid" hosiery. Silk, cotton, and nylon were in short supply, so why not "paint" hosiery on the legs? Thus were born such products as Velva Leg Film Liquid Stockings (an invention of Elizabeth Arden) and "Victoray."

```
O.P.A. Odd Lot Release of Ration Shoes
          NOW ON SALE
         RATION FREE
      LADIES' DRESS AND SPORT OXFORDS
  $2.98 Values, Now  . . . . .  $2.23
  $3.98 Values, Now  . . . . .  $2.97
  $4.98 Values, Now  . . . . .  $3.73
      CHILDREN'S SCHOOL AND DRESS SHOES
  $2.98 Values, Now  . . . . .  $2.23
  $1.98 Values, Now  . . . . .  $1.47
       MEN'S DRESS AND WORK SHOES
  $3.98 Values, Now  . . . . .  $2.97
  $4.98 Values, Now  . . . . .  $3.73
       Rountree's Cash Store
```

TURN SCRAP INTO VICTORY

IS THERE A [tank] IN YOUR BARN?
A [shell] IN YOUR BASEMENT?
A [gun] IN YOUR GARAGE?

America's War Production needs Scrap Metal, Old Rubber, Old Rags

Make a thorough-going search of your home or farm for the waste materials our war industries need. Search attic, basement, closets, garage, backyard, barn, and field. From rubber bands to old iron rails, every ounce of usable scrap you turn in is scrap for tanks, planes, ships, and guns—scrap for Victory!

What to Save . . . *Scrap metals*: garden and farm implements, discarded tools, iron beds, old stoves, heaters and boilers, lengths of pipe and hardware, metal roofing, drain pipes, tire chains, batteries, fencing, pails, washboards, pots and pans, tablewares, metal gadgets, and anything else made of iron, steel, brass, copper, zinc, lead, aluminum, and tin, except tin cans (unless you live in a community where these can be reclaimed) . . . *Old rubber*: tires and tubes, rubbers, overshoes, rubber soles and heels, swim caps, rubber raincoats, rubber tubing, hot water bottles, rubber sheets, rubber gloves, rubber sink mats, old garden hose and all rubber goods . . . *Old rags*: all cast-off clothing, shirts, underwear, sheets, towels, mattresses and bedding, carpets, flour, sugar, and feed bags, and burlap bags. *Do not* dispose of materials still in use or which might have to be replaced, *but* do not throw away any article which can be salvaged.

How to Save . . . Keep rubber, metals, and rags separately. Roll fencing and barbed wire into tight rolls or coils. Return cotton and burlap bags as clean and free from holes as possible. Clean rags are more useful.

How to Dispose of Waste . . . Give your collection to a charity or to your local Salvage Committee . . . or sell to a dealer (junk man). Call the dealer when you have an accumulation or, if possible, take your scrap to the dealer's yard yourself. Make saving scrap a regular habit—every day, every week—and turn it into Victory!

General Salvage Section
BUREAU OF INDUSTRIAL CONSERVATION, WAR PRODUCTION BOARD, WASHINGTON, D. C.

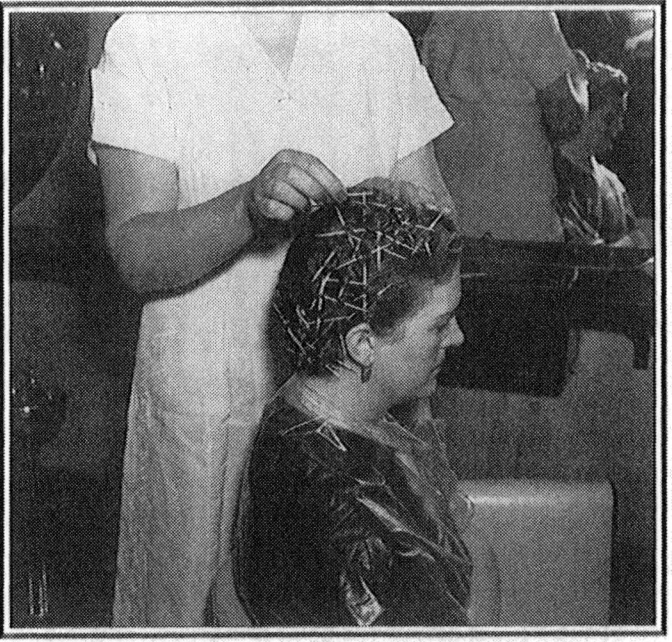

One beautician, anticipating a shortage of hairpins, stocked a supply of toothpicks to be used as substitutes. (Institute of Texan Cultures, *The San Antonio Light* Collection)

Victoray is an example of the countless ingenious ways that the war theme was worked into the advertising of the times. The message was never subtle; the ads were designed to make the reader (and user of the product) aware of how patriotic the firm was.

Make do or do without! Texans learned both lessons well.

The Winter 1942-43 "Dallas Edition" of the Sears catalog tells the story. At the beginning of the index, Sears regretfully advised its friends and customers that many items had been deleted from the "book." A glance at the list reveals the reason. The products were made from metals and other raw products that were imported and/or needed for war production. Filling an entire page, the list included electrical appliances, copper tea kettles, accordions, rifle ammunition, rubber flooring, nylon hosiery, lawn mowers, safety pins, plows, tennis shoes, mandolins, and saxophones—altogether more than 100 items make up the list.

On page after page, customers were advised that items were rationed and required a certificate or rationing certificate for purchase—tires, for example. Customers were cautioned that an empty tube must accompany a toothpaste order. Plumbing supplies totaling more than $5.00 had to be certified as replacement parts or for emergency repairs—no remodeling of the family bath.

What was true at Sears was true at the dime store, the hardware store, and the lumber yard. Making do or doing without was a part of the "effort," and Texans were no slackers. In the words of the Sears catalog, Texans did what they had to so that "the men who are fighting our battles have the guns and planes and tanks and ships they need."

Fixing up, reusing, or learning to get along without was just one way of filling in the gaps in living that Texans came to know. In March 1942, Lone Star Gas Company proclaimed the housewives of Texas and the nation to be the "guardians of the nation." Housewives were asked to pledge that they would buy wisely and waste nothing.

Children participate in a rubber hunt.
(Institute of Texan Cultures, *The San Antonio Light* Collection)

Lois and Madge Doyle are shown "attempting to balance the aluminum supply . . . as an aid to national defense."
(Institute of Texan Cultures, *The San Antonio Light* Collection)

Contemporary Texans, with short memories, might believe that recycling is new. Not so. Recycling was born out of the necessities of World War II. A Texan could not pick up a newspaper or magazine, ride a bus, or listen to the radio without being reminded to save, save, save. Everything was needed for recycling—newspapers, toothpaste tubes, tin cans, scrap metal in any form, old clothes. The list went on and on.

The Boy Scouts, Cub Scouts, Rotary Clubs all pitched in for one kind of scrap drive or another. With raw materials scarce, the cause was obvious. Texans learned about the value of using it up or saving it for reuse.

Communities found ways to make scrap drives an event. Citizens dismantled an old, unused bridge near Elgin in Central Texas and had a parade afterward to celebrate their achievement. In Giddings, a contribution of scrap metal could get a kid into the Saturday afternoon matinee at the local theater. Bob Stevens of Denton recalls that his school challenged the students to contribute their weight in scrap metal.

The students at St. Mary's University in San Antonio joined with the faculty in removing ornamental iron from campus buildings. Texas farms were littered with worn-out implements (mostly left over from the Depression) that found their way into military vehicles and airplanes. An ad in the Sears catalog asked everyone to look in their basements, garages, and attics for scrap that could go to war.

Communities prided themselves on the successes of their local drives for used materials. The need to conserve and reuse had been taught by the rigors of the Depression, and now Texans saw it as a matter of patriotic duty to throw nothing away.

Everyone had something to contribute to scrap metal collection so that Adolf Hitler could receive an "early Christmas present." (Texas A&M University Archives)

The local scrap drive frequently became an occasion for having a good time, for letting off steam and celebrating patriotism. Slogans such as "Bury A Jap With Scrap" or "To Hell With Hitler" said it all. The antagonism toward the enemy was never subtle or understated. A Texan's scrap metal or wastepaper might wind up killing the enemy.

It was a good war, a "just" war.

The third "essential" of normal living—shelter—likewise presented problems for Texans. Many moved to work in defense plants or to be near a family member stationed at a Texas post, only to find no housing. Building new homes was out of the question—lumber, copper, and lead had more important uses.

The housing shortage was particularly felt in the larger cities. Texans, never at a loss for ingenuity, found ways of creating "apartments" or rooms for rent in their homes where none had existed before.

The less patriotic sometimes tried to gouge would-be tenants, but the strong arm of the Office of Price Administration usually controlled rentals effectively. Every building that could be converted to housing was used. In Dallas, one entrepreneur thought of converting vacant gas stations to housing. Hotels and tourist courts (today's motels) were always full. Everything was tried, but the housing problem remained unsolved until the end of the war.

Scrap metal collection outside Municipal Auditorium (Institute of Texan Cultures, *The San Antonio Light* Collection)

The rationing of gasoline and tires and the absence of new automobiles made getting around in Texas a challenge. The 35-mph speed limit made highway travel at best unattractive and tiresome. Dale Odom, who grew up in Sanger, recalls that it took 15 hours to travel from Dallas to Texarkana, a distance of less than 200 miles.

Sometimes those fortunate enough to have a little gasoline and willing to put up with the speed limit made extra cash by hauling "passengers" who had signed up for the trip, perhaps at some "travel bureau." These agencies specialized in matching drivers and passengers for a small fee.

Buses and trains became the substitute for the family car. Commercial aviation had not yet made its appearance in Texas on a large scale (the *Texas Almanac* gives no statistics on air travel during World War II), but Texas already possessed a good highway system and led the nation in railroad miles.

The statistics for the war years speak loud and clear. In 1941, more than 17 million passengers traveled by bus; in 1943 the number had soared to more than 88 million. The same was true for rail passengers—in 1941 slightly over 5 million Texans caught the train; in 1943, nearly 25 million were riding the rails.

Bus fares were lower than rail fares, and virtually every community in Texas was served by the bus lines. Tires and gasoline were available to common carriers. Texans by the tens of thousands commuted by bus to work in the cities from rural areas.

At the outbreak of the war, all major and most minor rail lines had passenger service; even during the Depression, the railroads had maintained an extensive passenger service. After Pearl Harbor, the problem for Texans was not in finding a train for Memphis, New Orleans, or Denver but in finding space on those trains. Railroads were so burdened by military traffic that they could scarcely begin to accommodate civilians.

Trains were the fastest and most reliable form of transportation. But during the 1930s the railroads bought little new equipment and faced World War II with what they could muster. Railroad shops in Denison, Cleburne, Marshall, Fort Worth, Childress, Palestine, and Houston were stretched to capacity to return to service cars and locomotives that had been sitting sometimes for years in the scrap line or had been "stored unserviceable." And, of course, the war made the purchase of new equipment impossible.

Union Station in Dallas was the busiest railroad terminal in the state, serving all major lines offering passenger service. Its concourse and waiting rooms were jammed with the travelers who hoped to get on the next train. The daily scenes in Dallas were repeated all across the state.

A train at the station and a ticket in hand did not guarantee a ride. The lack of equipment severely limited space. It was almost impossible to buy a berth on a Pullman, and the coaches and chair cars were jammed. The weary Texan often stood or sat on a suitcase in the vestibule.

Railroads made certain that service personnel received the most attention. Soldiers and sailors were always boarded first and were served first in the dining car. Everybody else ate later—if at all. Sometimes the diner ran out of food before all the civilians were fed, prompting many travelers to pack a lunch before setting out on a trip.

Long freight movements of tanks, jeeps, and artillery were common sights. And they had the right-of-way over all regular scheduled passenger trains. Troop trains often pushed passenger service onto a siding and caused delays. Trains were held out of the larger terminals simply because there was not an empty track for their arrival.

The 1941-42 edition of the *Texas Almanac* had 575 pages; 1943-44 edition, 334 pages. Many statistics, available upon request, had been omitted to save paper.

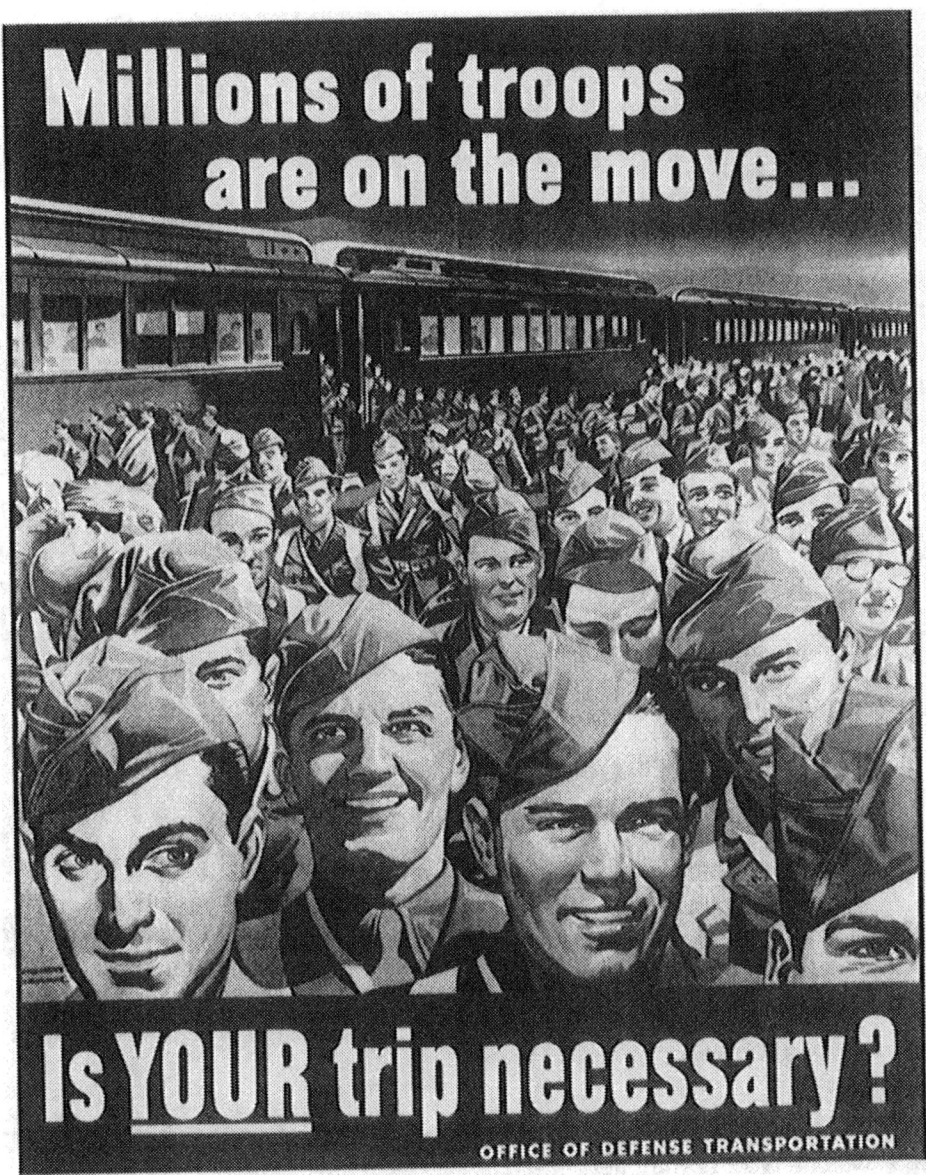

Mostly Texans were urged to restrict their travel. The question was always—"Is This Trip Really Necessary?" Less travel by civilians eased the strain and saved resources.

Getting to and from work was a problem as well. Dallas was daily thankful that it had kept its nearly 100 miles of streetcar lines. Houston, San Antonio, and Fort Worth had abandoned the trolley in the 1930s for the more modern, efficient bus. El Paso had the only other street railway—and it ran for less than twenty miles! The Office of Defense Transportation controlled public service and did its best to keep Texas cities supplied with buses, tires, and gasoline. When a new bus appeared on the streets, it had a familiar legend giving its Office of Defense Transportation (ODT) permit number.

"Work or Fight"

World War II prolonged the life of Texas's only major interurban system. The Texas Electric Railway was the last of a number of such lines, but it had been reduced before the war.

With its own building and terminal in downtown Dallas, the Texas Electric's hourly service to Waco and Denison gave access to the city for wartime workers. The big red and cream cars were as crowded as any bus or train, and the rush hour around the Interurban Building strained the patience of every commuter.

The Texas economy, which had staggered through the Great Depression, was stimulated, as was the nation as a whole, by the rapid and phenomenal growth of war-related business and industry. Large segments of the Texas population migrated in search of "war work." On August 5, 1944, the state comptroller reported that Texas was "in the black" for the first time since March 18, 1933.

Texas farmers and ranchers knew prosperity for the first time since World War I. Ranchers made good profits on their livestock in spite of federal regulations and short feed supplies. The ready market for their produce increased the income of Texas farmers by $183 million between 1942 and 1943.

World War II created a number of defense-related industries that came to Texas and stayed. General Dynamics in Fort Worth, Pantex near Amarillo, and the old North American Aviation plant (now LTV) still fill orders for the modern military.

Between 1939 and 1943, it has been estimated that the Texas economy tripled with the investment of billions in new industry or in the revamping of old technologies. Texas was vital to the production of aviation gasoline, synthetic rubber, and TNT.

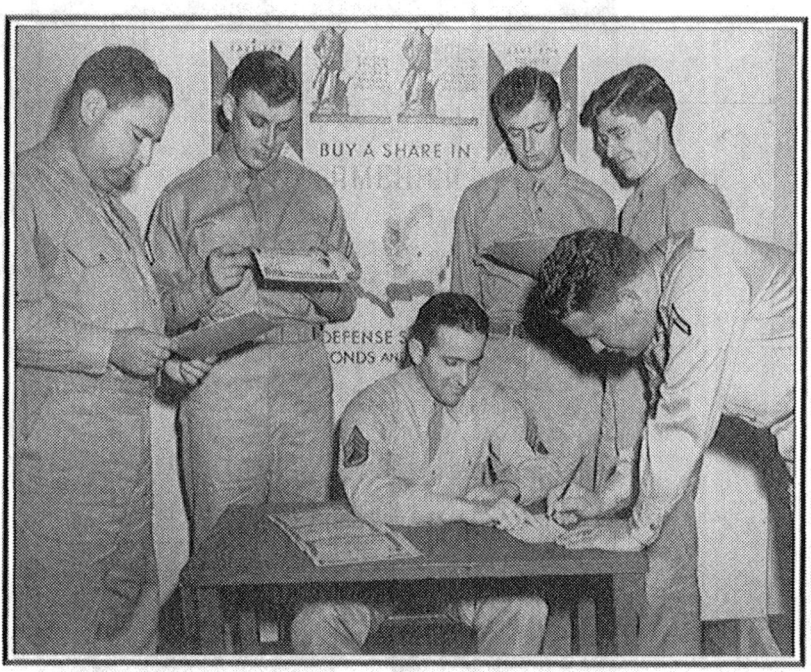

Troops buy war bonds on a "pay as you fight basis."
(Texas State Archives)

Slogan for Labor Day 1943:
"Every day is labor day until victory"

> Urban population grew by 450,000 between 1940 and 1943.

The Texas economy and its natural resources played a major part in the overall war effort. The need for oil was crucial. The difficulty for the nation was getting the supplies from the richest of all oil states to the East. The solution to the problem was the construction in 1943 of the "Big Inch" pipeline from Texas to New Jersey. Before its construction, the railroads of Texas had tried to fill the need with endless tank trains.

The success of the "Big Inch" pipeline was quickly followed by the completion in 225 days of the "Little Inch." This second pipeline carried refined petroleum products to the East.

World War II gave Texas 44 army and navy bases or stations. Because of its near-perfect climate for flying, the air force established 65 air fields or bases in Texas after 1941. Bexar County alone had eight major military facilities.

The building and supplying of these military establishments gave tens of thousands of Texans work and endless dollars to spend. The irony was that there was often not much to spend the money on, and Texans learned to save.

Since Texans could not spend their newfound wealth on luxuries, the duty to buy war bonds and/or war stamps became a theme of advertising in all imaginable forms. If you went to the movie, there was a slogan on the screen urging you to buy war stamps in the lobby on your way out.

TEXAS GOES TO WAR

The advertising in newspapers, magazines, catalogs, and on the radio never let Texans forget where their dollars should go. In the *Dallas Morning News*, for example, nearly every column or story was headed by a "Buy War Bonds and Stamps" legend. Dairies, optometrists, utility companies, banks, title companies, and department stores all found ways to couple their message with the advice to save to support the fighting men.

As in so many areas of life during wartime, schoolchildren took a special part. As much a part of the curriculum as the three R's, kids were taught to save and contribute to the war through small sums of money used to buy 10-cent or 25-cent war stamps, carefully pasted in an attractive booklet. Contests and challenges among classes and schools made for great competitive fun.

The country engaged in a series of war bond drives throughout the duration. Texas was always proud to announce that it had exceeded—sometimes handsomely—its quota. In the fourth drive in 1944, Texas went over its quota by 16 million dollars.

At the beginning of the war, President Roosevelt announced that baseball and the World Series would continue. After all, the sport was our national pastime. But in Texas sports did not fare as well. The Texas League, which had

Children put on a Defense Stamp skit to inform the audience how the purchase of stamps helps their country.
(Institute of Texan Cultures, *The San Antonio Light* Collection)

Students line up to buy defense stamps.
(University of North Texas Archives)

always fielded good teams and commanded loyal fans, had to suspend operations. The burden on trains would have been too great. So the League—and the Dixie Series that it played with the Southern Association—had to wait out the war while places like LaGrave Field in Fort Worth, Steer Stadium in Dallas, and Mission Stadium in San Antonio stood empty and silent. The Dallas streetcars no longer carried the familiar sign "BALLPARK—GAME TONIGHT."

Professional baseball was not the only athletic competition affected by the war. The difficulties of travel forced many school districts to curtail or suspend their sports competition. Schools in some of the larger cities continued to play football and basketball, but district play was limited to the local schools who often played each other twice or more to fill out a season's schedule.

College athletics were affected as well. The Cotton Bowl game continued throughout the war, and the Southwest Conference survived, but some schools, such as Baylor University, dropped out of the football scene simply because they did not have enough male students to field a team.

Even before the outbreak of war, the federal government had made plans to construct internment camps to accommodate up to 100,000 "enemy aliens." Some of these campsites eventually became prisoner of war camps, and 21 POW camps were located in Texas.

German POWs stationed near Alvin, Texas, work on the construction of a canal for nearby rice farms. (U.S. Army photograph)

German POWs stationed in the Prisoner of War Side Camp near Alvin, Texas, seal cans of sweet peppers. (U.S. Army photograph)

In Angelina County, POWs cut logs to required lengths for pulpwood and lumber. (U.S. Army photograph)

Clothing and Equipment Section at Camp Swift, Texas. Prisoners of war repair worn field kits and leggings.
(U.S. Army photograph)

Prisoners at Camp Swift present a band concert for the benefit of other prisoners.
(U.S. Army Photograph)

Prisoners rest under shelters and listen to the radio (most speak English).
(U.S. Army Photograph)

TEXAS GOES TO WAR 93

This cemetery, where 11 POWs are buried, was designed by a POW architect from Hamburg, Germany.
(Texas State Archives)

The camps were built to standard plans by the Corps of Engineers, and many were situated near military bases. Camp Maxey, Camp Wolters, Camp Hood, Camp Swift, and Fort Sam Houston all had POW facilities classified as "major." The internees almost exclusively were German.

The camps were carefully operated in accord with the Geneva Convention, which allowed the captors to employ POWs. In Texas many were used to work crops, mostly cotton, at 80¢ a day. They were also employed in canning, cutting and hauling logs, and even doing war-related jobs for the military.

At Camp Swift, near Bastrop, the POWs designed and built a cemetery for their dead. At Camp Maxey, German prisoners published three newspapers in their native language. Bands and choruses were common recreations.

The POWs in Texas were a familiar sight as they were transported to farms to work. Local residents had a normal fear and suspicion of their strange neighbors, but there were no major incidents. The POWs were more of a curiosity than anything else. They were just another face of the war as Texans saw it.

Food, clothing, shelter, the everyday pleasures—all that Texans took for granted was changed by the war, and some of the changes were permanent. Texas probably was affected by World War II no more than the rest of the country. But the scale seemed to be grander. Texans did not do things in a small or modest way. Then as always, they did things the Texas way. The state that remembered the Alamo and Goliad was not likely to forget Pearl Harbor.

THE WORDS & PICTURES OF WAR

by
CAROLYN BARNES

Texans, like most other Americans, willingly heeded the call to arms in their outrage over Pearl Harbor. But only a few months of shortages, sacrifices, and general disenchantment later, Americans weren't at all certain what, who, or why they were fighting.

National polls conducted in 1942 reflected their confusion and pessimism: one-third of the respondents had no clear idea of the war's purpose; another one-third favored a separate peace with Germany. To Franklin Roosevelt, who was trying to convince Congress to fund the war and to convince the American people to fight it, arm it, and do without for it, this clearly would not do.

On June 13, 1942, FDR signed an executive order creating the Office of War Information (OWI), which was to be responsible for all propaganda, domestic and foreign. Its chief was Elmer Davis, journalist, author, and popular radio commentator. Davis and the OWI were charged with bringing order to and expanding the propaganda, official and otherwise, that had begun in the United States in support of the Allied war in the mid-'30s.

In many ways it would prove to be an impossible task. Davis was a better journalist than politician, and he would lose skirmishes and territory to more skillful military and governmental bureaucrats. The OWI would be disrupted internally by philosophical quarrels between and within its domestic and foreign branches. But by war's end, Davis and the OWI would have a profound effect on what Texans and all Americans had come to see, hear, think, feel, and say about the war.

The poster became one of the most prolific instruments of the propaganda war. Posters were produced by the hundreds throughout the war years, not only by the government but by corporations and private organizations as well.

I AM TALKING TO YOU

"I am talking to you, Ed Murrow. And what I have to say to you is this—that you have accomplished one of the great miracles of the world...

"How you did this, I do not know. But that you did was evident to anyone. You spoke, you said, in London. Sometimes you said you were speaking from a roof in London looking at the London sky. Sometimes you said you spoke from underground beneath that city. But it was not in London really that you spoke. It was in the back kitchens and the front living rooms and the moving automobiles and the hot dog stands and the observation cars of another country that your voice was truly speaking. And what you did was this: You made real and urgent and present to the men and women of those comfortable rooms, those safe enclosures, what these men and women had not known was present there or real. You burned the city of London in our houses and we felt the flames that burned it. You laid the dead of London at our doors and we knew the dead were our dead—were all men's dead—were mankind's dead—and ours. Without rhetoric, without dramatics, without more emotion than need be, you destroyed the superstition of distance and of time—of difference and of time."

—Archibald MacLeish, at a dinner honoring Edward R. Murrow

Lt. Elton P. Lord, attached to the Signal Corps at Fort Sam Houston, Texas, looks at a poster of himself and an American worker. Victor Keppler, New York photographer, selected Lt. Lord as a "typical American soldier" while Lord was attending officer candidate school.
(Texas State Archives)

Posters were ideally suited to the wartime lifestyles of Texans, most of whom were busier than they had ever been before. Hung on the walls at bus stops, train and bus stations, factories, schools, and stores, posters cleverly—and colorfully—combined words and images calculated to stir the emotions necessary to sustain the war effort: pride, anger, determination, caution, sympathy, and a dose of guilt for good measure. Everyone noticed them, and hardly anyone failed to get their message.

Texans were urged to "Produce for victory" because "Every rivet is a bullet." Car-sharing was promoted with the warning that "When you ride alone you ride with Hitler." Those with the time and ration stamps for a trip were urged to "Vacation at home."

98 THE WORDS & PICTURES OF WAR

In what might have been a flight of fancy even in wartime, Texans also were encouraged to "File your tax return early." In a surprisingly frank admission that factory thefts occurred, workers were told to "Stop stealing tools. That crew will need them in combat." More ominous to Texans with loved ones overseas was the warning that "A careless word" meant "another cross" and another GI's life lost.

War required money as much as manpower, and Texans were exhorted in poster after poster to purchase war bonds and stamps. Usually they were reminded not of what good would come from buying bonds, but what evil would occur if they didn't. An innocent mother and child menaced by dark hands bearing the *swastika* and rising sun was typical of the appeals, which featured family images more than any other.

As television is today, radio was the medium of the masses during World War II. Almost every Texan, indeed every American, had one in their home or knew someone who did, giving radio access to 90 percent of the population. That it should become the most obvious and effective propaganda tool of the war years was a given.

None used it more effectively than FDR. He had taken to the airwaves in 1933 to sell the New Deal in the first of his immensely popular "fireside chats." He would use the same technique to steel the national spine for the rigors of war.

His mastery of the medium was absolute. The patrician New Yorker spoke to the farmer in the Piney Woods of East Texas, the rancher on the Panhandle plains, the welder in the Houston shipyards in calm, subdued tones and simple phrases, sharing his thoughts, hopes, and fears as a friend or neighbor might do. When FDR spoke, the Lone Star State listened.

In February 1942 the national networks began broadcasting the 13-week series *This is War*. Its programs, with titles such as "The Enemy," "America at War," and "Mr. Smith Against the Axis," reached an estimated 20 million people every Saturday night, informing and building morale.

OWI radio officials created a series of one-minute messages that were recorded by well-known personalities and sent to radio stations around the country. OWI-produced campaigns included those for war bonds, victory gardens, the Red Cross, rationing, salvage collection, student nurse recruitment, and victory loans. The OWI claimed each adult in America heard at least four war messages a week, and the two-week appeal for glider pilots that resulted in 30,000 volunteers goes a long way to prove that point.

As effective, if not more so, at sustaining the war effort were the radio entertainment programs: the comedies, dramas, adventures, soap opera serials, and variety shows that were a part of every Texan's daily life.

The OWI fed messages to all the most popular programs, from "The Lone Ranger" to "Terry and the Pirates." Nigel Bruce, in his best Dr. Watson voice, urged his audience to buy war bonds at the end of an episode of the "Adventures of Sherlock Holmes." Fibber McGee and Molly helped the drive for skilled workers by reminding their listeners, "It's your sons of toil that'll help put those Nazis under tons of soil."

The OWI also managed to have war-related themes incorporated into scripts and storylines whenever possible. Ma Perkins, who as part of the storyline lost a son in the war, was forever telling housewives to save fat and tinfoil. By March 1943, fat and grease salvage had increased more than 7 million pounds. On Jack Benny's "Victory Parade," Mary Livingston spoke of her dieting uncle, who lost 23 pounds by eating only soup. Benny, as straight man, said her uncle "musta had a lot of will power," setting up Mary's punch line: "No, my aunt gave his teeth to the Rubber Drive."

After radio, the most popular entertainment in Texas and the nation was the movies. At the outbreak of World War II, an average of 85 million movie tickets were sold weekly. Almost everyone went to the picture show at least one afternoon or evening a week to see the feature, a cartoon, newsreels, and perhaps a serial or "short" feature. When called to the war cause, Hollywood played its part with gusto, fighting the war in the air, on land, and at sea.

A special Signal Corps unit was established to create propaganda films for the military and industry. Some 132 members of the Screen Directors Guild and more than 437 other industry personnel were commissioned officers in this unit. Master directors Frank Capra, John Ford, John Huston, George Stevens, and William Wyler, *Citizen Kane* cinematographer Gregg Toland, and Darryl F. Zanuck, head of production at 20th Century Fox, were among those enlisted, in some cases literally, to make documentaries for the military.

With no experience in making documentaries—Frank Capra said he'd "never even been near anyone who's made one"—they applied their knowledge and understanding of feature film-making techniques to the task. The results were sometimes mixed when judged by documentary standards: situations were dramatized, footage from one battle found its way into a film about another, scenes were shot on studio sets using professional actors, and the action often was overwhelmed by the din of blaring trumpets or syrupy strings. But the Hollywood film makers also did what Hollywood film makers have always done best: they combined words and pictures that touched the minds and hearts of men and women, young and old, at a time when it was needed most.

The most famous World War II documentary was Capra's *Why We Fight*. Capra had enlisted in the army as a colonel shortly after Pearl Harbor, and it was for the army that he produced the seven-part epic to instill and maintain morale among the troops.

> *Carmen Adams had not heard from her brother in Europe for some time until she learned from watching a Movietone newsreel that he had been wounded.*
> —Austin Adams

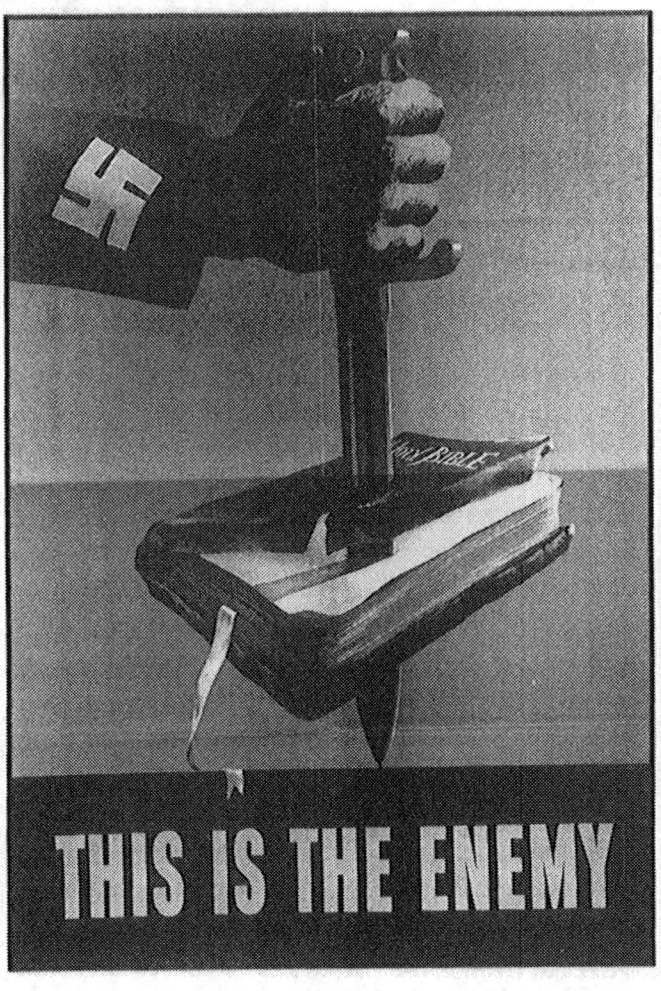

As he often did in his films, Capra divided the world into good—democracy—and evil—fascism. His touch was as sure as ever: *Prelude to War*, the first installment in the series, won the 1942 Academy Award for best documentary. Winston Churchill and Joseph Stalin were so taken with the installments on the battles of Britain and Russia that they had them shown in their countries.

The army and the War Department were equally impressed with *Why We Fight* and with its larger propaganda potential. They pressed for its distribution in movie theaters, but Hollywood and the theater owners resisted. Hollywood feared military encroachment into its territory. Theater owners said the 50- to 60-minute installments were too long for shorts, too short for features, and thereby unprofitable all the way around.

The military eventually won, and Hollywood and the owners agreed to show *Why We Fight*. Improbably billed as "The Greatest Gangster Picture Ever Made," it was a resounding flop. Some disgruntled army officials charged sabotage, claiming that Hollywood was capable of drawing "large audiences to lousy pictures when it felt like it."

John Huston's documentaries included *Report from the Aleutians*, about combat in a forgotten corner of the war, and *San Pietro*, which documented the fierce fighting and casualties in that Italian village.

John Ford contributed his efforts on the Academy Award-winning *Battle of Midway* and *December 7th*, made with Gregg Toland. *Midway*, the first documentary to find favor with movie audiences, was a case of being in the right place at the right

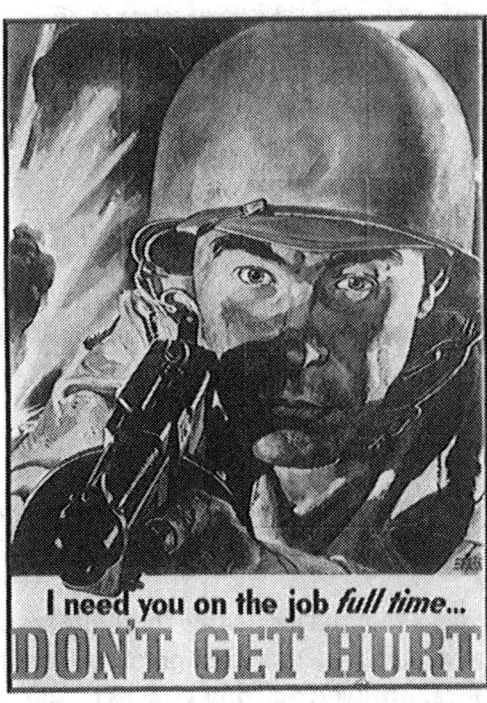

time. A navy commander, Ford was on the island when it was attacked by the Japanese. He placed three cameras in the sand, shooting the action as it happened. Much of the film was unusable, and Ford was wounded during the fighting, but the resulting documentary was a huge success.

December 7th was a classic example of the blurring of fact and illusion in Hollywood documentaries. Working in 1943, Ford and Toland had to stage most of the action in the studio using actors, miniatures, and camera tricks. Highly emotional, intended to build morale more than to inform, *December 7th* won the 1943 Academy Award for best "documentary."

Darryl Zanuck weighed in with *At the Front*, about the North Africa campaign, while William Wyler made two famous documentaries, *Memphis Belle* and *Thunderbolt*. *Memphis Belle* chronicled the final combat mission of a Flying Fortress of the same name. Shot from inside the plane, it made combat vividly frightening. *Thunderbolt* followed the 57th Fighter Group during a mission to destroy supply lines deep in German territory. Also shot from inside the planes as they darted and dived through the air, it presented some of the most exciting sequences ever filmed.

Hollywood also turned its attention to the making of motivational and training films and by 1944 was cranking out 20 per week. Distributed to soldiers and war workers, to schools, churches, and community groups, these non-theatrical films were another link in the overall propaganda chain.

Katharine Hepburn narrated *Women in Defense*, which informed women about the jobs awaiting them in defense plants and the armed forces. Bette Davis appeared on camera in a film for the Red Cross, while Jimmy Stewart and Clark Gable made recruitment films for the air forces.

Walt Disney lent Donald Duck to the cause in a series of animated films that included *The New Spirit*, in which Donald pays his income tax; *Get in the Scrap*, about scrap metal drives; and *Victory Through Air Power*, about the role of the air corps in the war.

I FOUND IT AT THE MOVIES

For grade-school children the war was a great adventure. And for us the greatest adventure of all could be found in the movies. For 25¢ I could take a bus downtown, buy a ticket, a box of popcorn, and spend all day in the theaters. I saw every sort of movie that played in Port Arthur—double-feature cowboy shows at the Peoples Theater on Saturday, double-feature films noir and other B-films at the neighborhood Port Theater during the week, and first-run shows at one of the two downtown houses on Sunday.

I remember war movies well. Robert Taylor and Lloyd Nolan defending Bataan against the dirty Japs. The Japanese bombing Peking. The Chinese laborer crying when some of the American flyers died in Thirty Seconds Over Tokyo. *The Japanese soldiers executing Dana Andrews in* The Purple Heart. *The speech by the war correspondent in* Objective Burma *that suggested the Japanese were sub-human and should be wiped off the face of the earth.*

Even after the war ended, it was the sneaky Jap soldier who popped out of the trap-door and shot a relaxing John Wayne in the back in The Sands of Iwo Jima.

Why then can I remember no movies about Nazis that condemned Germany as a failed society? Instead, I remember movies on the European theater that featured American outfits composed of a wiseacre from Brooklyn, a sharpshooter from Texas, a slow-talker from the South, a farmer (blond) from the Midwest, an intellectual (probably Jewish) from an unidentified city, a hyphenate American (usually Italian), and a volunteer from an occupied country (Polish or French). The multicultural outfit drove tanks/sailed boats/flew planes/landed on beaches or something like that and had one officer, such as Randolph Scott, who gave great patriotic speeches. One member of the outfit died while saving another's life. I don't remember any African-Americans in these polyglot units. An occasional Mexican-American slipped in, however.

But most of all I don't remember these outfits suffering the extreme cruelties at the hands of the German soldiers that those movie heroes in the Pacific did when they fell into the clutches of the Japanese. For example, I don't remember a Luftwaffe pilot turning his plane and shooting any American flyer who bailed out of his burning aircraft the way the Japanese Zero did in Wake Island.

We kids hated the Gestapo, who tortured valiant French/Danish/Norwegian/etc. members of the resistance. We even feared and mistrusted members of the SS legions. But not Germans.

I do remember being shocked at the war's end when the newsreels showed the horrors of the concentration camps. The scenes of the Nuremberg trials, with the narrator recounting the war crimes, horrified me more. If Japan had exterminated Jews, I would have understood; but not Germany. The U.S. government may have deliberately separated the Nazi party from the Germans themselves because leaders wanted no anti-German hysteria to spread across the country in World War II as it had in World War I. It may also be that war propaganda that bashed Orientals was culturally acceptable, but that which condemned a European nation and not just its leaders was not.

In either case, I wonder if my time spent at the movies helps explain why I still refuse to own a Japanese automobile?

—Robert Calvert

Manpower, Fuel Conservation, and *Salvage and Food for Fighters* reminded Texans of all ages and occupations of the contributions they could make. *Doctors at War* was not a radio serial, but a film on the medical treatment of the wounded.

Patriotic themes also found their way into feature films. The major studios spared no expense in presenting movies that depicted the war effort in the most stirring light. Americans and their allies were courageous, tough, and noble. Nazis were intellectual but brutal. The Japanese were sneering, leering barbarians.

Those who kept the home fires burning saw the importance of their efforts reinforced on the big screen in *Mrs. Miniver*, starring Greer Garson. Although it dealt with the dignity, grace and quiet courage of a British family at war, *Mrs. Miniver* in a larger sense was about all families who watched their loved ones leave, then pitched in, coped with adversity, and waited as best they could. The film won Academy Awards for best picture, actress, supporting actress, direction, and screenplay. Its closing lines struck deep chords in the audiences of darkened theaters everywhere:

> This is not only a war of soldiers in uniforms. It is a war of the people—of all the people—and it must be fought not only on the battlefield, but in the cities and in the villages, in the factories and on the farms, in the home and in the heart of every man, woman and child who loves freedom. Well, we have buried our dead, but we shall not forget them. Instead, they will inspire us with an unbreakable determination to free ourselves and those who come after us from the tyranny and terror that threaten to strike us down. This is the people's war. It is our war. We are the fighters. Fight it then. Fight it with all that is in us. And may God defend the right.

Action films such as *Wake Island*, *Air Force*, *Guadalcanal Diary*, *Action in the North Atlantic*, *Destination Tokyo*, *Sahara*, *Objective Burma*, and *Thirty Seconds Over Tokyo* brought the fighting on all fronts and all terrain home to America. Their credits featured stars of the first rank—Humphrey Bogart, Errol Flynn, Cary Grant, Spencer Tracy, John Garfield, Raymond Massey, Brian Donlevy—who left no doubt about the courage and integrity of the Allied fighting men.

Joe Smith, American celebrated the courage of another kind of fighting man. Robert Young was an average "Joe," a factory worker kidnapped by the Nazis because he knows the plans for a new bombsight. Subjected to torture, he refuses to betray his secrets and country. He escapes and leads the FBI to his captors.

The nurses of the armed forces, who cared for the wounded while enduring hardships and facing capture and death only slightly less often than the fighting men, also found themselves portrayed on screen. *So Proudly We Hail*, starred Claudette Colbert, Paulette Goddard, and Veronica Lake as nurses trapped on Corregidor Island. *Cry Havoc* featured Margaret Sullavan, Ann Sothern, and Denton's Joan Blondell caught up in the Bataan retreat.

TEXAS GOES TO WAR   105

Many films also dealt with those displaced and made desperate by war, none more memorably than *Casablanca*. Lone Star audiences were enthralled by the pairing of Bogart and Ingrid Bergman as former lovers whose paths cross when she and her husband, a noted resistance leader, arrive in Casablanca pursued by the Nazis. Bogart was never more cynical or honorable, Bergman never more alluring. Rounded out by Paul Henreid, Sydney Greenstreet, Peter Lorre, Tyler's own Dooley Wilson singing "As Time Goes By," Conrad Veidt as the quintessential Nazi villain, the incomparable Claude Rains, crackling dialogue, and more atmosphere than a half-dozen movies, *Casablanca* won Academy Awards for best picture, director (Michael Curtiz), and screenplay.

The decade of the 1940s was a busy one for Humphrey Bogart. He made 11 films, including *The Maltese Falcon* and *High Sierra*, and fought the war in more movies than any other major star. In addition to playing Rick in *Casablanca*, he was an army officer pretending to be a traitor in *Across the Pacific*, a merchant marine in *Action in the North Atlantic*, a tank commander in *Sahara*, an escaped Devil's Island convict who joins a bomber crew in *Passage to Marseilles*, and, in a sizzling pairing with Lauren Bacall, a cynical gun runner on the island of Martinique in *To Have and Have Not*.

Movie cartoons, written as much for adults as children (if not more so) took advantage of the good/evil conflict presented by the war to build morale while lampooning the Germans and Japanese at every opportunity.

In a series of cartoons produced throughout the war, Warner Brothers championed the Allied effort by pitting the hapless enemy against the wily, wacky antics of Bugs Bunny and Daffy Duck.

In *Daffy the Commando*, Daffy Duck is shot down behind the German lines. Far from being afraid, the irrepressible Daffy tweaks, terrorizes, and generally humiliates the pompous German General Rooster, whom he derisively refers to as "Herr Von Limberger." Bugs Bunny delivers a similar treatment to Hitler himself in *Herr Meets Hare*. In *Russian Rhapsody*, Hitler decides to bomb Russia personally, only to have his airplane bedeviled by "Gremlins from the Kremlin."

In *Super Rabbit*, Bugs Bunny championed the cause of the marines in a cartoon that no doubt brought laughs to Texan audiences. Fortified by super vitaminized carrots, Bugs flies—literally—to Deepinaharta, Texas, to thwart a jack rabbit hunt. When his carrots fail him, Bugs announces, "This looks like a job for a real superman" and dashes into

A Marine posts notice: Jap hunting licenses issued here.
(Institute of Texan Cultures, *The San Antonio Light* Collection)

a telephone booth. He emerges wearing a marine uniform and singing "From the Halls of Montezuma," then says, "I can't play anymore because I've got important work to do."

The Ducktators was a web-footed Warner Brothers parody of Hitler, Mussolini, and Hirohito. Midway through the cartoon, a note from "The Management" appeared on the screen in the form of an apology to the "nice ducks and geese who may be in the audience."

Fifth Column Mouse, another Warner Brothers product, warned against the dangers of appeasement. An evil cat promises cheese to a weak mouse if he will induce his fellow mice to come over to the cat's side. To the tune of "Blues in the Night," the mouse makes his case, singing, "He came here to save us, not to enslave us, appease him." The other mice agree, but soon regret their decision when the cat begins to cast an eye over them for dinner. Told, again in song, to "Grit your teeth, show some fight; we did it before and we can do it again," the mice revolt and drive the cat out.

Dozens of references to the war found their way into other Warner Brothers cartoons as well. In *Little Red Riding Hare*, Granny leaves a note tacked to her door telling her granddaughter she's working the "swingshift at Lockheed." In *Sooner Crooner*, Porky Pig is the owner of the "Flockheed Eggcraft Factory."

World War II was the best reported war in history. American correspondents wrote their stories from the beachheads and frontlines, from the decks of battleships and the cockpits of long-range bombers. Wherever the war was to be found, so too were the men and women of the press.

> *"This is London at 3:30 in the morning....Again the Germans have been sending their bombers singly or in pairs. The anti-aircraft barrage has been fierce but sometimes there have been periods of 20 minutes when London has been silent. That silence is almost hard to bear. One becomes accustomed to rattling windows and the distant sound of bombs and then there comes a silence that can be felt. You know the sound will return—you wait, and then it starts again. That waiting is bad. It gives you a chance to imagine things."*
> —Edward R. Murrow

> *"Berlin was a kind of orchestrated hell, a terrible symphony of light and flame. It isn't a pleasant kind of warfare—the men doing it speak of it as a job. Yesterday afternoon, when the tapes were stretched out on the big map all the way to Berlin and back again, a young pilot with old eyes said to me, 'I see we're working again tonight.'"*
> —Edward R. Murrow

Reporting from London beginning in the 1930s, Edward R. Murrow set the standard for war coverage. He assembled a team of journalists who reported war as it had never been done before, bringing an immediacy and haunting sense of reality to his listeners across the Atlantic in America. Standing on rooftops during the long nights of German bombings, riding on minesweepers in the North Sea and on RAF bombers over Berlin, Murrow made war all too real.

Reporting "on the spot" were dozens of American radio, wire service, and newspaper correspondents. Attached to military units throughout the European and Pacific fronts, they went unarmed into battle. Many were wounded—one received 29 wounds in a single naval landing—and more than 30 were killed.

Texan Walter Cronkite, then reporting for United Press, described a bombing raid over Germany as "an assignment to hell—a hell 26,000 feet above the earth." Larry Allen of the Associated Press reported the sinking of the British battleship HMS *Barham*, which vanished before his eyes. "It happened so quickly that it was difficult to believe....

Ernie Pyle two days before leaving Guam. This picture was taken by Capt. Edward J. Steichen, USNR. (U.S. Navy)

Five minutes previously the *Barham* had been steaming majestically. . . . Now she didn't exist."

Stanley Johnston of the *Chicago Tribune* was aboard the carrier USS *Lexington* when it was sunk during the battle of the Coral Sea. Five torpedo hits on the port side had set the ship ablaze, Johnston wrote, when an officer, assessing the damage, reported to his captain, "I would suggest, sir, that if you have to take any more torpedoes you take 'em on the starboard side."

Hugh Baillie of United Press reported the war from the viewpoint of a single group of men: Pete Peterson, the fighter pilot who didn't come back from a mission over Germany, and his waiting squadron. "Finally, after hours of waiting as long as they thought they could, Pete's crowd fueled up their fighters. They went back over the area where they had fought. The boys flew around, hunting and looking, hunting and looking, until their gas ran low. That night there was a vacancy at the head table in the mess—a vacancy but no mourning. Pilots aren't like that."

Of all the war correspondents, none was more idolized by the average GI than Ernie Pyle, whose columns reflected a self-described "worm's eye view" of the war. His dispatches spoke volumes about the loneliness of boys far from home who became men all too quickly.

Reporting from the battlefields of Tunisia, Pyle wrote of the "ghosts" that kept sleep from coming to weary soldiers:

Concussion ghosts, traveling in waves, touched our tent walls and made them quiver. Ghosts were shaking the ground ever so lightly. Ghosts were stirring the dogs to hysteria. Ghosts were everywhere, and their hordes were multiplying as every hour added its production of new battlefield dead.

Ten days before that dispatch was printed in the *New York World-Telegram*, Ernie Pyle was killed by a Japanese sniper on the island of Ie Shima. GIs placed a marker where he died:

> At this spot the
> 77th Infantry Division
> Lost a buddy
> ERNIE PYLE
> 18 April 1945

Most Texas newspapers relied upon the wire services—Associated Press and United Press—for their war coverage. The *Dallas Morning News*, however, sent its own correspondent, Wick Fowler, to the field.

Fowler described the war in a language any Texan could understand—often using metaphors from Friday-night football. George Patton's drive on Metz was "nothing more than an off-tackle smash run from the double wing formation." When the French battled back after four years of Nazi humiliation, "they drove with the same resolve that Lubbock tears into Amarillo—or vice versa—if one has beaten the other for four consecutive years." Winston Churchill elegantly described Britain's stand against Hitler as his nation's "finest hour." Fowler saw it as a classic "goal line stand."

Fowler's dispatches—usually datelined simply "With the 36th Division," "Third Army Front" or "Southern France"—were filled with vignettes about his fellow Texans. He told of a sergeant from Austin repairing vehicles at the frontline, a Dallas infantry officer who broke through the German lines at Verdun, a colonel from Fort Worth who led the rebuilding of the Port of Marseilles, and the reunion of two brothers from Mount Vernon who hadn't seen each other in three years. These men, and thousands like them, were the husbands, sons, fathers, brothers, and friends his readers held close in their hearts and prayers.

Fowler, like all correspondents, led a nomadic life. His expense records failed to meet the requirements of *Morning News* accountants, who wanted an explanation of how he spent the paper's money. Fowler sent back a piece of paper sack on which he had written:

Covering War: $500.

As important as the words of war were its pictures. And nowhere were the pictures of war more eloquent than on the pages of *Life* magazine. Barely a half-decade old in 1941, *Life* almost seemed to have been created with war in mind. Its large size and emphasis on photographs made it perfect for recording the events and images of war.

Life's roster of staff and free-lance photographers during the war was impressive: Alfred Eisenstaedt, Edward Steichen, Margaret Bourke-White, Robert Capa, George Strock, and W. Eugene Smith.

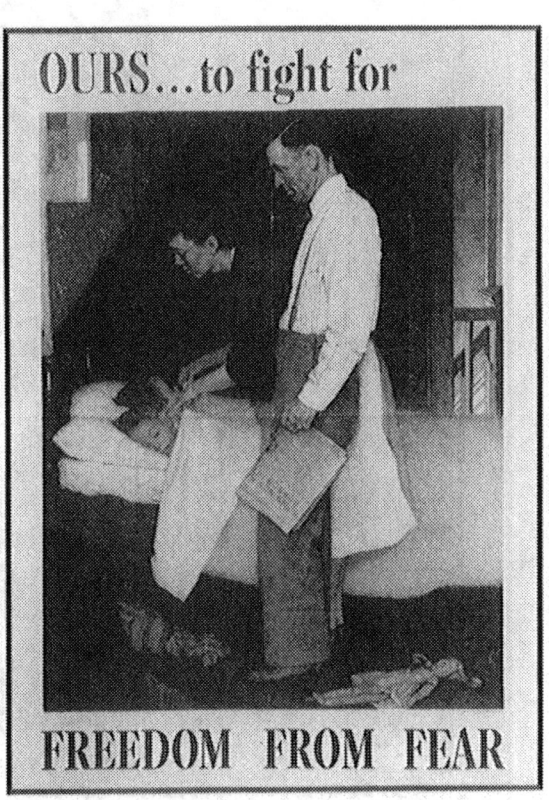

Steichen immortalized the men of the aircraft carrier USS *Lexington*, recording images of victory, fatigue, and anxiety. Bourke-White photographed air force bombing missions over Tunisia, the siege of Moscow, the Italian campaign, and accompanied the army into Berlin. Strock's photo of three dead GIs on the beach at Buna was one of the first photos of American casualties to be approved by the censors.

Robert Capa, born Endre Friedmann in Budapest, already was famous for his photographs of the Spanish Civil War. During World War II he became even more famous for his photographs of the battles of Salerno and Bastogne, the D-Day landing at Normandy, the liberation of Paris, and the taking of the city of Leipzig, where a soldier he was about to photograph was killed by a sniper. Sickened, Capa took pictures of the young man's blood pooling on the floor. Less than 10 years later, Capa would die after stepping on a land mine while photographing French troops in North Vietnam.

Around the world in the Pacific, Eugene Smith covered 13 invasions as American troops fought their way toward Japan. He landed at Tarawa, Saipan, Guam, Leyte, Iwo Jima, and, finally, Okinawa. Smith's photographs were stark and uncompromising—twisted Japanese dead at Tarawa, wounded Americans on Saipan—and he often risked his life to be at the frontlines. On Iwo Jima, he was pinned down by the crossfire between an American

Hellcat taking off from the deck of the USS *Lexington*, photographed by Edward Steichen (U.S. Navy)

IWO JIMA FLAG

It was 1959, and I was having lunch with Bernard Holly, Keith Wells, and another man or two in the Hotel Wooten Coffee Shop in Abilene. The Hotel Wooten was famous for the fact that once the big neon sign atop its 15 stories shorted out and read "Hot— Woo—."

Bernard and Keith were oilmen—petroleum engineers, geologists, whatever. I was a columnist for the Abilene Reporter News. *Keith and Bernard had been marines in World War II, as I had been, but Keith had been a captain and Bernard was the gung-ho type who eagerly volunteered for suicide missions. In 1959 marines still talked a lot about "The War," and when I mentioned Iwo Jima, that 1945 island landing that cost 50 percent of every unit that made it, Bernard said, "Hey, you want a story? You know the flag raising on Iwo? On top of Suribachi? That picture that's in every book about the war?"*

"Well," Bernard continued, "that was the second flag raising. Keith and I were part of the first flag raising on Iwo Jima."

Keith laughed. "I almost wasn't. I'd been wounded earlier—pretty badly, as it turned out—but a bunch of us fought our way up Mount Suribachi and drove out most of the Japanese from the top. When what was left of my platoon and I finally made it, there was ol' Bernard Holly with what was left of his squad. The top of Mount Suribachi wasn't the pleasantest place in the Pacific right then."

Keith from the Panhandle and Bernard from Abilene had known each other on Guadalcanal, but hadn't seen each other for several months, being with different outfits. But there wasn't time for playing old home week or even shaking hands, with bullets flying. One of Keith's GIs carried a small American flag he'd brought off the troop ship, about 3 x 4, and Keith said, "Hey, let's put it up so the rest of the island will know we've got Suribachi." The heights of Suribachi had been the dominant Japanese position, overlooking the whole island.

Keith explained, "Some general or admiral aboard the command ship saw that little flag through his binoculars, and he called ashore for a party to be sent up Suribachi with a larger flag and a proper flagpole to officially show the colors. Joe Rosenthal, a photographer with the Associated Press, went with the party. They made their way up, and Rosenthal shot that photo, and as they say, the rest is history."

Even the second flag raising was dangerous; many of the men of both parties died before the fighting ended. Bernard Holly and Keith Wells didn't see each other for the remainder of the war (Keith spent weeks in a hospital), and it was years later they discovered they were both living in Abilene—not quite as surprising as meeting on Suribachi where two marines out of the thousands who hit Iwo Jima ran into each other in an unscheduled episode that involved a handful of men from two different outfits—and 14 years later found themselves telling about it.

Wars do a lot of funny things like that.

—A. C. Greene

---

tank and a piece of Japanese field artillery for more than an hour. At Okinawa, his last assignment of the war, Smith was wounded by shrapnel on the mouth, face, and hand.

One famous photograph that didn't make its way into *Life* was taken, ironically, on Iwo Jima on the day that Smith was caught in the crossfire. It was there that wire service photographer Joe Rosenthal took the photo of marines raising the American flag during the heat of battle. *Life* refused to publish the photo because it had been staged.

Along with the photographers and writers whose work filled the pages of *Life* each week were a small group of artists who provided sketches and paintings from the frontlines. Among these was Texan Tom Lea.

Lea made four trips overseas for *Life*, one annually from 1941 to 1944. On his second assignment, he spent 64 days aboard the aircraft carrier *Hornet*, leaving just three days before it was sunk by the Japanese. Often providing the text accompanying his paintings, Lea's words were equally affecting:

Around us the air is full of black popcorn. ... Men look up at the sky and read how close they are to death. A bomb hits off our stern—a near miss—throwing a towering, white, slow column of water high above the flight deck. The bomber that dropped it zooms up, as our anti-aircraft guns converge on him. He climbs into the crossfire and in the roar and confusion we see suddenly a burst of flame on his starboard wing and his climb slows, reaches the top and suddenly he is slipping back sideways. You find that your teeth are clinched so hard that you can hardly get the words out that you want to say— "Fall, you bastard, fall."

The July 11, 1945 issue of *Life* carried Lea's final assignment: a seven-page spread on the marine invasion of Peleliu Island, a speck on the map of the Pacific heavily fortified by the Japanese. Lea described in words and drawings what the first 32 hours of invasion was like for an individual marine. He knew what it was like, because he'd done it—landed on the beach under fire. He passed a bomb crater and saw that it had been converted into a field hospital by a doctor who was performing surgery. Lea and another correspondent took cover in a foxhole and became aware of someone crawling toward them: a corpsman who thought they were dead. He saw a dying marine staggering along the beach, his face bloody, one arm barely attached to his body. Another marine, shell-shocked, stood quietly, waiting, his eyes staring into the distance at nothing.

"You are so afraid," Lea wrote, "that you come out the other side finally, and you are not afraid any more."

Newspaper and magazine advertisers attached their own unique perspectives to the war effort. Aside from the usual urgings to buy bonds, save scrap, and produce more, merchants couched their sales pitches in the language of the times.

(*Brief*)

Texas Ranger
(Texas State Archives)

Not only did pilots and crewmen name their planes fanciful names, they painted elaborate pictures on the noses and sides of bombers and fighters. These photos reproduce some of the "nose art" to be found on navy, air force, and marine aircraft.

Belle of Texas
(*Brief*)

Texas Goes to War 113

An optometrist stressed the need for workers to achieve "visual efficiency." Drinking milk produced "vitamins for victory," according to a dairy. Adults were told to conserve their clothes by having them dry-cleaned regularly. Department stores offered tips on smart buying. Telephone callers were told to make their conversations "fewer and shorter" to clear long distance lines for war-related calls. Women were encouraged to buy a series of dress patterns at their local stores, then learn to sew by radio as part of the "McCall Sewing Corps."

Cartoonist Bill Mauldin's popularity with the American public was exceeded only by the affection of the GIs he portrayed. First published in the *45th Division News*, Mauldin's biting cartoons eventually made their way into *Stars and Stripes*, the official armed forces newspaper, and numerous stateside publications including *Life*.

His most frequent subjects were two classic "footsloggers," Willie and Joe. Weary, dirty, and tired, they endured the misery of war and more than their share of army snafus and rules. Mauldin, an infantryman himself, knew of what he drew: he spent most of the war on the battlefields of Europe and had first-hand knowledge of the indignities soldiers often were subjected to, not by the enemy but by their own.

One cartoon showed an officer refusing Willie and Joe admittance to a club because they were not dressed according to regulations. "Them buttons was shot off," Willie says, "when we took this town, sir." Mauldin received a minor shoulder wound and, by regulation, was awarded a Purple Heart. In a subsequent cartoon, Willie was shown at an aid station, where a medic was attempting to give him a medal, too. "Just gimme th' aspirin," he tells the medic. "I already got a Purple Heart."

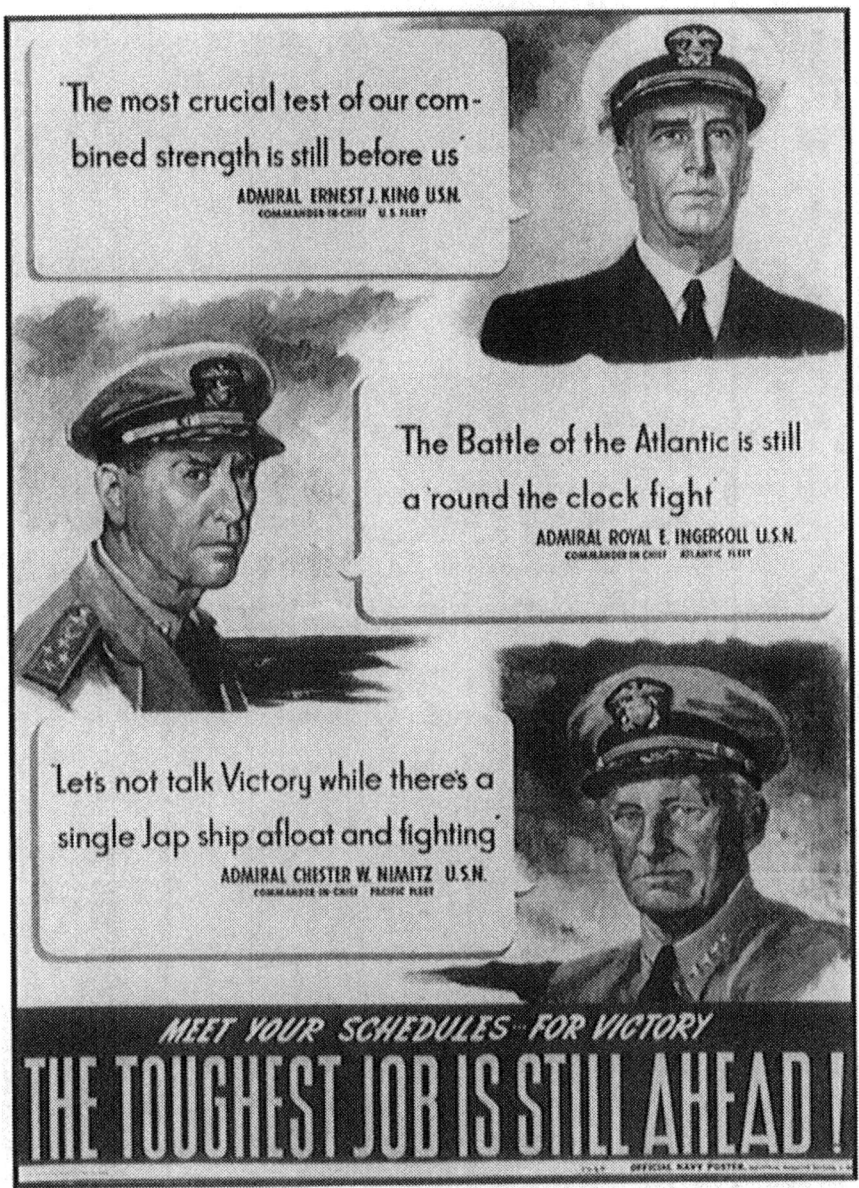

Though popular with the dogfaces, Mauldin's cartoons drew the wrath of many commanding officers. The fastidious General Patton, who ordered his men on the front fined for sloppy dress, once summoned Mauldin to his headquarters and berated him for lacking respect for authority and discipline. Others, however, including General Eisenhower, viewed Mauldin's work as a necessary and useful venting of frustration.

While reading *Stars and Stripes* in 1945, Mauldin learned that he had won the Pulitzer Prize. Prizes and medals meant little to him. What mattered to him was that the real Willie was buried in a grave near Anzio.

TEXAS MINORITIES WAGE WAR

> If Hitler wins, every single right we now possess, for which we have struggled for more than three centuries will be instantly wiped out. If the Allies win, we shall at least have the right to continue fighting for a share of democracy for ourselves.
>
> —W. E. B. DuBois, Editor
> NAACP's *Crisis*

by
DAVID ZIMMERMANN

Steward First Class Leonard Harmon died while evacuating wounded from the USS *San Francisco* during a naval battle in the Pacific. The U.S. Navy posthumously decorated Harmon with the Navy Cross and named an escort destroyer in his honor.

Sgt. José M. Lopez singlehandedly held off a German assault, providing K Company with enough time to safely withdraw before being overrun. Lopez received the Congressional Medal of Honor for his heroic defense of his unit.

Platoon Leader Saburo Tanamachi was killed as he tried to aid a wounded buddy during the 442nd Regimental Combat Team's desperate attempt to save the 1st Battalion of the "Texas Army." Tanamachi, posthumously awarded the Silver Star and Purple Heart, was one of the first two Japanese-Americans buried at Arlington National Cemetery with full military honors.

The courage and determination of these men was matched by many others during the war. Both on the home front and in battle, Americans fought to destroy the threat of the Axis Powers. However, these three men shared a common trait that makes their contributions to the war effort especially significant: each was a member of a minority group that suffered the brunt of American prejudices at that time.

U.S. Naval policy prevented Leonard Harmon from serving in any capacity other than steward or messman because he was an African-American.

As a Mexican-American, José Lopez would be denied service in a South Texas cafe after he had received the Medal of Honor.

Because of his Japanese ancestry, Saburo Tanamachi was classified as unfit for service by the armed forces until January 1943.

AFRICAN-AMERICAN TEXANS

> The first crack to appear in the Hitlerian foolishness was the theory of racial superiorities. It wasn't the intellectual George Washington Carver—or the great men of Poland and Russia. It was the brute force of physical contact—the only thing the Nazi psychology can understand. Joe Louis liquidated Max Schmelling in two minutes and eleven seconds, and the Master Race wondered.
>
> —Sgt. Bill Davidson, *Yank*
> February 13, 1944

(Mountain Empire Historical Society, Col. Morris H. Marcus Collection)

Chaplain's assistants—9th, 27th, and 2nd Cavalry Division Headquarters Troop
(Mountain Empire Historical Society, Col. Morris H. Marcus Collection)

> In 1939, there were only five black officers in the U.S. military. Three were chaplains.

But many Americans didn't wonder. They didn't rethink their own theories of racial superiority. "Hitlerian foolishness" was not a product solely of Nazi Germany. It was also a part of American life—and it would shape the role that many Texans played in World War II.

Many African-Americans saw the Second World War as an opportunity to prove themselves. According to Tuskegee Airman Lt. Melvin Sikes, "We thought if we could prove that we were patriotic, if we could prove that we could fight, we would be accepted as first class citizens. But, they didn't want to let us fight."

At the outbreak of the war, African-Americans were not allowed in the marines or the air corps. In the navy, blacks were allowed to serve only as messmen and stewards. The army had some "colored combat units," including the 9th and 10th Cavalry Regiments.

Texas Goes to War   119

Ninth Cavalry soldiers practice firing with .50-caliber water-cooled gun. Although the 9th and 10th Cavalry did spend time touring the U.S. to help sell war bonds, both units were trained for combat duty.
(Mountain Empire Historical Society, Col. Morris H. Marcus Collection)

DALLAS BOOSTS WAR BOND SALES

Dallas editor Felix McKnight recalls a rally at the Good Street Baptist Church, which included Mayor Bob Thornton and boxing great Jack Dempsey. McKnight says the all-black crowd, many of whom were very wealthy, got excited, and the rally turned into something of a revival meeting. He says Thornton would call out to a crowd member: "Maceo Smith, what are you gonna buy?" Smith would quietly respond, "Twenty thousand dollars worth." Thornton would then yell to the crowd, "Maceo Smith says he's gonna buy forty thousand dollars worth." McKnight says this rally yielded tremendous sales.

During the war, five African-Americans graduated from West Point.

When the 9th and 10th Regiments were transferred to the 2nd Cavalry Division on October 10, 1940, it became the first multiracial unit in what had been a segregated army. Second Cavalry was headquartered at Fort Clark, Texas, the former home of MacKenzie's raiders, the Negro Seminole Scouts, George Patton, and George Marshall. Like the 9th Cavalry which also was stationed there, Fort Clark had a long and proud history.

The soldiers in the 9th and 10th Regiments were equipped in traditional cavalry uniform: riding boots and breeches, campaign hats with broad brims, and spurs. Each soldier was assigned two horses, although some of the men purchased their own mounts. According to Lt. Albert Bly, "we took care of our horses before ourselves, because they checked on the horses more than us."

In an army of draftees, the 9th and 10th Regiments were professional soldiers. Their predecessors, "the Buffalo Soldiers" had served in the Indian Campaigns, saved Roosevelt's Rough Riders in the Spanish-American War, and accompanied "Black Jack" Pershing into Mexico. Yet during the Second World War their duties were limited to performing in stateside bond drives.

Gen. James Walker, last commander of the 5th Cavalry Brigade before the brigade was sent to North Africa
(Mountain Empire Historical Society, Col. Morris H. Marcus Collection)

In 1944, the white units of the 2nd Cavalry Division were transferred and, like most white cavalry units, transformed into armored divisions. Almost a year later, 2nd Cavalry was dismounted and systematically deactivated. The once-proud Buffalo Soldiers of Fort Clark became service units in a North African port.

The deactivization of the 9th and 10th Cavalry Regiments sparked a controversy in Congress over the military's delay in assigning larger numbers of African-Americans to combat duty. As a result of the criticism by politicians, newspapers, and African-Americans themselves, two black divisions, the 92nd and 93rd, were sent to Italy and the Pacific. The regimental flags of the 9th and 10th Cavalry, though, had been unfurled for the last time during the war.

Prairie View A&M had one of the few Reserve Officer Training Corps for African-Americans in this country at the beginning of the war. The program had been organized in 1918.

African-American and Anglo cavalry troops participate in ceremony
(Mountain Empire Historical Society, Col. Morris H. Marcus Collection)

The navy, like the army, was reluctant to assign blacks to combat duty. Although it had once again begun to accept African-Americans for service in 1932, the navy continued to establish regulations that excluded blacks from serving in combat. Only a few of the 150,000 African-Americans who served in the navy during World War II saw battle. Of those who did, four won the Navy Cross, and two of those were Texans.

The first hero of the war was a black navy messman from Texas, whose washing was interrupted by torpedoes exploding against the hull of his ship docked in Pearl Harbor.

Col. Marcus (right), last regimental commander of the 9th Cavalry
(Mountain Empire Historical Society, Col. Morris H. Marcus Collection)

Ninth Cavalry baseball team, champions of the 2nd Cavalry Division, 1943
(Mountain Empire Historical Society, Col. Morris H. Marcus Collection)

"Dorie Miller, Texas-born, Texas-raised."
(Institute of Texan Cultures)

Mess Attendant Doris Miller, the son of a Waco sharecropper, had joined the navy in 1939 to help support his family. His mother, Mrs. Henrietta Miller, recalls that "We were kinda hungry in those days. He wanted to help out."

When the USS *West Virginia* was hit in Pearl Harbor, Doris Miller and Lt. Frederick White, whose shoes it was Miller's duty to shine, met on deck and began to help evacuate the wounded. They were then ordered to the bridge to help move the ship's fatally wounded captain. Once he had carried the dying officer from the bridge, Miller returned to the deck with White. There, amid enemy gunfire, Miller manned a .50-caliber machine gun and began firing at the Japanese fighters. Although he had attended battery school, Miller had not been allowed to touch or operate the guns because of his race. Despite his inexperience as a gunner, some sources credit him with as many as four kills. Miller once said, "It wasn't hard. I just pulled the trigger and she worked fine. I had watched the other guys with these guns."

Stories of "an unnamed Negro hero" were circulated for almost four months before Miller's name was publicized by the Pittsburgh *Courier*. The press and navy masculinized his name to "Dorie," and he was eventually dubbed by the navy and the press as "Dorie Miller, Texas-born, Texas-raised."

At first the navy would only award Miller a letter of commendation. Bills to award him the Medal of Honor were presented to Congress and defeated. Finally in May 1942, acting on orders from President Roosevelt, the Secretary of the Navy presented Doris Miller with the Navy Cross, the navy's highest medal.

Doris Miller went on to serve on the USS *Liscome* and died on November 24, 1943, when the ship was lost with all hands. He was still a steward. On June 30, 1973, a destroyer escort was named in his honor.

On July 10, 1943, the destroyer escort USS *Harmon* was christened by Mrs. Naunita Harmon Carroll, mother of Leonard Harmon, and launched at Hingham, Massachusetts. The first fighting ship to be named for an African-American, the *Harmon* was assigned to the 3rd Fleet in the South Pacific, where it earned three battle stars. A navy promotional poster with pictures of the *Harmon,* the Navy Cross, and Leonard Harmon bore the inscription "a fighting ship named for a fighting man."

Leonard Roy Harmon, an African-American from Cuero, Texas, joined the navy the same year as Doris Miller and eventually became a messman aboard the USS *San Francisco.*

Near the Solomon Islands, the *San Francisco* engaged a Japanese naval group. During the battle, Harmon's ship destroyed three smaller ships and disabled a battleship, but the *San Francisco* was badly damaged.

Harmon began to help evacuate the wounded while the ship was still under attack. According to the navy citation:

Harmon rendered invaluable assistance for caring for the wounded and evacuating them to a dressing station. In addition to displaying unusual bravery in behalf of the injured executive officer, he deliberately exposed himself to hostile gunfire in order to protect a shipmate and as a result of his courageous deed, he was killed.

Steward First Class Leonard R. Harmon was posthumously awarded the Navy Cross.

One year later, a submarine chaser and the destroyer *Mason* were staffed with black crews. It would not be until 1945 that the first black naval officer would report for duty.

More restrictive than the navy, the army air corps had entirely excluded African-Americans from its ranks on the assumption that blacks would not make competent fighter pilots. When the Civilian Pilot's Program was initiated by Congress in 1939, African-Americans were among those who began pilot training at air fields across the country. In 1940, with the passage of the Selective Training and Service Act, the air corps was forced to begin recruiting and training African-American pilots.

Three Tuskegee bombardier cadets pose for a graduation photo at the San Angelo air field.

On January 16, 1940, the army air corps initiated what the Commanding General of the Southeastern Air Corps called the "Tuskegee Experiment." The 99th Pursuit Squadron, made up of African American pilots was formed and began its training at Tuskegee, a small town east of Montgomery, Alabama.

Sam Daniels had entered the military as a musician, playing the saxophone in an army band. Forced to join the air corps, he was reluctant to join the Tuskegee Experiment because he knew that he wouldn't be able to use his pilot's skills after the war. Daniels had been taught how to fly before the war at Stinson Field in San Antonio. He was interested in airplanes and had gotten some odd jobs at the field to learn more about them. Eventually, Daniels approached Chuck Woodchick, who had a flight school at Stinson, about lessons. Despite the warnings of his friends that teaching a black to fly would hurt business, Woodchick agreed to teach Daniels. After his training at Tuskegee, Sam Daniels went on to fly with the 99th Pursuit Squadron over Italy.

While in Italy providing flying artillery cover for the British 8th Army, the pilots of the 99th established an extraordinary record of combat service, even though they were often given hand-me-down planes that white pilots would no longer use.

The first squadron to down five enemy aircraft in less than four minutes, they were respectfully nicknamed the *Schwarze Vogelmencher* (Black Birdmen) by the Germans.

As more pilots emerged from Tuskegee, the 332nd Fighter Group was formed. It was composed of three squadrons—the 100th, the 301st, and the 302nd. The 332nd initially fought as attack squadrons and later served as bomber escort wings. The 332nd Fighter Group became the only bomber escort never to lose a bomber. A bomber pilot later told Lt. Sikes that he was always glad to see the black pilots because then he knew he would return safely. The 332nd also recorded the first destruction of a destroyer with fighter aircraft.

The 332nd Fighter Group finished the war with a Distinguished Unit Award. The 99th and 332nd had also received 155 Distinguished Flying Crosses.

Some Tuskegee airmen were transferred to Hondo Army Airfield to begin training as bomber navigators in Squadron 10, where they met whites in integrated classrooms, mess halls, and recreation halls, but were still assigned separate barracks.

In February 1944, amid a great deal of publicity, Squadron 10 began a final pre-combat training flight. The 21 cadets navigated six specially modified C-60 Lockheed Lodestars—one of which was aptly named the *Hondo Hound*—on a tour of several cities, including Chicago, New York, and Pittsburgh. Besides serving as a training flight, the stops provided publicity for bond drives.

Tuskegee Graduating Class

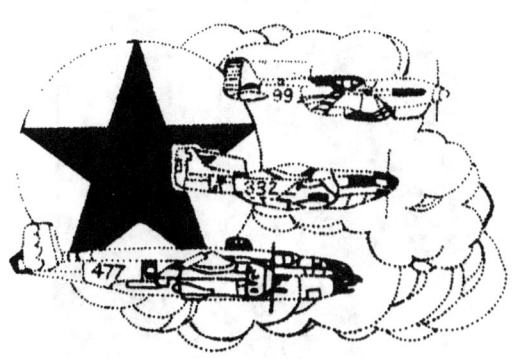

Later that month, the cadets were commissioned at Selgfridge, Michigan, as second lieutenants and flight officers and were assigned to the 477th Bombardment Group.

If the Tuskegee program was an experiment, it reinforced what blacks had proven throughout United States' military history. African-Americans could fight for their country if they were given the opportunity. Not only did they overcome the hardships and dangers of the battlefield, they proved that they would not be stopped by the prejudices of the country for which they fought.

TUSKEGEE AIRMEN COMBAT RECORD

	Destroyed	Damaged	Total
Aircraft (aerial)	111	25	136
Aircraft (ground)	150	123	273
Barges and Boats	16	24	40
Box Cars, Other Rolling Stock	58	561	619
Gun Emplacements	0	23	23
Destroyers	1	0	1
Horse-drawn Vehicles	15	100	115
Motor Transports	6	81	87
Power Transformers	3	2	5
Locomotives	57	69	126
Radar Installations	1	8	9
Tanks on Flat Cars	0	7	7

Total Missions:
- 12th Air Force 1,267
- 15th Air Force 311
- Grand Total Missions: 1,578

Total Sorties:
- 12th Air Force 6,381
- 15th Air Force 9,152
- Grand Total Sorties: 15,533

Total No. Pilots Sent Overseas: 450

Total No. Pilots Graduated at Tuskegee: 992

Total Killed in Action: 66

Awards:
- Legion of Merit 1
- Silver Star 1
- Soldier Medal 2
- Purple Heart 8
- Distinguished Flying Cross* 95
- Bronze Star 14
- Air Medal and Clusters 744

*Final total of Distinguished Flying Crosses awarded to Negro pilots estimated at 150
(Record through June 9, 1945)

MEXICAN-AMERICAN TEXANS

Today on the battlegrounds of the world, where free men are fighting for their dignity and honor and the cause of freedom, the names of Mexico-Texans stand out... Garcia... Longoria... Hidalgo... Lopez... Villarreal... Vasquez... Segura... Rubio...

Brownsville and the Valley stand out along with such cities and areas as San Antonio, Laredo, El Paso, and other border towns, for the fighting Mexico-Texas breed. Our boys have proved themselves.
—Clarence LaRoche, Brownsville *Herald*
January 21, 1945

At the opening of World War II, segregation in Texas was not limited to African-Americans. Mexican-Americans were often the victims of Jim Crow laws throughout the state. Many Texas towns had separate schools, churches, and cemeteries for their Hispanic citizens. Yet Tejanos retained a pride in their heritage, in their state, and in their country. When the Japanese bombed Pearl Harbor, Mexican Texans from across the state answered their country's call to service.

Ruben Moreno was 18 years old when he accompanied a friend to the navy recruiting office. Moreno recalls that he chose the navy because he didn't think they would take him, but take him they did. It was his friend who had to argue with the recruiting officer before being admitted.

Moreno was assigned to the USS *Chandler*, a 350-foot-long minesweeper in the Pacific. During his tour, Moreno saw several dogfights between American and Japanese fighters. He even watched a battleship sink a Japanese fighter plane that flew too close to the water on a suicide run. But it was at Iwo Jima that Moreno witnessed some of the most memorable events of his tour.

Two days before the marines landed at Iwo Jima, the *Chandler* arrived to begin its zigzagging sweep for mines. From its deck, Moreno had a clear view of the island as it was pounded by shells from battleships firing over the *Chandler* from five to six miles out at sea. After the battleships had finished, planes began bombing the island. When the marines landed, Moreno watched as they fought and

128 TEXAS MINORITIES AT WAR

Ruben Moreno

died on the beach: "Then came the marines and troops. And they still got killed because the Japs were deep in the ground. I wouldn't have wanted to be on the ground. I was glad I was in the water." As the ship patrolled the harbor that night, he could hear the cries for medics and supplies.

One of the troops who was on the ground during the landing at Ie Shima was Pfc. Joe S. Benavides. Benavides had grown up in Dallas and attended Tech High School before entering the army in 1943. As a member of the 77th Infantry, the "Statue of Liberty Division," he participated in several landings, including those at Guam and Leyete. At Ie Shima, acting as a litter bearer, Benavides retrieved the body of beloved newspaper columnist Ernie Pyle, who was killed by a sniper. Pfc. Benavides returned home with three Bronze Stars and a Bronze Arrowhead.

In Europe, Mexican-Texans were also proving themselves in battle against the Germans and Italians.

USS *Chandler*

TEXAS GOES TO WAR   129

SAN ANTONIO IN 1941

The San Antonio of 1941, where a branch of my family settled in 1731, was a place of "brown blood and white laughter," as I wrote in a poem years later, remembering the city's segregated schools and its English-only rules. Though the war transformed the city economically, a different kind of war would vanquish the barriers that had made San Antonio a divided community and strangers of Tejanos in their own land.

At war, Tejanos showed their mettle. Boys became men. The League of United Latin American Citizens (LULAC) suspended its annual conferences for the duration. On the home front, Tejanos built planes, subs, and gliders; handed out donuts and coffee to America's youth training at Fort Sam Houston, Kelly, and Lackland Air Force bases. Many became air raid wardens. On the West Side, Tejana mothers placed gold stars in their windows.

On the Day of Infamy, I went to the cathedral and prayed, wondering if I could pass for 17, hoping the war would wait for me, waiting for the dawn's early light.

I enlisted in the marines within days of my 17th birthday in 1943, and served in the American, Pacific, and China theaters.

—Felipe de Ortego y Gasca

Pfc. Cruz Benavidez had been assigned to the 75th Infantry when he joined the army. Ben—a nickname given to him by his buddies—served as a scout and rifleman in an attack patrol.

While on patrol near the Belgian town of Velsan, Ben's platoon came upon a small farmhouse. From behind a fence, the soldiers saw that the area around the house had been cleared, giving anyone in the house a clear view of the road. If the troops were to pass in safety, the house had to be checked for German soldiers. One of them would have to move around to the front door within clear view of the window that overlooked the road.

As the first soldier left the cover of the fence, he was killed by a blast of machine-gun fire. The second man was knocked to the ground by another burst. Now, it was Ben's turn. When he stepped from the protection of the fence, he was hit by a bullet that passed through his hand and into his chest, knocking him to the ground. As machine-gun fire ripped into the shrubbery behind him, Ben slid into the tracks a tank had left in the snow. Unable to open his first aid kit, he stuffed snow into his wounds in an attempt to medicate them and staunch the flow of blood.

Jesse Espinosa participated in both the Normandy and Rhineland campaigns.

>
>
> **S/Sgt. Lucian Adams**
>
> Sergeant Adams's company was stopped in the Montagne Forest while attempting to reopen the supply lines to the embattled 3rd Battalion. The company had to stop after losing nine men and only gaining ten yards. They were under attack by a special unit of German soldiers equipped with automatic weapons and grenade throwers. Adams borrowed a Browning Assault Rifle (BAR) and charged into the forest firing the gun from his hip. Having moved within range of a machine gun nest, he killed the gunner with a grenade before shooting another German soldier who was throwing grenades at him. Adams continued moving forward surrounded by the machine-gun fire of another German emplacement. He killed the gunner with a grenade and captured two German infantrymen. Adams resumed his trek through the forest amid the concentrated fire from what remained of the German force. He killed five more Germans before reaching and destroying yet another machine gun.
>
> The Port Arthur native had singlehandedly eliminated a specialized German force and reopened the supply lines. S/Sgt. Lucian Adams received the Medal of Honor for "conspicuous gallantry and intrepidity at the risk of his own life."

When the machine gunner was silenced, the platoon sergeant yelled to the fallen private, "Come on, Ben," thinking that Cruz had merely been diving for cover. After the sergeant discovered that Ben was wounded, he had the private transported to a field hospital behind the lines. The next morning Benavidez woke up to find the man who had gone before him in the next bed suffering from a leg wound.

Benavidez refused to allow the doctors to amputate his hand. Instead, he was sent to a Paris suburb for skin and bone grafts before returning home with corporal's stripes and the Purple Heart.

Tejanos participated in the war effort in various ways at home, and the war transformed their lives just as it did the lives of their fathers, brothers, and sons in the battlefields.

Leon Moreno of Dallas, Texas, is awarded the Bronze Star by Brig. Gen. James Lewis.

The lives of many of the Mexican-Texans in San Antonio were transformed by Roosevelt's call for "50,000 planes with 50,000 pilots." Kelly Field, which had been a fighter base, began to provide essential services in the production and maintenance of airplanes. To meet their production demands, Kelly began hiring and training unskilled labor, including the Tejanos of the west side barrios. Of the 35,000 people working at Kelly during the war, 10,000 were Mexican-Americans. Later, civil rights groups would accuse base officials of discrimination because no Hispanics were employed in positions higher than mechanics' assistants or laborers. At the time, however, it offered impoverished Mexican-Americans an unprecedented opportunity to obtain on-the-job training, with substantial increases in pay.

E. Martínez helps collect donations for British War Relief.
(Institute of Texan Cultures, *The San Antonio Light* Collection)

Sgt. José M. Lopez

When the flank of K Company was in danger of being overrun by German troops, Sgt. Lopez carried a machine gun to a shallow hole and began laying down a protective fire. Although the hole offered Lopez no protection above the waist, he continued to fire as an approaching enemy tank began to shoot at him. Seeing that the enemy troops had begun to outflank him and his company, Lopez moved back and again set up the gun. He was knocked down by the concussion of an exploding shell. Dazed and shaky, Lopez held off the German advance until K Company was able to safely withdraw from the area. Carrying the machine gun in the midst of enemy fire, Lopez joined some members of the company attempting to set up a defense. He fired until he was out of ammunition, and then withdrew to the safety of a nearby village.

José Lopez had originally wanted to join an airborne division, but was refused because he was a father. Sgt. José Lopez of Mission, Texas, was awarded the Medal of Honor for "gallantry and intrepidity on a seemingly suicidal mission," which saved his company from being destroyed.

Pfc. Cleto Rodriguez

During the Battle of Manila, Pfc. Rodriguez's unit was ordered to capture the heavily defended Paco Railway station. To reach the station, his platoon had to cross an open field. One hundred yards from the building, the platoon was pinned down by enemy gunfire. Rodriguez and a buddy moved forward to a house within 60 yards of the station. There, they fired at the Japanese for two hours, killing 35 men. They then moved closer and discovered Japanese replacements attempting to reinforce the fortifications. The two men wiped out the reinforcements. Rodriguez moved closer and threw grenades into the building. With their ammunition running low, the two soldiers began their dash back to the platoon, alternately providing cover for one another. Before reaching the platoon, Rodriguez's friend was killed. Later that same day, Rodriguez would attack a machine gun nest, enabling his companions to advance.

For "gallant determination to destroy the enemy and heroic courage in the face of tremendous odds," San Antonian Cleto Rodriguez was decorated with the Medal of Honor.

Jesucita Casteñada in her Civil Air Patrol Cadet Uniform

Some San Antonio businessmen also were angered because a large, unskilled, cheap labor force had been lost to them. But for many of the city's Tejanos, Kelly Field was an escape from the poverty of the barrios. It was during this time that a corrido (a ballad), became popular on the west side. The song was entitled "*No te me acabes Kelly*" or, loosely translated, "Don't let Kelly die."

Unlike African-Americans, Mexican-Americans were not segregated once they entered the military and were not denied service in any of the three branches, though some of the prejudices of civilian life followed them into the military. An African-American recruit remembers that Fort Hood had three sets of outhouses labeled "Whites, Coloreds, and Mexicans." Nevertheless, many Tejanos discovered what it was to be treated as equals. And when they came home, they brought that realization with them.

TEXAS GOES TO WAR

S/Sgt. Marcario Garcia

Company B was pinned down on a hillside with meager cover. German artillery had begun to concentrate its fire on their position. Although wounded, Garcia refused to be removed for medical treatment. Instead, he crawled up the hill into enemy fire. Having moved within a few yards of an enemy machine gun emplacement, he hurled grenades at the position, destroying the gun, and shot three German soldiers trying to escape. After returning to his company, another machine gun opened fire on their position. Garcia once again moved up the hill alone and destroyed the gun. He then accompanied his unit until they had achieved their objective before allowing himself to be removed for medical treatment.

Marcario, who had been born in Villa de Castano, Mexico, entered the service in Sugarland, Texas. In recognition of "conspicuous bravery" on behalf of his adopted country, S/Sgt. Marcario Garcia was awarded the Medal of Honor.

In 1919, José Garcia settled in Mercedes, Texas, with his family after having fled the revolutions of Mexico. He named two of his children after Aztec emperors and one after the Trojan hero Hector.

Hector Garcia joined the military in 1942 after completing his medical training in Omaha, Nebraska. Garcia fought throughout North Africa and Italy, winning the Bronze Star and six battle stars, but he would win national recognition only after he had returned from the war and begun the battle for equality.

After helping veterans fight discrimination in housing, education, and employment after the war, Garcia formed the GI Forum in 1948 to organize his defense of Mexican-American civil rights. A year later Garcia and the GI Forum came to the aid of the Longoria family when the funeral home in Three Rivers refused to bury the remains of Pfc. Felix Longoria, a Mexican Texan killed during the war. The funeral home refused to allow his family to use its chapel because he was a Mexican-American. Garcia brought the matter to the attention of Sen. Lyndon B. Johnson and the national press. As a result, Longoria was buried with full military honors in Arlington National Cemetery.

Pfc. Silvestre S. Herrera

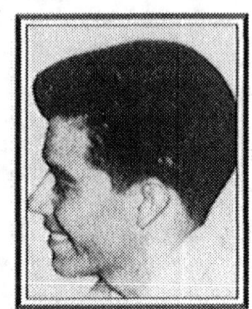

Pfc. Herrera and his platoon were advancing along a wooded road near Mertzwiller, France, when a machine gunner opened fire on them. Although the rest of his platoon dove for cover, Herrera made a frontal assault on the position, capturing eight German soldiers. When the platoon resumed its advance, it was halted by machine-gun fire for a second time. Again, Herrera continued forward alone. He was stopped when an exploding mine tore off his feet, knocking him to the ground. He continued firing on the German position. With cover provided by Herrera's accurate shooting, another squad was able to avoid the minefield and flank the Germans to capture their position.

Pfc. Silvestre Herrera of El Paso, Texas, was awarded the Medal of Honor for "magnificent courage, extraordinary heroism, and willing self sacrifice."

JAPANESE-AMERICAN TEXANS

> We affirm a historic truth here—that loyalty to
> one's country is not modified by racial origins.
> —Inscription on a monument in Bruyères,
> France, dedicated to the 442nd. RCT

Mutsuo Kawamura traveled to San Antonio in order to enlist after having been refused in San Benito. He was the first Japanese-Texan inducted in San Antonio.
(Institute of Texan Cultures, *The San Antonio Light* Collection)

On October 22, 1944, the remnants of the 1st Battalion of the Texas Division were cut off behind German lines during a drive to capture La Houssière. Trapped on a small hill with dwindling supplies, the unit radioed for help. The 442nd Regimental Combat Team was called forward to the rescue.

The 442nd was made up of Japanese-Americans, known as Nisei, sons of Japanese immigrants. Composed primarily of Hawaiians, the 442nd had adopted the motto "Go for broke," Hawaiian gambling slang for betting all the money on a single throw of the dice.

Members of the 442nd Regimental Combat Team relax at a USO club in New York before leaving for the European front.
(Institute of Texan Cultures, courtesy of George R. Kitamura)

The 442nd RCT was "the most decorated regiment in the history of the U.S. Army in relation to time spent in combat."

Although the 12th Air Corps had begun dropping supplies to the men of the 1st Battalion, radio messages continued to describe an increasingly desperate situation. Time was running short when the 442nd started out in the predawn darkness of October 27th, five days after the 1st had been cut off.

The forest separating the 442nd from the 1st Battalion was rugged and heavily defended by German troops. Trees exploded from artillery fire and mines, adding to the danger from German snipers and ambushes. The 442nd slowly pushed forward through the forest, fighting from tree to tree. After two days of costly battle and a night of chilling rain, the 442nd encountered the Germans' main defenses. They had dug in along a narrow ridge, blocking the path to the 1st Battalion.

As the men of the 442nd listened to the cries for help from the 1st, they received word from the rear that the battalion would not last much longer: "Relief must be effected immediately." An attempt to flank the Germans was easily rebuffed. They then attempted to infiltrate the German position with the supporting fire of tanks, but were pinned down. The 442nd was trapped when the order to "fix bayonets" was passed from soldier to soldier. They were going to go for broke.

Two companies led the charge through the narrow path leading to the German position. Firing from the hip, the Nisei advanced directly into enemy fire. The Germans finally broke and ran. The 442nd had captured a position in 30 minutes that would have normally taken two days. The German defense had been broken, but at an incredible cost in casualties to both sides.

The next day the 442nd helped to overcome the final German defenses and finally reached the trapped battalion. The 1st Battalion later recognized the courage and determination of the Nisei of 442nd by declaring them "honorary Texans."

There were a limited number of Japanese-Americans in the U.S. military because of a Selective Service classification that prohibited people from enlisting in the military because of their ancestry. Many Japanese-Americans in the service before the outbreak of war with Japan were discharged after the bombing of Pearl Harbor. However, some Japanese-Americans who remained in the service were not assigned to the 442nd.

U.S. Army Pvt. Shigeru Imai
(442nd Regimental Combat Team)
of Houston, Texas, in Italy
(Institute of Texan Cultures)

A STATEMENT OF LOYALTY

"We were stunned and horrified as we learned of the unprovoked attack on American territory. We have been and are now loyal to the United States of America, the country of our choice, a country of democracy and freedom. We regret that we cannot become American citizens. However, each and every one of us is ready and willing to perform our duty in rendering our service to the United States of America."

—*Statement presented to the FBI by Japanese-Americans of San Antonio, Texas, December 8, 1941.*
(Institute of Texan Cultures, *The San Antonio Light* Collection)

San Antonio's Dodd Field served both as a temporary prisoner of war camp and a debarkation center for returning troops. When the officials at Fort Sam Houston received word that Japanese soldiers were en route to Dodd Field, the officers assumed that the soldiers were prisoners of war. MPs were sent to the rail station to meet the soldiers and escort them to the prison camp at Dodd Field. The "prisoners" were actually Japanese-American soldiers assigned to duty at Dodd, but they were being held prisoner. One of their men escaped that night and carried word to their commanding officer that they were not AWOL.

Anti-Japanese sentiment had been a fact of life for Japanese-Americans long before December 7, 1941. When the Japanese bombed Pearl Harbor, many Americans believed that their hostility and suspicions had been justified. Japanese-Americans were immediately associated with the enemy. On December 7, a roundup of Japanese aliens throughout the country was ordered. In San Antonio, the *Express* reported:

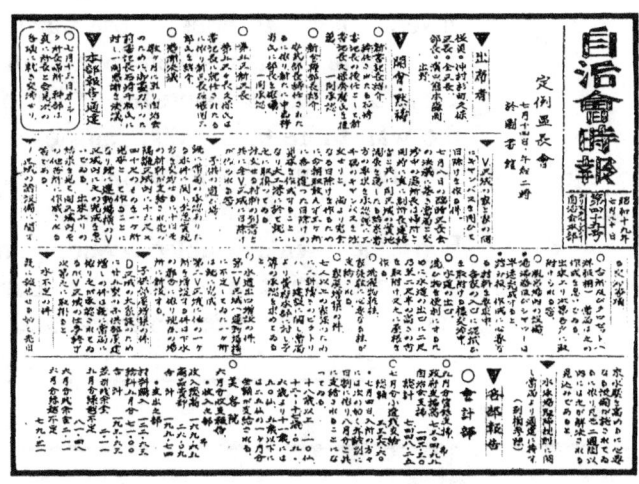

Newspaper printed in a Japanese-American Internment Camp

>Mayor C.K. Quin issued directions to Patrol Capt. Dave Cruz to order city policemen to round up every person of Japanese nationality or descent for questioning.
>
>Quin said that those released would be kept under close surveillance for the duration of the conflict with Japan. All Japanese will be required to report to police headquarters every day, he said, to give accounts of their activities.

Guard rides the fence at the Crystal City, Texas, Internment Camp
(Institute of Texan Cultures, Courtesy Mona Baskin)

On February 19, 1942, Franklin Roosevelt issued an executive order allowing the military to move and intern any group of people it perceived as a threat to national security. Although the order would affect the lives of Germans and Italians, it was mainly directed at Japanese-Americans living on the West Coast.

TEXAS GOES TO WAR 139

The Immigration and Naturalization Service (INS) opened and operated several camps to house those displaced by the Western Defense Command. Three of these camps were located in Texas at Seagoville, Kenedy, and Crystal City. In 1940, there were fewer than 500 Japanese-Americans in Texas. During the war, more than 5,000 Japanese from around the U.S. and various South American countries were confined in Texas camps.

Kenedy was one of the few cities to actually petition for a camp. Hoping to boost the town's troubled economy, the Kenedy Chamber of Commerce asked the government to convert a Civilian Conservation Corps facility to an intern camp. A women's reformatory in Seagoville was used to house female aliens

The graduating class of 1945, Federal High School, Crystal City Internment Camp (Courtesy R. C. Tate, Crystal City)

"FOREWORD"

Though it is not in a true sense a melting pot, Federal High School has in the past two years certainly proved to be a melting pot. Students from near and far—the Pacific coast states, inland states, the territory of Hawaii, and South America—are gathered here in this spot in lower Texas. Homework, tests, basketball, football, baseball, assemblies, class meetings, elections, parties, and picnics—the highlights of a crowded school year—all are recorded in words and pictures in the following pages.

In future years may this annual help you to recall the many pleasant memories of Federal High School.

From the Crystal City *Roundup*, yearbook of the Federal High School, Crystal City Internment Camp.

arrested after the bombing of Pearl Harbor or those deported from other countries. In an attempt to prevent families from being broken apart by detention at separate facilities, the INS built barracks at Seagoville to house entire families. When these were filled by the Japanese from Latin America, the INS began construction of a third camp in Crystal City to house families. This camp would include a high school and grade school for children.

The internment camps operated as small cities. The internees worked at various jobs throughout the camps and battled boredom by playing volleyball, chess, and attending movies. Federal High School at Crystal City had football and volleyball teams.

Late in 1947, Crystal City Internment Camp closed, the last of the three camps in Texas to shut down. The other two camps had been deactivated in the final months of the war. Crystal City remained open because it still contained Japanese from South America. INS classified them as illegal aliens, although they had been brought to the United States by the government, and their immigration papers had been seized by U.S. officials. Many ended up being sent to Japan because the South American countries refused to allow them to return, and the INS would not allow those who wished to stay to remain in the U.S.

Japanese-Americans not interned in the camps were subject to having their homes searched periodically by the FBI. They were also forbidden to own cameras, guns, short-wave radios, and binoculars. Their bank accounts were frozen, and travel was restricted by the government. In some areas, Japanese Texans were aided by their neighbors, who petitioned for their release from internment camps. On the

---

"PROPHECY"

Dusting off my crystal ball I see a vision crystallizing out of the mist—Now I see bright lights and tall buildings. Can it be New York? No, it's Crystal City—1960.

Ah, there's Mayor Shoji Kanogawa going into a dress shop owned by Ayako Hosaka and Doris Kawahira. The mayor explains that he came to check up because they were using up too much material in girdles.

Now we see a beauty shop operated by Emi Uyehara, assisted by Thomas Ikeminya and Albert Matano, finger wave specialists. A few doors down we see Kyoko Uyeshima and Ruth Akata running a lunch room with the aid of Harry Kawaguchi, who handles the job of soda jerk.

In front of the lunch room we see the most-likely-to succeed Bob Uno, now head of the Engineering Department of Sanitation, and better known as a garbage collector. He is ably assisted by Manfred Jacobi.

The crystal is getting murky, and the future is going away slowly. Sigh—now I can go back to bed, for there is no more snooping to do for awhile. See you next semester.

—From the Crystal City Roundup, *yearbook of the Federal High School, Crystal City Internment Camp.*

whole, though, Japanese-Americans were the focus of much of the public's anger and frustration. Indeed, the hostility directed toward the Japanese-Americans was so great that other Asians began wearing buttons to distinguish themselves from the Japanese.

Sgt. Frank Fujita heard the news of the attack on Pearl Harbor aboard a troop transport ship that had just set sail from Hawaii. A member of the 36th Division, Fujita was from Abilene. His mother was an "Oklahoma girl" and his father was from Nagasaki, Japan. When news of the government's roundup of Japanese reached the ship, some of the men began asking if there were any "Japs" on board. Fujita decided that he had better answer the question himself: "So I told them they didn't have a Jap on board. As far as I knew, there was nothing but Americans. But, there was a sergeant on board that was half-Japanese if that made a difference. After that, I didn't hear anything else."

Not all Japanese, though, were able to disarm the hostility directed at them. Instead, they became victims of the nation's fears and ignorance.

In 1918, San Antonio had transformed an old limestone quarry into the Japanese Tea Garden. In an attempt to create an authentic atmosphere, a Japanese family was invited to live at the garden. Kimi E. Jingu, an artist who had painted in the lobby of the Gunter Hotel, and his family moved into two-story house located at the garden. The Jingu family ran the concessions for the park for the next 32 years.

Mrs. Jingu and her five-year-old daughter, Mary, roamed the gardens in traditional kimonos. Mary was constantly being fed by enchanted tourists. Finally, Mrs. Jingu had a small plaque made to hang around Mary's neck that read "Please do not feed me."

Japanese tea gardens
(Institute of Texan Cultures)

Kimi Jingu
(Institute of Texan Cultures)

Helen Eiko Jingu making iced green tea at the Japanese sunken gardens
(Institute of Texan Cultures)

Lillian Jingu, representing the Japanese Junior Red Cross, gives a "good will" packet of seeds to Preston Dial, Jr. The seeds are to be planted by the Alamo in celebration of Armistice Day, 1936.
(Institute of Texan Cultures)

Kimi Jingu died in 1937, but his family continued to live at the Tea Garden until 1941. In response to anti-Japanese sentiment, the city of San Antonio decided to change the name of the garden to the Chinese Tea Garden and evict the Jingus. The Jingu sisters found various jobs to help support their mother, and brother Jimmy dropped out of the University of Texas to join the Army. As a Nisei, he was assigned to the 442RCT—the regiment that would save the 1st Battalion of the 36th Division. Before the end of his tour, he received the Purple Heart and a citation for combat bravery.

In 1984, with members of the Jingu family present, the garden was finally renamed the Japanese Tea Garden.

Women at WAR

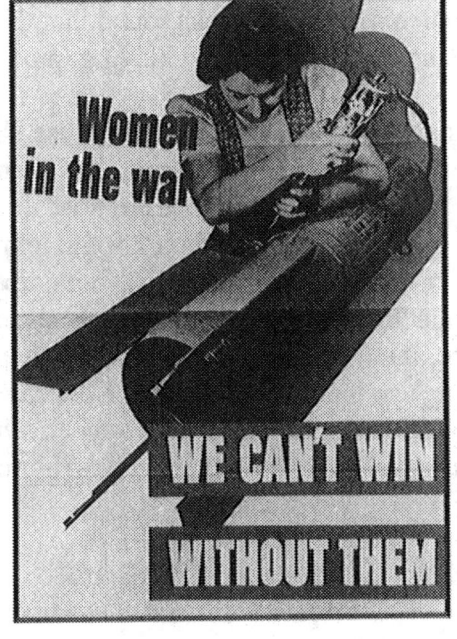

by
CYNTHIA GUIDICI

"This is Edna Bly speaking . . . speaking earnestly to the housewives of Liberty, Texas. I'm a housewife, too . . . never worked outside my home until this year. Feeding my family and buying war bonds just didn't seem enough. So I got an eight-hour-a-day job, and manage to run my home besides. My husband's proud of me . . . and I've never been happier. I feel I'm *really* helping to make the war end sooner . . . and maybe saving the life of just one boy from home."

This one-minute spot from the United States War Manpower Commission's "Womanpower Spots Series" showed Texas women they were needed as never before when war broke out in 1941. But venturing out of the home wasn't easy: women stood to gain independence and experience in the work force, but the idea of leaving the home threatened and intimidated some women. The radio series worked to overcome that fear as part of the federal government's intensive campaign to recruit women for the workplace and the military. The fictional housewife—the name and city changed to reflect the location—was "speaking earnestly" to get women to take on another job.

Rosie the Riveter offers an encouraging word. (Poster commissioned by the War Production Coordinating Committee.)

The country needed working women to help win the war. Ads were designed to make a woman feel proud as she did her patriotic duty, perhaps saved a life, certainly shortened the conflict. But there was another side to consider: taking a full-time job—six days a week, eight hours a day—didn't relieve or excuse a woman from her household duties. And with a war on, domestic help became as scarce as nylons when maids and cooks found that they could make bigger salaries by moving into industry.

"Edna Bly" could do her bit because she had the support of her husband, but many women faced stiff opposition from husbands, fathers, and brothers when they left the home for the arsenal or war plant. We remember "Rosie the Riveter" and her wartime sisters and take them for granted 50 years later, forgetting how hard it was for working women during World War II. These were women who had trained and believed in their work as homemakers, wives, and mothers.

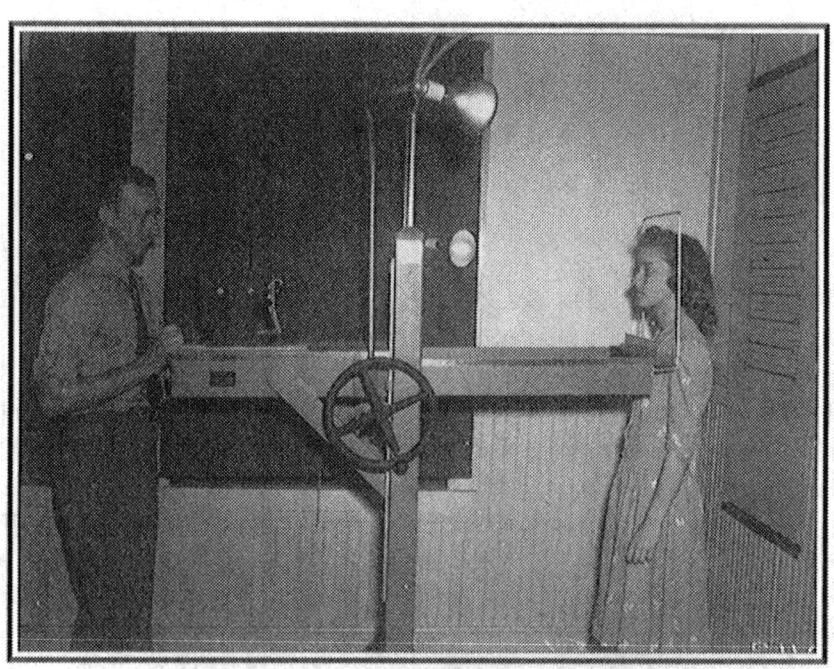

To protect defense areas, identification tags were prepared for all workers.
(Institute of Texan Cultures, *The San Antonio Light* Collection)

Women and men dismantling airplanes at Kelly Field
(Institute of Texan Cultures, *The San Antonio Light* Collection)

Ignition and carburetor specialist
(Institute of Texan Cultures,
The San Antonio Light Collection)

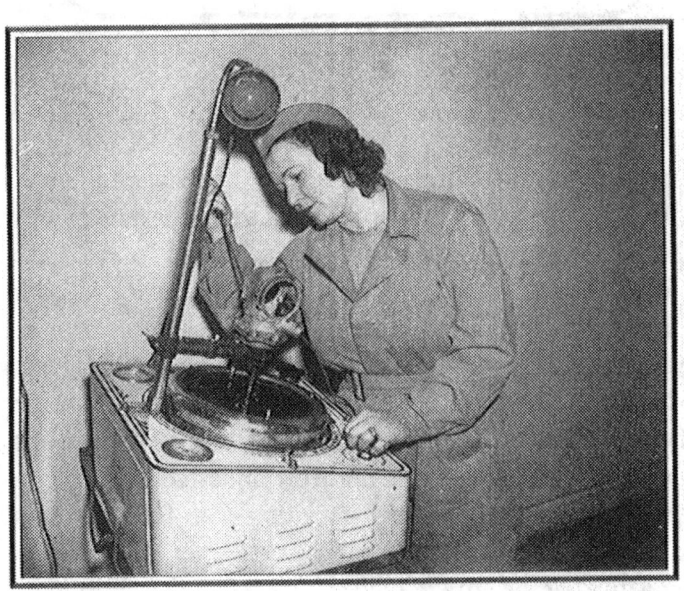

Those 12 million working women on the job when war broke out in 1941 were mostly working under economic duress, often brought on by the necessities and debts of the Depression. The great majority had fewer ties to home because they were still single. But as the war drained away the "manpower" needed to run the stores, factories and schools, everyday housewives who never imagined that they'd leave their homes to work did just that. The newness of their situations, the challenge of learning an unfamiliar skill, the exhausting drudgery, and the often open hostility they faced called for a special sort of courage.

TEXAS GOES TO WAR   147

On May 1, 1942, the U.S. Senate passed the bill that brought the Women's Army Auxiliary Corps (the WAACs) into being.

For the first 15 months of our existence, we were an outside arm of the army and lacked the full privileges accorded male soldiers. But late in 1943, we became a part of the Army of the United States and dropped the term "Auxiliary" from our name. We became the Women's Army Corps (WAC).

We civilians who entered the Auxiliary, and later the WAC, were taught to respond as soldiers in basic training, where marching, physical exercises, the Articles of War, military courtesy, gas warfare, and sometimes gunnery practice taught us the proper discipline required of soldiers.

Women in the army served at ports of embarkation sending and receiving overseas troops. We labored in postal battalions, at rail and motor vehicle maintenance, in photo, map, and camouflage departments, at food and supply depots.

WACs were multigraph operators, tailors, projectionists. We served in medical, athletic, and entertainment occupations.

By the war's end, we could be found in every corner of our country, its possessions, and all locations of warfare overseas.

Although not a deliberate goal on our part, we found ourselves clearing a path toward women's liberation.

—Clarice Pollard

WAAC/WAC "Change of Station"
(drawing by Clarice Pollard)

Maximum Enlistment of Women During the War

WASPS	over	1,000
WACS	over	140,000
WAVES	over	100,000
SPARS	over	13,000
Women Marines	over	23,000
Army Nurse Corps	over	60,000
Navy Nurse Corps	over	14,000

Different motivations urged women to face that challenge. About half the women who took jobs or joined the armed forces had husbands or brothers serving in the military. At first, the military worried about the problems that might arise if both spouses worked for the government, but it was soon proven that military wives responded better to the unusual demands (such as high mobility) of the military. And for the wives of men in the war theaters, who were three times as likely to work as other women, there was great comfort in actively helping a husband's cause rather than simply waiting with folded hands for news.

About a third of the enlisted women said they joined for adventure or for economic benefit. A number of single women with college degrees wanted to take on a challenge before set-

WASPs in uniform
(Texas Woman's University Library)

Members of the first WAC company
(Texas Woman's University Library)

tling down. In this, they were like many single men who enlisted for adventure. Economically, although military pay could be considerably lower for women than for men, women in the services drew a higher salary than they had in civilian life; for some women, that money fed children, supplemented a husband's military pay, or made it possible to continue higher education. Other women simply enjoyed the novelty of bringing home a paycheck, both for the extra spending money and for the feeling of independence it brought.

One young Brownwood woman was looking for adventure when she got an older brother to drive her to Fort Worth so that she could get a job. Look-

ing back, Sylvia Boyd remembers thinking very little about the war at all:

> We didn't have even a radio at home, and, since we lived out in the country, news reached us slowly. We really weren't so concerned about the war. I wanted to work, and the city had work, so I went to the city. But I remember watching my brother drive away after he dropped me off at the boarding house. I almost ran after his truck to stop him. I was a little scared of being on my own.

Some women entered the service to get revenge on the enemy for the death of a family member. A few who joined had no sons, brothers, fathers, or

TEXAS GOES TO WAR   149

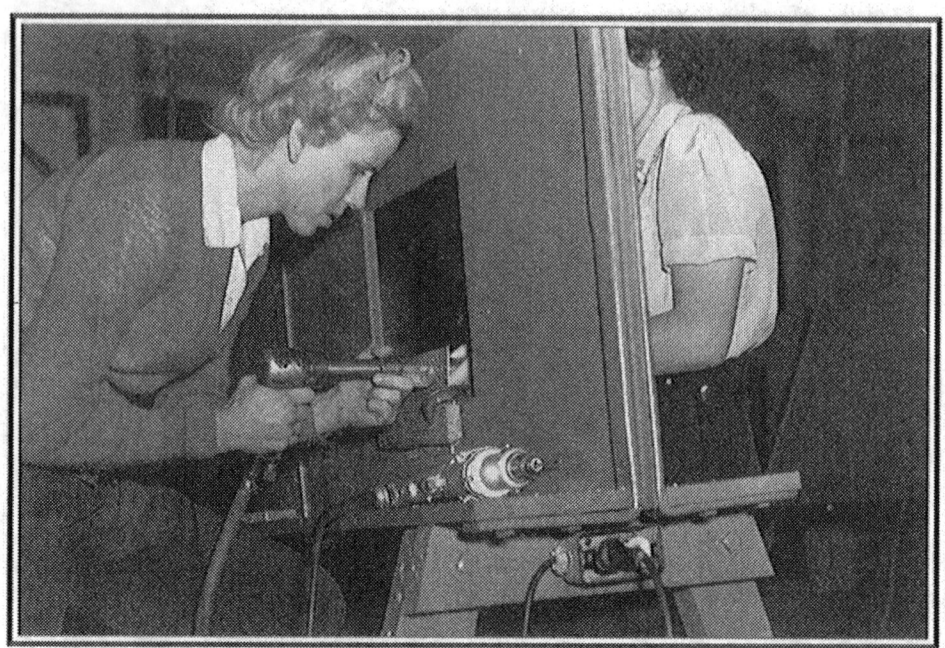

Students at North Texas State Teachers College learn important job skills to support the war effort
(University of North Texas Archives)

husbands to send to the war, so they served in place of the absent men in their lives. Other parents with no sons encouraged their daughters to serve. But a quarter of the women in the services said they joined up because they were tired of housework, they wanted to escape domineering parents, or they were bored with the routine of their lives.

Women in the factories, offices, stores, and even those in volunteer work, added other reasons to those that military women gave. Patriotism, of course, called numbers of women up for service, as it did many men; certainly the various ads aimed at women stressed the red, white, and blue of the work issue. Many women also developed a strong sense of purpose as they engaged in productive work with their hands in the factory. Finally—and not just for women but for all civilians—working outside the home provided social interaction when it was badly needed. The loneliness brought on by loved ones serving abroad, the anxiety of waiting and scanning the newspapers and mail for any word, and the chance to share hardships with co-workers each day meant that women didn't have to face the uncertainties of wartime alone.

> Women teachers of the city schools can now marry men in the armed forces of the United States and still keep their jobs with the Dallas Board of Education. The ruling is applicable for the duration of the war to any teacher who marries a soldier, sailor, or marine. When the husband returns and is discharged from the forces without physical disability, the teacher's marriage shall be considered a resignation and cancellation of her contract without further notice . . .
>
> *The Dallas Morning News,* March 18, 1942

Despite the great numbers of women who responded to the government's call for action, some women held back. A few were apathetic, but most just wanted to care properly for their children and refused to abandon them to others' care. Other women had husbands at home who made good money, so no economic need pushed them into the job market. And the husbands of working wives had to put up with ribbing and ridicule from friends and co-workers about the man of the house who couldn't do his job by himself. (Much government advertising targeted these men.) Some men feared that women who worked out of the home had an unruly and unnatural sexual drive; this was especially the case for women who enlisted in the services. Statements such as "I wouldn't let my sister join the WACs; she'd be ruined forever" discouraged some unmarried women from enlisting. A woman's chances of postwar matrimony and employment might be adversely affected if she had a military record.

Often, women feared the type of work they would have to do, afraid it might be dirty, repulsive, and too difficult. There also was the possibility of hostility from male co-workers, as working friends had warned them. Many feared that their femininity might be threatened. A few feared that if they became pregnant they might have to continue war work even at the risk of their health and that of the baby. One worker at a Boeing defense plant in Texarkana, Helen Stafford Pennington, on discovering that she was pregnant, asked for a release from her job without giving the reason. The plant managers would not let her quit until, a bit embarrassed, she told them why she needed to be absent from the job. Promptly, the plant made the necessary arrangements for her, proving that women's worries on the last count were quite ungrounded. But horror stories about poor working conditions and unpleasant treatment persisted. Many of the stories were true, and the more hesitant women had to be lured past their worries by the very successful advertising campaign engineered by government and industry.

That campaign accounted, at least in good part, for the 47 percent increase in women in the workforce from December 1941 to July 1944. The campaign was no haphazard affair. Planned carefully by the War Manpower Commission, it reached out to involve business, advertising, and entertainment as well. Hollywood glamorized the WAC or the WASP (and, of course, the housewife, too). Cosmetic ads in *Vogue* encouraged women to help their men fight for every woman's right to be lovely, while appliance ads in magazines like *Good Housekeeping* stressed the manufacturer's contribution to the war effort while admonishing women to do their part as well.

At first, most ads, government posters, and radio spots also glorified work as a service to the country. The WMC's "Basic Program Plan for Womanpower" of August, 1943, stressed that war work "will have to be glorified as a patriotic service if American women are to be persuaded" to take jobs and stick to them. Advertisers produced sales pitches covered in flags and silhouettes of soldiers in battle; government promotions went so far as to threaten women that a soldier might die if they didn't take up the work burden. Slackness on the part of women, some ads said, contributed directly to a longer war. One ad compared the woman with any free time on her hands to the draft dodger—an ad that had to be dropped because of its threatening approach.

In time, the government found that women, who had for decades been traditionally shielded from politics and had accepted the "hand that rocks the cradle" as their participation in nation-building, didn't respond as fully as men did to simple calls to patriotism. Far more successful with women were ads that appealed

The Women's Motor Corps practice with hose to be prepared to fight fires on the home front if necessary.
(Institute of Texan Cultures, *The San Antonio Light* Collection)

Members of the Women's Motor Corps learn auto mechanics. They also participate in military drill.
(Institute of Texan Cultures, *The San Antonio Light* Collection)

to personal relationships, ads that said, "Save your man" rather than "Save your nation and your rights." Another poster warned, "Longing won't bring him back sooner, take a war job and help him come home," and showed a woman clutching a letter to her breast.

The mobilization campaign also addressed women's fears about the types of work they'd have to do. Over and again, ads compared riveting with sewing, filing with sorting laundry, and caring for the injured with caring for sick children. These campaigns persuaded timid women to try outside work, but one ad comparing factory work to "pleasant and easy housework," as one woman wryly observed, was obviously the work of a male ad campaign planner.

Ads let women know that beauty and factory work, femininity and a military uniform, could go hand-in-hand and stressed the importance of setting aside a few minutes for personal care each day so that the men who came home would find the lovely face and form they had left behind. Some ads insisted that women could look great even while working in a factory. A July 6, 1942, *Life* magazine article on a "typical" factory girl praised the ability of working women to maintain their personal care standards:

> Now, at day's end, her hands may be bruised, there's grease under her nails, her makeup is smudged, and her curls out of place. When she checks in the next day at 6:30 A.M. her hands will be smoother, her nails polished, her makeup and curls in order, for Marguerite is neither drudge nor slave, but the heroine of the new order.

The Sears Catalog for Fall and Winter 1943 (Dallas issue) stressed "neat appearance," "clever"

> To prepare for their war-time assignment— whether in a factory, on a farm, or in civilian defense activities—UT women enrolled in a special war-conditioning course which met three times a week on campus to hurtle through, around, and over a city-block maze of obstacles scientifically designed to put all muscles of the body into play.
>
> from *The University of Texas: A Pictorial Account of Its First Century,* by Margaret Berry. (UT Press, 1980)

This photo was published in "The Smart Set Magazine" section of *The San Antonio Light* with a caption informing the reader that "recruits are needed."
(Institute of Texan Cultures, *The San Antonio Light* Collection)

design, and "trimly tailored" details in its two-page spread advertising "Sturdy, comfortable clothes . . . for factory, for farm and home." And women considering enlistment were even told that the flattering uniforms designed by top designers would turn heads and attract dates.

Still, once women got to work or took on volunteer jobs, they learned quickly that most of the glamour was in Hollywood, but that the challenge and the excitement of the new, the fatigue and the determination to do their best, were with them in the coastal shipyards, county Red Cross chapters, farm fields, and waiting for them at home, too.

As they adjusted to their busy new schedules, many working women squeezed in a few volunteer hours a week as well. Volunteer work also provided an outlet for women who were too old or too young to work, or who couldn't get work for other reasons. In a war that called for total commitment of the nation's citizens, volunteer work brought citizens together and strengthened the community and individuals in it.

The Civil Air Patrol provided many civilians with the opportunity to help on the homefront. Cadet Jesusta Casteñada, at the urging of a friend, joined the Civil Air Patrol when she was 18. Jesucita, as her friends called her, attended lectures on the use of Morse code and helped fold parachutes for the Army Air Force. At night, her unit practiced marching exercises at Crozier Technical High School.

This picture of members of the British War Relief Society appeared in the *The San Antonio Light,* April 26, 1941, with a caption informing readers that "boxes have been placed in stores, schools, and offices over the city for collection of tinfoil." (Institute of Texan Cultures, *The San Antonio Light* Collection)

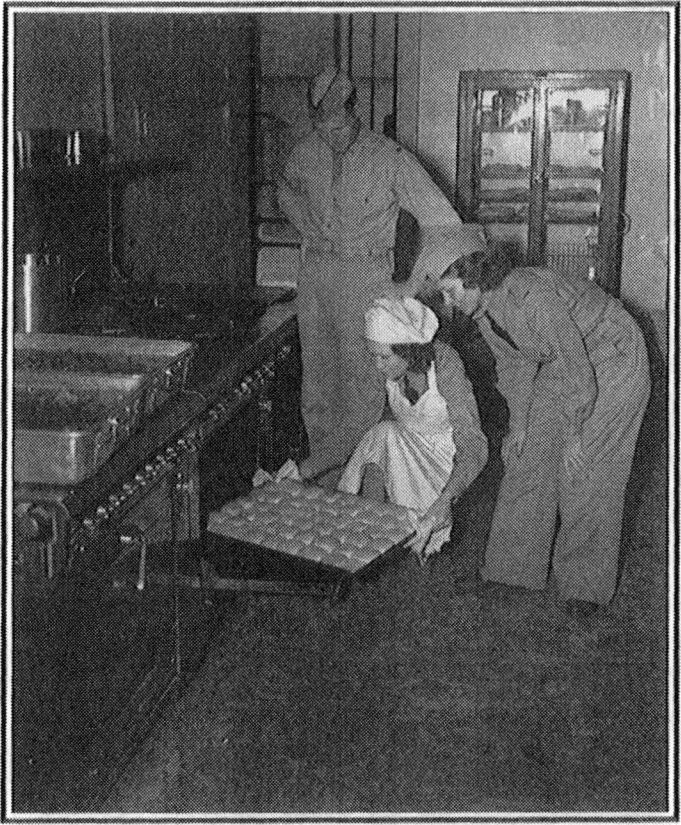

Members of the Women's Motor Corps learn to be canteen cooks at Sam Houston's school for cooks and bakers
(Institute of Texan Cultures, *The San Antonio Light* Collection)

> Mrs. Ernest Wadel of the Civilian Defense Council volunteer office said women are being recruited to staff the Dallas area warning center . . . The warning center will be operated on a full day and night schedule. More than 100 volunteer women serving without pay are needed to staff the four-hour shifts. Women of American citizenship between the ages of 20 and 48 years who have good health, eyesight, and hearing are eligible.
>
> *The Dallas Morning News,* December 3, 1942

Women had a wide variety of community service groups to choose from. Some, especially minorities, who were barred or discouraged from working in many organizations, devoted their time to local church-sponsored activities or to national organizations like the Salvation Army. And almost every city had clubs that fought the moral ravages of war. Dallas, for instance, was home to the "Little Below the Knee" club, formed at the end of the war to protest the new, higher hemlines that fashion designers hoped young women would wear.

TEXAS GUARDETTES

In October 1942, a women's auxiliary unit of the Texas Defense Guard was formed in Fort Worth and called the Texas Guardettes. This organization, which had no official standing, grew to over 100 women. They wore attractive blue uniforms with Sam Browne belts and trained themselves in military drill and courtesy, providing administrative support for the Texas Defense Guard.

They took first aid courses so they could work with Civil Defense and Red Cross authorities in times of disaster. The Guardettes were responsible for many war-effort drives, collecting cigarettes for the men overseas and junk jewelry to be used for native barter in the South Pacific campaign.

Service personnel in the local area could find these women also helping run the Service Men's Center on weekends. Because of their association with the Guardettes, several of these women would go on to join active military organizations before the war's end.

—*Bill Block*

Lucy Wilson receives an air medal for combat flying, August 21, 1944

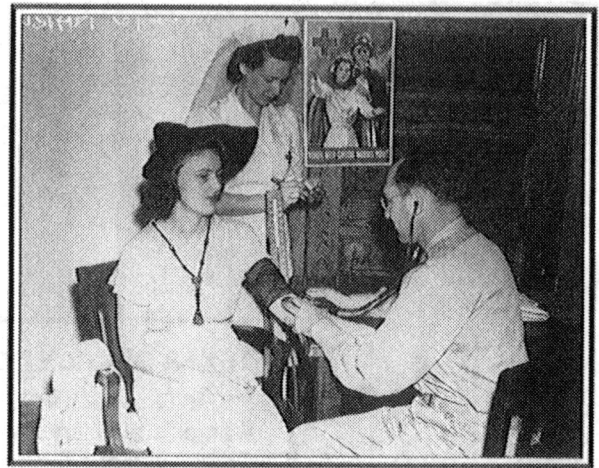

Applying as a Red Cross volunteer
(Institute of Texan Cultures,
The San Antonio Light Collection.)

> A total of 119,755 work hours were given by 14,068 Red Cross volunteers in the last four weeks.... Production services turned out 47,378 surgical dressings for the United States Navy and local hospitals' reserve stocks and 13,312 garments for the armed forces and war victims.
> *The Dallas Morning News*, March 17, 1942

Many women worked in government-related volunteer groups such as the Civil Air Patrol. In some places, 20 percent of the city air raid wardens were women. And in Texas, civilian women kept watchful eyes on the various bases, practiced evacuation techniques, and held fire drills. Women also served as watchdogs for the Office of Price Administration, jobs that were taken seriously since any price change affected what they could or could not buy for their own households.

The USO (United Services Organization), created in 1941, recruited the talents of women for entertaining the soldiers at home and abroad. Women staffed recreational centers for bases and for men on furlough, smoothed the way for soldiers being transferred from one area to the next, and organized activities from dances to library services for servicemen. To qualify as a USO Cadette, a woman had to be single, have some college education, and dress according to regulation. She acted as hostess and dance partner for the soldiers. The USO was one of the organizations that did allow women of color to participate, but they were not allowed to dance with white soldiers.

The American National Red Cross, the largest of the volunteer organizations, was hesitant to accept women at the beginning of the war. But as war needs grew, the Red Cross gladly welcomed the women. The organization developed a series of associated programs that eventually used a billion-and-a-half hours of volunteer work. Women contributed millions of those hours, learning and practicing first aid, water safety, home nursing, proper nutrition, and accident prevention. The Red Cross also provided services for canteens, both in the states and abroad. Sally Craighead Marcus went abroad with the Red Cross as a young, single woman. Her mother had been a Gray Lady, so Sally knew what she was getting herself into—or so she thought! After volunteering in Dallas for duty, she was shipped to Europe and taught to drive a 2-1/2–ton mobile canteen truck named "Old Glory." She worked close to the front lines, serving up countless cups of coffee, thousands of donuts, and many encouraging words to soldiers. Mrs. Marcus spent two years in Europe with the Red Cross. She recalls:

> It took someone with a sense of dedication, commitment, and adventure. It took someone who wasn't afraid to bathe in a creek or sponge off in water heated in a helmet; someone who could drive a big truck one hour, wrap bandages around a German prisoner's hand the next; then console a crying young soldier who's homesick and afraid to die. There was heat, humidity, rain, and cold. There was gunfire, cannons, and land mines. We were experiencing a lot of what the soldiers experienced.

An emergency call for one hundred quilted flannel pneumonia jackets in a week for a military hospital in Texas was received by the sewing service of the Dallas County Red Cross chapter.
The Dallas Morning News
Februrary 2, 1944

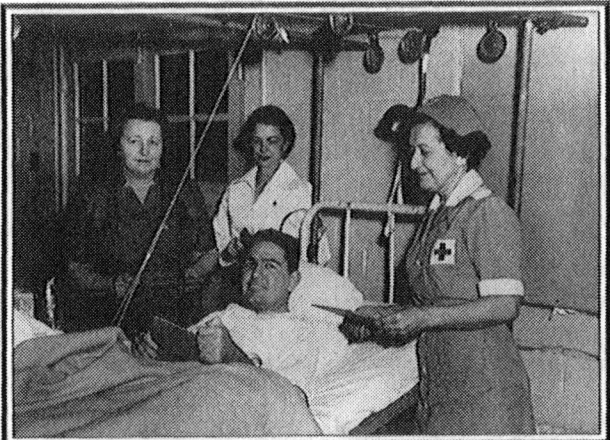

Volunteers lend assistance
(*Brief*)

WARRIOR IN WHITE

East Texan Lucy Iris Wilson signed up to be a Red Cross nurse in 1940 and became one of the 104 "Angels of Bataan and Corregidor."

Four days before Corregidor fell, she and 11 other nurses left the Philippines and were taken by boat and submarine to Australia. She left behind Dan Jopling, the man she was to marry, on the day that Bataan fell.

After returning to Big Sandy as the first decorated heroine of the war, Lucy Wilson joined the 13th Air Force in the Pacific and flew C-47s with wounded soldiers through 1944.

In February 1945, she saw Corregidor liberated and helped fly out the prisoners of war.

In November of that year, she was reunited with Dan Jopling, who had been presumed dead all through the war. Jopling had spent 42 months as a POW and was in an Army hospital in New Mexico when he and Captain Lucy Wilson married. They lived happily until his death in 1985.

It wasn't until 1991, when she returned to Upshur County to autograph copies of her book, Warrior in White, *that her hometown friends learned many of the details of Lucy's wartime experiences. The submarine escape from Luzon had been a military secret, and the rest of the story needed a half century's perspective.*

—*Sarah Greene*

The work that Mrs. Marcus and her co-workers did helped the Red Cross maintain its international reputation, but more important, it brought a taste of home to the soldiers.

Back in the States, the Red Cross Production Corps employed 45 million women to knit millions of garments and roll billions of surgical dressings for soldiers. Later, some critics complained that machines could have done the work faster; but again, there was a hint of home in a hand-knitted article of clothing that machine production could never have included. The women benefited, too, from the time they invested in each garment. Volunteer work was simply very good for morale, at home and in the field. As Mrs. Marcus said, "We were just glad to be there to help."

Being there to help meant a full-time commitment to the nation's food production for women who had to take up the heavy farm work left behind by servicemen. Women had always been farm workers, just as they had always been involved in the Extension Service and the Fed-

(Texas A&M University Archives)

"Toughen up, girls!"

War demands something from everyone—the men from the farms to the firing line and the women to lend a hand with farm work. When this call comes Texas 4-H Club girls won't be unprepared. But if they need a pattern, we'd like to recommend Evelyn Young, 4-H Club girl, who has become "rather handy" around the family farm in Carson County since her father died two years ago. Last winter she saved the expense of a hired man by milking and running the separator, feeding hogs, calves and chickens, and doing a "few other things." During the harvest season she hauled grain and, her mother says, always brought in better loads than her older and younger brothers. There is little within the house or on the farm that Evelyn cannot do. She can remodel rooms and make her clothing. And she can also keep her hair curled and her print dress fresh while cleaning a chicken house. There is much women and girls will have to do on the farms while their men face the enemy. Their grandmothers did it. That kind of women make victories—brave hearts, stout muscles, and faith in their ability to give and do.

The Extensioner,
magazine of the U.S. Agricultural Extension Service
February 1942

A woman takes over the reins so men in the household can fight the enemy
(Texas A&M University Archives)

Learning the fine points of operating a tractor
(Texas A&M University Archives)

eral Agricultural Program. War changed the level of involvement and the type of commitment for women on farms and ranches across Texas. They had been "Home Demonstrators," teaching each other the best methods of preserving food and performing other household tasks. But with the war, women shouldered the responsibility of large-scale food production on many farms. The goal they set was "to feed the world." And they did it. Together, men and women working their farms with reduced labor pushed production up dramatically during the war years. As women in urban areas tended their victory gardens, they thought of rural Texas women, hauling grain, working cattle, and harvesting the important cotton crop. 4-H Clubs encouraged girls as well as boys to take an active role on their farms and praised the children in publications. In agriculture, the entire family got involved in the war effort.

By 1942, unfilled jobs outnumbered available single women. In 1943, for the first time in American history, married women outnumbered single women in the workforce. The 2.75 million women working by the end of the war had 4.5 million children under the age of 14. But child care programs, mostly run by the government, could handle only a fraction of the children of working mothers.

Days were long for women who worked and ran the home. The woman had to rise before dawn, fix breakfast and lunch buckets for her family, and clock in by 6 A.M. After eight hours of work—if overtime wasn't demanded—women had to deal with shopping in a time of shortages and wartime rationing. Because of gas shortages, many women faced a long drive in a carpool or on public transportation. When they got home, women stepped back into their roles as homemakers. If they were lucky, they had the help of older children.

Some women, like Mrs. Coy Davis, worked late shifts. Mrs. Davis, with five other people, drove each day to Grand Prairie's North American Defense plant to print blueprints on the second shift—from 6 in the evening till 2 in the morning.

For most women, taking on an outside job meant doubling the work load, not leaving half of it behind, which explains in part higher rates of absenteeism. Of the husbands who were home, only a few helped with household duties; more than one working wife left her job because, as one woman said, "My husband likes his meals on time, so he persuaded me to quit."

Not only did women find it hard to work and maintain a home, but they often found hostile attitudes at work. They expected to be tired, to wonder how long it would be before they got used to the new routine, but they did not expect the unfriendly attitudes of male co-workers. In some instances, a man who was responsible for training a female "partner" simply ignored her, so that when the supervisor came around to inspect her at her job, she was not prepared to do it correctly. Other women complained that plant managers assigned them to do work that was not in the job descriptions. Stories of women hired to work the line but instead were put to cleaning latrines by foremen were common. And,

Neighbors team up for the war effort
(Institute of Texan Cultures, *The San Antonio Light* Collection)

> Dallas Kiwanians were urged to plant victory gardens to help the drastic need for food. Ernest Duke, branch manager of the Federal Crop Insurance Corporation, told the club of the heroic work done by women on Texas farms in the face of a labor shortage. The fairer sex, he added, are driving tractors, hauling produce to town in trucks and doing other jobs formerly taken care of by men.
>
> *The Dallas Morning News*, April 5, 1944

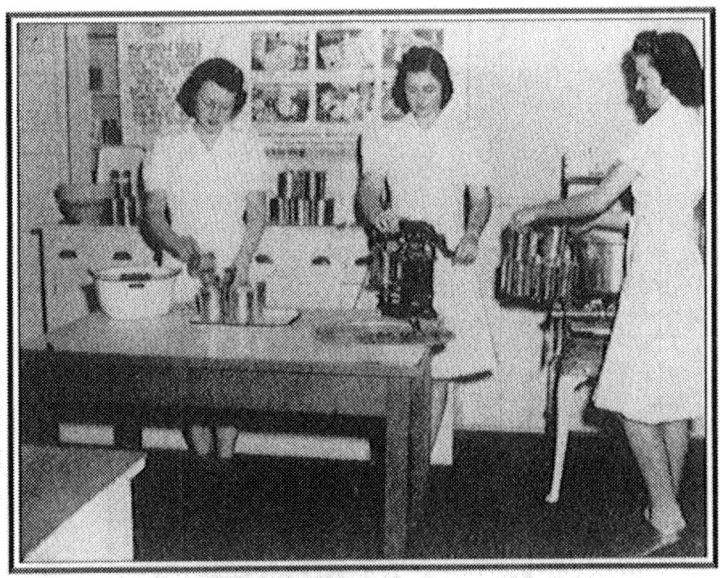
TWU students learn war-time food preparation
(TWU *Bulletin*)

Despite these discouragements, minority women volunteered much more readily than white women, and they worked persistently to break through the double barrier of race and gender; but by the end of the war, black women made up only two percent of all working women.

As more and more women went to work, employers and employees found much to praise about women's contributions. Employer after employer documented the precise and accurate work done by women, noted their willingness to learn, and pointed out that female employees were doing "a man's job" right alongside the men. As for the women themselves, the hard work and sometimes frantic schedule paid off in self-respect, in pride in their accomplishments, in a place among the home-front soldiers, and in a long-term reassessment of women's accepted social

despite legislation requiring equal pay for men and women, most women's paychecks were only 40 to 60 percent of their male counterparts'.

Black women had a particularly tough battle as they tried to get jobs in a white marketplace. The government decreed equal pay and insisted that all Americans, regardless of race, should be able to participate in the war effort. Businesses found "unofficial" ways to avoid hiring black women: by pointing out, for instance, that with increased production needs, there was no time to build separate restroom facilities. Or a business might claim that it would hire women of color just as soon as it had enough applicants to staff a segregated shift—then the required number never materialized. Some employers claimed that white employees would "walk off the line if Negroes were hired."

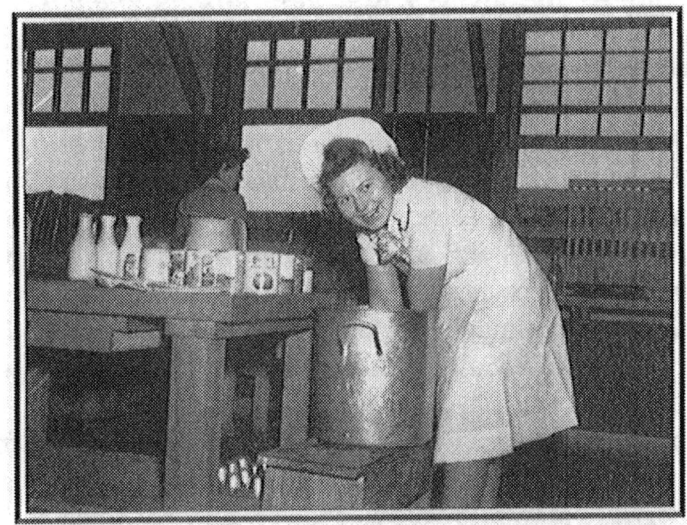
(Institute of Texan Cultures,
The San Antonio Light Collection)

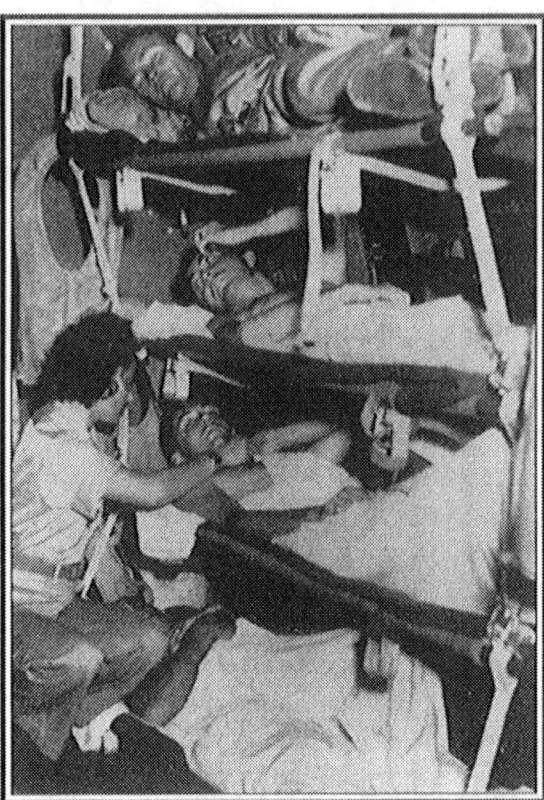

Lt. Edna Brackett evacuating wounded
(*Brief*)

roles. Though many women returned to homemaking after war production dropped off, 3.8 million women who joined the labor force during the war stayed on, holding open the door for younger women to follow them.

For women in the professions, the war provided opportunities for advancement that would permanently change the status of women in music, education, medicine, and law. For women in music, the war meant a chance to move out of all-female, amateur, and community orchestras and to compete for chairs in nationally-known symphony orchestras, playing not only harp and violin, traditionally "feminine instruments," but also "masculine" instruments such as trombone and French horn. Once women began to play with the symphonies, they continued to compete with men for prestigious chairs. Even during the postwar years, women held about a dozen chairs in leading ensembles, and orchestras nationwide were peppered with women sitting in various sections.

For women who practiced law or taught in colleges and universities, the war meant the chance to move into more secure positions. It wasn't just that men away at war left vacancies to be filled. The war itself produced legal work for both men and women to deal with; and thousands of soldiers, some of them women, would take part in the GI Bill after the war, ensuring a greater need for college professors.

The nursing profession benefited significantly from the war. Even before America entered the war, at least 40,000 nurses had volunteered to work with the Allied forces under the aegis of the Red Cross. When America declared war, more than 100,000 nurses volunteered for military duty, and 76,000 served. Nurses were stationed in every theater—often close to enemy lines. Some were captured in the Pacific theater. Nurses lived under the same conditions as the soldiers, gained the respect of the servicemen, and won over the military establishment, receiving equal pay, benefits, and full military rank. (Army nurses of both sexes earned $150 a month and could rise to the rank of major, with a pay of $166.67 a month.)

Even black women served as nurses, and by the end of the war, 500 African-American nurses had completed their training. Still, they could treat only men of their race and had to live separately from other nurses. But given the fact that, before the war, few colleges would accept women of color as candidates for medical training, their war work takes on added significance.

Not only did nurses advance in prestige during the war, they also gained in technique and expertise. Nurses trained with physicians in the field, learning pharmaceutics, medical technology, and physical therapy. Equally important to the servicemen, though, was the nurses' effect on morale. The nurses exhibited professional attitudes and the courage to tend the wounded under enemy fire. They emerged from the war a strong, organized, respected group, more so than any other military auxiliary.

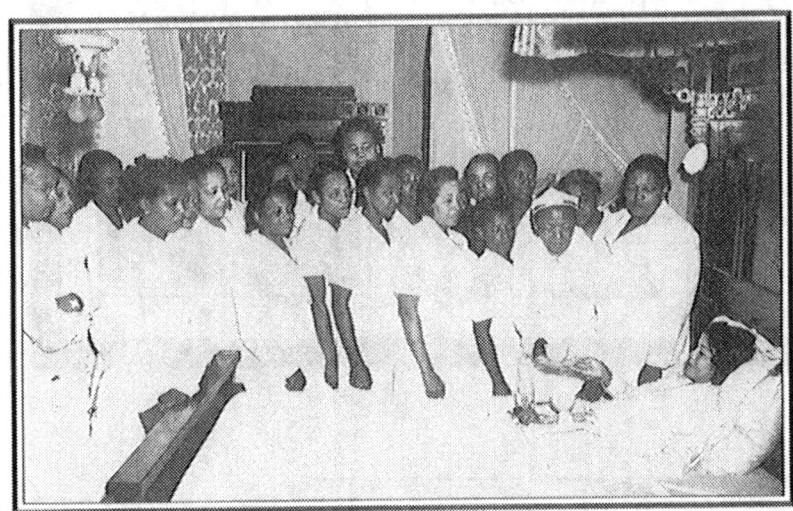

Home Nursing Class
(Institute of Texan Cultures,
The San Antonio Light Collection)

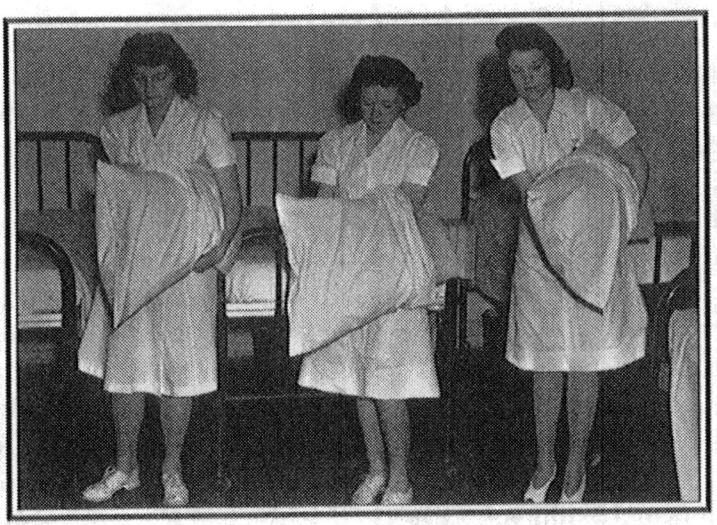

Nursing class at North Texas
State Teachers College
(University of North Texas Archives)

When I joined the WAVES in May 1943, it was as if I were at the end of a pendulum, suspended from a fixed point but swinging freely from the part of my life in a small town in deep south Texas to a tiny speck lost in 5,000 WAVES at boot camp on the Hunter College campus in the Bronx. To and fro. I was suddenly changing from a very frightened wide-eyed girl in sturdy black oxfords into a real person.

The 5th Regiment at boot camp was a shakedown, transforming a flighty bunch of civilians into Navy personnel, even though the Navy Department hadn't yet spelled out the requirements. In three weeks, we became trim and sharp, using Navy slang like bulkhead, porthole, deck and field day. I still smile when I sing the beautiful Navy hymn: "Eternal Father, Strong to save—protect us from these RESTLESS WAVES!"

After three weeks at Hospital Corps School in Long Beach, California, I was assigned to Oak Knoll Naval Hospital, Oakland, California, where I was a secretary in the pathology lab then later worked in occupational therapy. Pay scale ranged from $54 a month for hospital apprentice ("h.a. duce") to $96 for pharmacist mate, second class. Even so, it was enough for weekend liberties in San Francisco, payments on $5,000 GI insurance and to buy an $18.75 War Bond every month.

The fellows in the orthopedics ward took great delight in making new WAVES blush by yelling "I needa DUCK!" (male urinal) and wanting their backs rubbed each evening. It wasn't all fun and games, however. I went in navy ambulances to meet hospital ships at Pier 9 in San Francisco, watching kids "ship out," returning as leather-hard men. On litters. Even worse was going to the morgue to transcribe autopsies.

The bomb. The victory. The peace. Finally, it was all over. Thanks to the GI Bill, I earned a journalism degree from the University of Texas where I faced more discrimination and harassment than ever in the Navy. A few years ago I found a box of letters and journals my mother had saved and I published The Way of the WAVES, *and later a collection of* Old WAVES Tales. *Under the same conditions, I would do it all over again!*

As in the book of Ecclesiastes, "To everything there is a season and a time to every purpose . . . a time to kill, and a time to heal . . . a time to weep, and a time to laugh . . . a time of war, and a time of peace."

—Marie Bennett Alsmeyer

One group of women who took part in the war faced unique problems when they chose to participate in the most staunchly masculine of all American institutions: the military. Ideas about masculinity and femininity, about social roles, were shaken for both men and women by the military's decision to enlist women for certain duties. Some men perceived the military's invitation to women a slight to their manhood, as did one senator when he objected to the bill that established the Women's Army Auxiliary Corps: "Think of the humiliation! What has become of the manhood of America?" Other men questioned the ability of women to contribute anything to the military's needs.

"Why, bless you," another senator objected when the Women Accepted for Volunteer Emergency Service bill was under debate, "how do you know that they are not going to spend $200 dollars to dress up a girl and then put her in the kitchen?" Even the women who joined had their concerns. One cartoon from the period of the WAAC debut shows a couple sitting on a park bench, the woman dressed in her uniform. "I love it when you look at me that way," she explains. "It makes me feel like a woman again."

But the generals who got the bills for the women's auxiliaries through Congress believed, like Gen. H. H. Arnold, that "in the fields for which a woman's civilian training best fits her, a woman can do the job

"Morning Cleanup"
Clarice Pollard

WAAC prepares for day's work
Daedalian 1943
(Texas Woman's University Library)

of two men." Women in the military branches, at peak about 271,000 strong, carried the bulk of the clerical work, releasing men from desk jobs for combat (as the women were occasionally reminded by individuals whose loved ones had been so "released"). WAVES, the Navy branch, SPARS (for "*semper paratus*," the Coast Guard motto), and Marine Corps Women's Reserve were almost entirely clerical. In fact, by 1945 women marines made up about 85 percent of enlisted personnel at Marine Headquarters and somewhere between one-half and one-third of permanent personnel at all large marine posts and stations. Some women in the naval branches worked in specialty fields; the SPARS, for instance, took pride in their part in the top secret LORAN (Long Range Aid to Navigation) project. It was in the WAACs, however, that the greatest variety of duties occurred before the war ended.

The WAACs became the WACs, Women's Army Corps, in June 1943, the name change pointing out the change to full military status for the group. This branch of the service boasted the largest number of volunteers: the army wanted 150,000 WACs; they recruited 140,000 by war's end.

Oveta Culp Hobby, the Texan who led the WACs, was determined to give the branch the chance to prove itself. She labored constantly against biased reporting and frivolous rumors, insisting that the media refer to WACs as "women," not "gals," and downplaying the constant questions about beauty practices among WACs. Of Hobby, who took the WAC helm at the age of 37, one general said, "In all of these duties she displayed sound judgment and carried out her mission in a manner to be expected of a highly trained staff officer."

Hobby's WACs had to be 20 years old to enlist; they were not given dependency allowances for children, so many were still single. Forty-two percent had high school diplomas and another 11 percent had gone to college. Six percent were African-Americans and served in segregated units. WACs served in the States and abroad, many as clerical and support staff, but others in specialized areas. WAC recruits had an advantage over new, young male inductees in that they usually already had a skill. Many women got the chance to work in weather observation, radio and cryptographic jobs, control tower operations, aircraft reconnaissance, laboratory technology, chemical clean-up, and mechanical repair. A small group of highly trained WACs became chemists, pharmacologists, and toxicologists. Also, 422 WACs were employed within the Army Corps of Engineers on the Manhattan Project. The program director, Gen. Leslie Groves, complimented the women at the conclusion of their work, saying that "no one outside the project will ever know how much depended on you."

WACs served in Ordnance Installation, the Quartermaster Corps, the Transportation Corps, and the Corps of Chaplains. They had more mobility than other military auxiliaries, more chances to work abroad, and more opportunities to prove themselves as soldiers of a sort. But as with all the military branches, WACs faced derision from detractors in the press and government, sexual advances from misinformed soldiers who had the wrong idea about the role of the unit, and pressure to resign from returning military men toward the end of the war.

"WAC cook"
Clarice Pollard

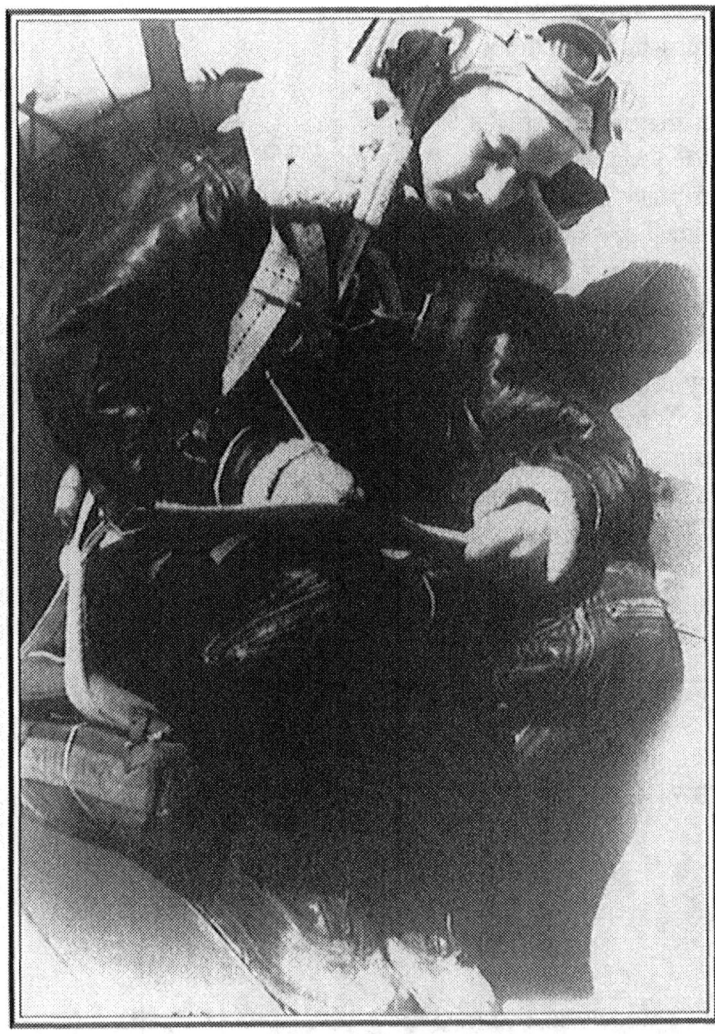

WASP completing flight records
(Texas Woman's University Library)

The story of another group of women who saw military service but weren't acknowledged for it until 1977 belongs to the WASPs (Women's Airforce Service Pilots) and a smaller but related group, the WAFS (Women's Auxiliary Ferry Squadron). Both groups drew women who wanted to fly for the war effort. The WAFS, headed by Nancy Love, consisted of trained pilots who ferried war planes. The WASPs, directed by Jacqueline Cochran, trained slightly more than one thousand women in Sweetwater, Texas, to fly in various Air Corps assignments. When Cochran put her program together, she called for 2,000 women to enlist. Twenty-five thousand applied. Cochran selected the best 1,830 of them and asked them to pay their own way to Texas. Before the war ended they had logged more than 60 million miles in every plane in the U.S. arsenal, from trainers to bombers to experimental fighters. One WASP flew the first military jet in its testing. WASPs' daily tasks included ferrying planes, testing cadet pilots, towing targets for air-to-air and ground-to-air practice, simulating strafing and smoke-laying missions, and jamming radar. Cochran's pilots were good at their jobs, and they should have been: they had to meet rigorous standards to apply. They were required to have a high school diploma at least (male pilots needed a minimum of three years of high school), and they must have logged five hundred hours (as opposed to the men's requirement of two hundred).

At first the WASPs, since they weren't in the air corps, didn't even have uniforms or mattresses for their bunks. In Houston and Fort Worth, WASPs bought their own beds; when the uniforms—all men's sizes—arrived at Avenger Field in Sweetwater, the pilots laughed and altered them.

These incidents, though they didn't dampen the pilots' spirits much, did indicate how much weight the WASP program had in Washington. Opposition to granting WASPs military status, pay, and benefits was stronger than with the other auxiliary branches, perhaps because these women were flying the latest in AAF warplanes, not just typing reports. By the time the bill to make the WASPs a military unit came to Congress, the war was coming to its satisfactory close, and the first of 200,000 military pilots were coming home. WASPs were unwanted competitors. When the last of their ferrying missions was complete, they went home, with no benefits, no veteran status, no recognition of the 38 pilots who had lost their lives in the line of duty. It was not until 1977 that their service to the nation was recognized fully.

WASP beside plane
(Texas Woman's University Library)

WASP plane towing a target
(Texas Woman's University Library)

The end of the war brought changes not only for WASPs and WAFS, but for all women in the military and in war work. The government and the advertising industry, a partnership that had once motivated women to go out and work, now thanked them politely and suggested they go home.

Many women were ready to do just that. Having deferred their marriage and family plans till after the war, they now wanted to begin another new life. Other women had always thought of their work as temporary and looked forward to the rest due them. They relished the thought of some years of stability after the Great War, the Great Depression, and this war. Family, to many, stood for that stability. Some women, however, found the idea of returning to the comparatively private and dependent life of wife and mother discouraging. But women who wanted to stay in the work force ran head-on into the nationwide conviction that all women wanted to go home (despite

Head nurse Francis Morgan, from Dallas
(*Brief*)

WACs disembarking find themselves engaged
in a minor skirmish with red tape
(*Brief*)

polls in which as many as 40 percent said otherwise). It was especially hard for single, divorced, or widowed women to give up their incomes; they needed jobs as badly as the men who were coming home by the thousands. Many women did find a way to stay at work, but in July 1945, women comprised almost half of unemployed Americans seeking work.

Women in the military faced varying situations. The WASPs and WAFS had already been disbanded; the WAVES and SPARS followed soon after, except for a small core of women who remained as clerks. But the success of the WACs, along with the continuing Soviet threat, persuaded the military to pass the Women's Armed Service Integration Act, allowing women regular and permanent status in the Army (with salary and rank limitations). No one expected women to become career military soldiers.

(Brief)

As they look back at women's involvement in the war, historians like to debate the long-term effects of the war on women's lives and the changes it brought, for a short time at least, to the accepted social roles and family structures. What can't be debated is the response of women, both in the home and in the workplace, overseas with the Red Cross or USO, or in the local Methodist Ladies' Auxiliary, to a war that threatened their way of life and their loved ones. When called to action, they answered. When asked to work, they worked, regardless of whatever other responsibilities they had. "Why did we do it?" Mrs. Sally Marcus asks herself. "We did it because we loved our country. There was NO reluctance. There was no question."

LOVE, MARRIAGE, & THE FAMILY

"Date Bureau in Action"
(Texas Woman's University Library, 1944 *Bulletin*)

by
SALLIE STRANGE

During World War II, Texas girls, listening to the strange accents of Yankee soldiers—soldiers who held girls' hands a little too tightly and seemed to back them into walls too eagerly and to press their knees under dirty wooden tables too quickly—could not believe what these foreign-sounding boys told them. Were girls up north, girls from Philadelphia and Toledo and Cincinnati, really "giving themselves" to soldiers, sailors, and marines under the guise of patriotism?

"Everything was intensified back then. Everything. The good feelings and the bad. That meant a kind of fierceness and desperation about people meeting. Like movie lovers, or something."
—*a woman from Texarkana*

USO Travelers' Aid Volunteers meet the train to hand out cookies to the troops
(Institute of Texan Cultures, *The San Antonio Light* Collection)

Boys—even Yankee boys—away from home, lonely, and without local ties, could be excused for some deception and minor exaggeration. And that's what USOs were for: to enable boys far away from home to find female companionship in an honorable and proper manner. USOs had been created by religious groups in 1941 for this specific purpose as well as for keeping up the morale of servicemen. Morale was very important in wartime, they were told, as important as training—even as important as equipment and ammunition. So USOs were established and flourished in Texas—in Dallas, Houston, San Antonio, and the smaller towns, especially those near the many bases.

"I grew up in Abilene, where there were mainly Baptists and a few Methodists and Presbyterians. I never knew a Jew before, though of course I'd heard some things. So when I was stationed at the Great Lakes and went into Chicago and met this girl I didn't think anything peculiar. Besides that, she was a redhead. Anyway, I saw her five or six times and things were heating up, when she out and tells me she's a Jew. I didn't know what to say."

—*a man from Abilene*

The USO in Texas had a population problem unlike that in any other state. Texas had an enormous number of bases and hence an enormous number of servicemen. Infantry training was done at Camp Wolters near Mineral Wells, which had a troop capacity of 24,973; at Camp Fannin near Tyler, which had 18,680 soldiers under canvas and plywood; at Camp Howze near Gainesville with its 39,963 infantry trainees; at Ford Hood between Killeen and Gatesville, an establishment with more than 95,000 troops; and at Camp Bowie near Brownwood, a base that trained men in the artillery, national guard, cavalry, engineers, and signal and chemical companies on its 120,000 acres. Over 150,000 men were training at these bases at any one time, and the list is far from complete.

> "Many of the old maids who went to the USO clubs met servicemen and married them."
> —a woman from Killeen

One of the service dances presented by Texas State College for Women, 1941–42
(Texas Woman's University Library)

In addition, Texas bases trained pilots at such places as Carswell Air Force Base in Fort Worth, Bergstrom Air Force Base in Austin, Goodfellow Air Force Base near San Angelo, Hondo Army Air Field, the Naval Air Stations at Dallas and Corpus Christi, and Sheppard Air Force Base near Wichita Falls. Anti-aircraft units were trained at Camp Wallace outside Galveston.

For soldiers and sailors stationed in Texas, USOs provided nonalcoholic beverages and snacks, and most had dances at least on Saturday nights. A few had dress codes for the girls (no slacks or shorts), and a few screened the girls, for there were "two kinds," and the local leaders of the well-run USOs saw themselves, like the nice Texas girls, as upholders of morality.

"We had a USO but I didn't go there much. I heard a lot of stories about what went on at those dances, but they were mostly rumors. A lot of my friends wouldn't date sailors because of their reputations. People thought you were a bad girl or something. But I dated one. Mostly I dated soldiers."
—*a woman from Waxahachie*

One of the consequences of immorality that frightened everyone and that the USOs were determined to help contain was the spread of venereal diseases. In 1942 the incidence of these diseases skyrocketed, compelling the army to make training films about the spread of VD and to show these as a part of basic training to the amusement of the more sophisticated servicemen. In addition, the army began dispensing prophylactics, causing controversy among the more religiously conservative Texans, and also began closing the most notorious red light districts adjacent to the bases, which to those Texans who valued their Wild West heritage seemed a breach of time-honored, heroic code. But prophylactics were dispensed and red light districts were closed.

National Catholic Community Service Center presented programs nightly for enlisted men. The center provided recreational facilities, a library, and writing facilities.
(Institute of Texan Cultures, *The San Antonio Light* Collection)

176   LOVE, MARRIAGE, & THE FAMILY

"My uncle ran the USO. He leased a building and hired this man who worked in a men's clothing store to run it. He called him the Director. After the war this man told my uncle those were the greatest years of his life. He felt he was doing something really important. I guess selling men's suits isn't very rewarding work."

—*a woman from Wichita Falls*

When questioned about sexual immorality among recruits, one general said that 25 to 30 percent of the soldiers in his command would deliberately seek out sexual partners, 15 percent would not have illicit sex no matter what the circumstances, and that some 70 percent were subject to temptation and could go either way, depending on the opportunity. It was this 70 percent that the general was concerned about, as were the directors of the USOs, the ministers and priests, the parents of young women, and the women themselves.

Troops enjoy a little relaxation and refreshment at a USO club.

Practice blackout becomes a social occasion
(Institute of Texan Cultures, *The San Antonio Light* Collection)

This debut tea and ball was turned into a benefit for the Red Cross.
(Institute of Texan Cultures, *The San Antonio Light* Collection)

A wealthy socialite in San Antonio gave tea dances every Sunday for the unmarried young ladies of prominent families to meet young officers stationed in Texas—decorous tea dances. Women's clubs in various towns followed suit. Churches issued invitations to servicemen to Sunday worship, promising Sunday dinner with Christian families as a bonus. Networks among gardening clubs, book clubs, church circles, among family and friends, were developed to take care of our "soldier boys" as they went on pass to Waco or Tyler or Dallas or Wichita Falls.

By the end of 1942 the informal and formal networks were well established to entertain the servicemen and give them the right kind of contact with Texas girls. And by the beginning of 1943 there was yet another way they found to keep our boys' spirits up and contribute to the war effort: the Army Specialized Training Program (ASTP) and the Navy Collegiate Training Program. These programs essentially gave potential officers in the army and the navy a free education at a university or college and a semipermanent connection with its community.

Young men, now subject to the draft at 18, could go to SMU or the University of Texas or any number of schools in Texas and get their degrees as they would have before the war. Except that in these programs the education, the housing, and the books were free. Upon graduation the cadets would be commissioned immediately or sent to Officers Candidate School.

"I knew these two boys from high school. Jerry was my boyfriend and Billy was his buddy. They both got lucky and went into the V-12 at some little school in Minnesota. Then this terrible thing happened. Jerry fell off one of those horses in the gym and fractured his skull, so they took him out of school and put him in a hospital. He got out in about a month, but by that time they had kicked him out of the V-12, and before he knew what was happening the army drafted him. He went to boot camp, then overseas, and was killed in the Battle of the Bulge. I was pretty near devastated, but Billy kept writing me, and when he came home after the war, we got married. It's kind of funny how things happen."

—*a woman from Houston*

Colleges and universities, having seen their enrollments drop by 20 to 40 percent, were eager to institute these new programs for soldiers and sailors. Faculties happily stiffened their math and science courses, accelerating the programs so that a degree could be obtained in three years rather than four. Fraternities welcomed this new pool of pledges. And girls at these schools were delighted. Now they could date boys they knew, boys they attended class with, boys that would be around next week, next month, even next year. These young women thought they had it made—a man in uniform they could trust and so could love. Many of them did.

In October 1940, the Selective Service Act had required all males between the ages of 21 and 36 to register for one year of service. Local draft boards as well as a state advisory board were established by the governors of each state with four classifications: I, indicating immediate service; II, indicating what was later to be called employment deferment; III, indicating deferment because of dependents; and IV, indicating physical or psychological deferment. The purpose of this bill was to raise an army of 900,000. By the summer of 1941, Roosevelt was calling for an army of 9 million. When the war draft was put into motion, the aim was 10.9 million. By December of 1942 there were actually more than 12 million in the armed services, with the navy and the marine corps relying primarily on volunteers.

"When my son was at Parris Island, two boys killed themselves because of basic training. It was really hard. My son wrote me about it and said that he wouldn't ever again do anything I told him not to do. He didn't realize it was going to be like that, you see. But he came out all right, I'm glad to say."

—*a woman from San Angelo*

A COUNTRY ANTHEM

When Wiley Walker and Gene Sullivan wrote and recorded "When My Blue Moon Turns to Gold Again" in Dallas in the spring of 1941, they never thought it would become the anthem for lovers separated by World War II. Written as a sad love ballad long before Pearl Harbor, the song captured the mood of loneliness, sadness, and separation of the war better than many of the songs written after the war began. As the war intensified, the song took on a deeper meaning, signifying the happiness that would come when the war was over and sweethearts were together again. The popular lines of "When My Blue Moon Turns to Gold Again"—"When the rainbow turns the clouds away," and "I'll be back within your arms to stay"—had young soldiers crying in their beer from New Guinea to New Boston and from Corpus Christi to North Africa.

—*E. Dale Odom*

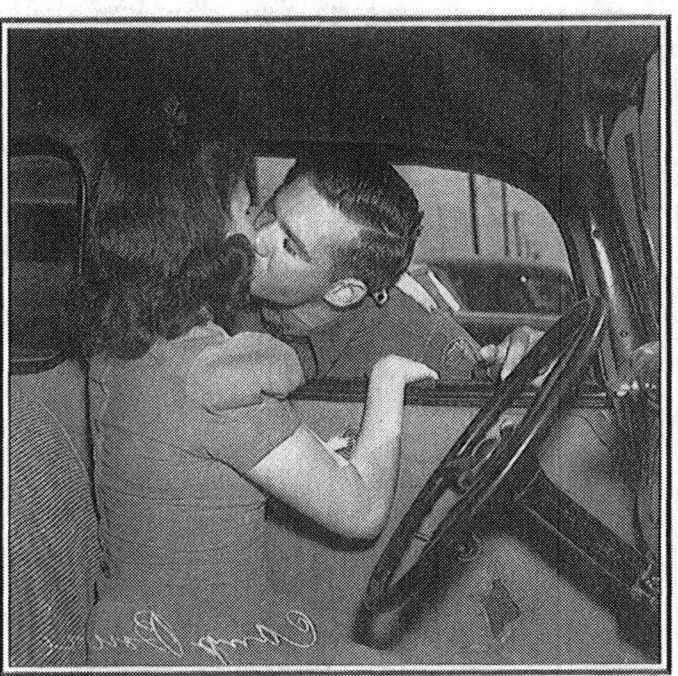

Visiting day at Camp Bowie
(Institute of Texan Cultures,
The San Antonio Light Collection)

This wedding took place only six months before Pearl Harbor.
(Institute of Texan Cultures, *The San Antonio Light* Collection)

With the threat of war looming in 1940 and with the mobilization of troops, the marriage rate had soared, 1941 marking the highest rate ever recorded in the United States. Ten percent of those marriages took place in December after Pearl Harbor. But the number of marriages grew during and even after the war. In 1940, 48 percent of women in the United States between the ages of 14 and 34 were married; by 1946, with marriages that had been postponed until after the war, the percentage of married women increased until six out of every ten women were married.

"I followed my husband because I was a part of a select group. I was a War Bride. I took a great deal of pride in that."
—*a woman from Odessa.*

What did these Texas women who married servicemen have to look forward to? What was on their minds when they married? Many of them felt the panic of the war. In newsreels they saw bombs drop on England; they saw the fall of Poland, Czechoslovakia, Austria; they saw the Maginot Line crumble. They were filled with dread. They said, "It can't happen here," but by those very words they were admitting that it could. Life was short, uncertain. One thing that was certain was that Joe or Bill or John or Harry would be sent overseas—to war-ravaged Europe or to an island in the Pacific or to India or Burma, who knew?—and there they would be in mortal danger, maybe never to return.

"My husband was given a ticket on the train for the naval base in San Diego. I went to the station to see him off. I'm ashamed to say it but I was jealous of him. He had his ticket, his meals would be paid for, he had a place to stay. Johnny and I had to make our own way out there. I hoped I could find a place to stay. Johnny was two at the time."
—*a woman from Marshall.*

LOVE, MARRIAGE, & THE FAMILY

It was in this frame of mind that many young women married. They married as an act of patriotism: a woman serves her country by giving of herself to a soldier, by loving him, writing him, waiting faithfully for his return. They married because it was romantic, because of *Mrs. Miniver*, because of Ingrid Bergman in *Casablanca*, because that's what women did. They married because they were lonely, because a soldier said he loved them, because a soldier said he didn't think he would be coming back. They married because their mothers had married their fathers in World War I. They married because they were in love.

New Year's 1943
(Institute of Texan Cultures, *The San Antonio Light* Collection)

J. B. "Jab" and Bobbie Owen

"During the war, Jab was in the navy and stationed in Hawaii. He was writing to two of us girls in Jacksboro. I didn't know about the other girl and she didn't know about me until Jab got the letters in the wrong envelopes. Was I surprised to read my best friend's name at the top of my letter! You see, my name is Bobbie. Anyway, I was really mad, so I didn't write him back. Then two years later I came in from a date with another boy, and there was Jab sitting on my doorstep. "I got three-days leave," he said. "Let's get married." That was nearly fifty years ago, and people told us that a wartime marriage would never last. Well, they were sure wrong."

—Bobbie Owen

TEXAS GOES TO WAR

CAMP FOLLOWERS

Because of the large number of people who had moved to Houston, housing was nonexistent. It was April 1942 before Daddy was able to find a permanent place to live so that my mother, sister, and I could join him. We lived at the Wayside Tourist Court, which was near the Buffalo Bayou and the Houston Ship Channel Turning Basin. I still remember lying in bed on foggy nights listening to the foghorns on the tugboats at the Turning Basin.

At first, we stayed in a cabin with only one bed that all four of us slept in. Luckily, it wasn't long until we were able to move into a cabin that had a living room, bedroom, kitchen, and bath. My sister and I slept on a rollaway bed in the living room. We thought we were fortunate to have so much space.

—Margie Burns Noneman

Did some marry for the $50 allowance given to servicemen's wives? That was the allowance—$50 a month. Apartment rent was around $35, leaving $15 for food, transportation, incidentals. Of the many brides who married during the war, one half stayed in the homes of their parents or their in-laws.

A young woman in Waco, Catherine Elizabeth, married a soldier at Fort Hood who was shipped to Pennsylvania. Should she follow him? Catherine Elizabeth could take what money had been set aside and take a train or bus. Lines were long, schedules erratic. One could miss connections, be stranded in St. Louis. Once she made it to the town near where her husband was stationed—if indeed she did make it—she had to draw on her savings to pay for a room in a hotel, a boarding house, or a private home, with or without kitchen privileges. There she would wait for him, sitting on the edge of the bed or in the wooden chair. She could take walks or go to a movie. She would have to put up with the wolf whistles of servicemen who lined the streets. She could nurse a cup of coffee in a diner. Maybe her husband would get a pass this week. Next week?

"Some of my girl friends lost their husbands and some of them came back so changed they really didn't know them. Betty had married this boy who liked to have a good time. A fun-loving person. Well, he came back a wreck, a mental wreck. I think they had to put him in an institution."

—a woman from Terrell

Almost half the married women followed their husbands, while a third stayed at home and saved their money until they were sure their husbands could get passes. Only then did they make the trek, sit in the aisles of trains, push off the advances of drunken sailors or soldiers. The rest stayed put, would not venture into the chaos, settled for writing letters daily, telling of what? Of boredom. Of idleness.

If a wife wanted to work, what could she do? She was only working for the duration, of course, and maybe not that long. If her husband thought

"Several of the girls I grew up with got into the Red Cross and went overseas. They were very excited. But I had to sit back and just watch them go. I had to stay home with the children."

—a woman from Amarillo

he could get a pass, she would go see him, at least meet him at some half-way point. What could she do? She could be a waitress. She might be able to work at her daddy's store or her uncle's. But part-time only. Subject to days off, even a week off, just in case.

Servicemen's wives who fared the best were, of course, the ones who had married before the war. Most had their own places to live, and some had jobs, friends, relatives, hobbies. To be sure, they were as lonely as their novice counterparts, but this was only one phase in their marriage, albeit a tragic one. They knew a marriage before the war, so they could imagine one after it. They knew their husbands as men, not just as soldiers—as partners, not just as lovers.

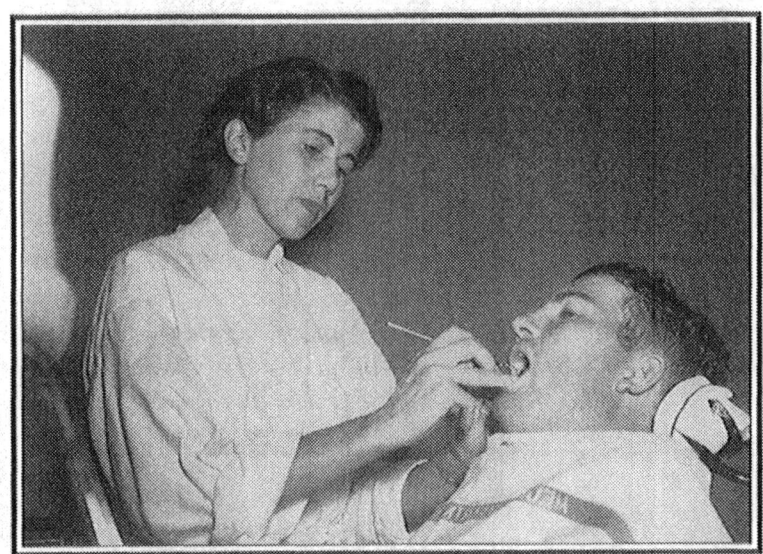
On June 5, 1941, *The San Antonio Light* ran this picture with the following caption: "Feminine dental hygienists add glamour to Fort Sam dental clinic."
(Institute of Texan Cultures, *The San Antonio Light* Collection)

But they were faced with the same problem as the brides: what could they do with their time? A woman in Abilene, Martha Ann, who had married in 1940, followed her husband, an ensign, to Boston and lived there for two months, during which time they spent three weekends together. Then she followed him to the Great Lakes near Chicago for six weeks, and then to Mobile, where they stayed in an elegant hotel. When he shipped out, she came back to Abilene, found an efficiency apartment, and got a job as a receptionist. Every Friday night she went to her cousin's house, where, with her cousin and two other "war widows," she played bridge and drank Cuba Libras. On Sundays, she ate dinner with her parents. That was Martha Ann's life for four years.

Many women did volunteer work. The two principal organizations to which they donated their services, besides the USO and their own churches, were the Office of Price Administration and the Red Cross. The OPA was run by volunteers all across Texas and was necessary in times of war—in times of shortages when landlords and merchants were tempted to raise prices and when consumers were tempted to supplement rationing by using the black market. Civilian male volunteers controlled the boards that enforced the OPA's rules, and women volunteers did the paper work.

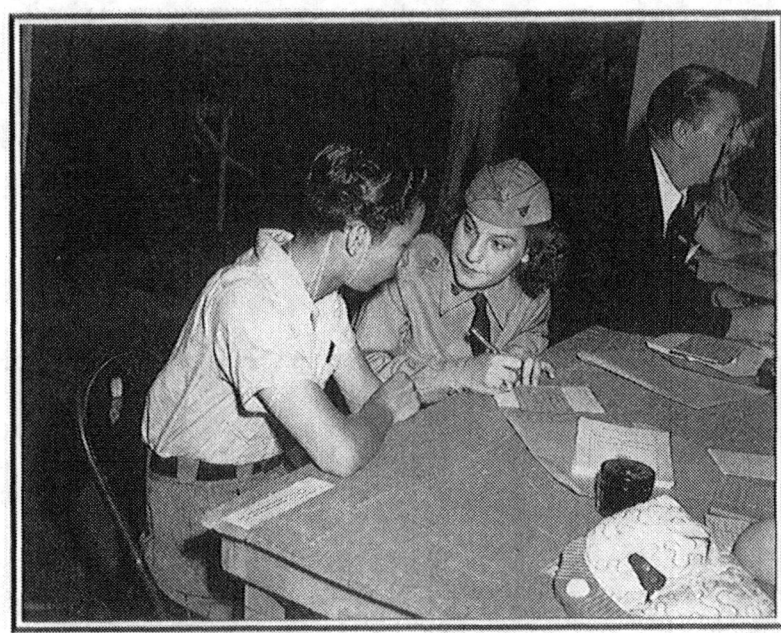
Woman's Motor Corps aid assists with registering for draft
(Institute of Texan Cultures, *The San Antonio Light* Collection)

> *"We had a first aid group at the office where I worked. We met every Friday after work and usually stayed at the office. One Friday we decided to go to my house. We met in the dining room, which we hardly ever used, and pushed the table against the wall. We were practicing artificial respiration, lying down on the floor, some people straddling other people, when my father came home. He looked in the door and said, 'What's going on in here?'"*
>
> —*a woman from Tyler*

The Red Cross burgeoned during the war years, sending its volunteers into civilian hospitals, using them as drivers to help stranded servicemen, overseeing the hand-knitting of garments for the troops, rolling bandages by hand, and collecting blood. In retrospect, some of this work was valuable but much of it was useless (the knitting and the rolling bandages, both more efficiently done by machines) and some of it revealed the prejudice of the time. The Red Cross segregated blood—blood from Negroes was marked and set aside for use on Negro troops only—and segregated volunteers on racial lines. Few Hispanics or African-Americans found their way into the service of the American Red Cross.

Many women sought paid employment. In 1940, 12 million women were employed; by 1944 the number was more than 18 million. Most employed women did not come from the ranks of the housewives. Of the 30 million housewives in 1941, seven out of eight were still at home in 1944, despite the urging of the War Manpower Commission. In fact, most of the employed women did not see themselves as working women, much less career women. They were helping the war effort by making a little extra money. Women workers were primarily part-time or temporary. Society and the women themselves would not have it any other way.

Volunteers fold bandages for the United States and British Armies
(Institute of Texan Cultures,

> *"When my husband was in Boston, I went there and worked three days a week at Massachusetts General. I did secretarial work as a volunteer, and they really needed me. Then at Corpus Christi, I worked for the Red Cross. I think I rolled bandages. I guess it was a kind of disruptive life, but also it was kind of fun moving around like that and meeting all those new people."*
>
> —*a woman from Chillicothe*

184   LOVE, MARRIAGE, & THE FAMILY

When we think of the women during those years, we are likely to think of Rosie the Riveter, who was certainly in the minority, and of the wives of servicemen, of Catherine Elizabeth and Martha Ann. But the wives of servicemen were also in the minority. In March of 1944, 2.5 million women—8 percent of all wives—were married to servicemen. Of wives under 20 years of age, 40 percent (still a minority) had husbands in the service. And of the wives from 20 to 44, only 11 percent were married to men in the service.

Such a woman was Mary Nell, who was married to a captain flying The Hump, a cargo route from India to Burma. Mary Nell lived in Dallas, but when she found herself pregnant with her first child, born in 1942, she alternated living with her parents in Fort Smith, Arkansas, and her husband's family in Baton Rouge, Louisiana. After her husband came home on leave, a second son was born in 1944, and she continued living with one or the other parents till the war was over and Captain McGuire came home for good.

> "When they sent Ed overseas, I decided to be a lady marine. I took the tests and went downtown to be sworn in. I was wearing my mink stole and my high heels, and the man who was swearing us in asked me, 'You sure you want to do this?' I told him I did. And then, that very afternoon, I heard that Ed was on his way home. I didn't know what to do, but Daddy knew this man who knew this man and pulled some strings, so they let me out. I guess you could say I was a lady marine for three days."
> —a woman from Dallas

The birth rate grew only slightly during the war—from 2.3 million in 1937 to 2.9 million in 1943 and down to 2.7 million in 1945. It was after the war before it climbed to 3 million, marking the baby-boom. War brides and wives did not alter their idea of the size of their families. There was too much confusion, too much chaos, too much danger.

Mothers of servicemen, half of all women between ages 45 and 75, were the largest category of women affected by the war. Blue Star Mothers had children in the service who were still alive. Those whose children had been killed were Gold Star Mothers. Many hung small banners, about 5 x 8 inches with blue or gold stars, in their windows. There were quite a few mothers with two gold stars, some with three or four, and at least one—a famous mother—with five, representing her five sons, who had served together and been killed on the same ship.

> "When the war started my sons were 31, 29, 26, and 18. They all went in the service."
> —a woman from Victoria

What then was daily life like for Texans during the war—for all the wives, all the mothers, all the families?

Part of it was good. Unemployment was 17 percent in 1939. By 1942 it was down to 5 percent, then dropped to 2 percent and stayed there till the end of the war. Not only were young men drafted from

> "We really felt no deprivation. If meat was low, Daddy would butcher a cow. Of course, some families lost sons, but that's just the way it was, and we kind of looked up to them, like they were celebrities."
> —a man from Iowa Park

TEXAS GOES TO WAR 185

JACKSBORO GOES TO WAR

Being born on the tail end of the Depression was fortunate for me. In the country town of Jacksboro, we all had plenty of nothing in equal proportions: no one had more of nothing than anyone else. The Depression was followed by World War II, and the war was even better. That the history books considered both occasions major catastrophes made me suspicious of historians ever after.

The reason for my pleasure in WWII was that I knew where everyone was and what we were all supposed to do. The entire National Guard unit from Jack County, Battery F, 131st Field Artillery was lost, the Lost Battalion. I remember being a little embarrassed about men from Jacksboro who got lost, but I knew they could take care of themselves.

My Uncle Glen, the oilfield giant, was chasing a fox named Rommel in Africa. Uncle Freddie was in a big boat, the USS Blackhawk, taking troops ashore at Iwo Jima.

They were there, we were here. My daddy was butchering beef at the grocery. My mother was in the kitchen. Mama Hartman was down on her knees asking God to smite the heathen, telling Him to save her boys, and putting two stars in the window. The citizens were on the square having parades or war rallies, saving coupons for sugar, hosiery, and tires, collecting tinfoil in big balls to make bombs, buying U.S. savings bonds to help lick the Axis, and giving the V-for-victory sign.

Before the war, I was aiming to be a cowgirl and practiced every day. The war gave me a change of costume. I donned a nurse's uniform, cape, and hat and played "In my arms, in my arms. Am I ever gonna' get a girl in my arms?" on the violin for programs. Sometimes I traded in my horse for a bicycle with spokes woven with crepe paper and handlebars fluttering with flags. War was pretty, fun, and safe in Jacksboro, Texas. I knew where everyone was and what to do.

—*Joyce Gibson Roach*

civilian jobs or prevented from taking them, but war work put a strain on the manpower of Texas, which was a boon for women who wanted jobs. The problem during the war was to do the necessary work with a shortage of people to do it, for Texas was experiencing an industrial revolution. Industrial revolutions uproot families, turn wives into factory hands, and work a hardship on children who are often left alone to shift for themselves till the parents come home from the mill or plant or shipyard.

In Corpus Christi, Southern Alkali expanded its plant. Dow Chemical came to Freeport; Carbide and Carbon Chemicals Corporation bought 200 acres for their plant in Texas City. Diamond Alkali, with its main office in Houston, built plants on the Gulf and in Dallas. In the Texas High Plains, three plants made sodium sulphate or salt cake. Shell Oil opened a new plant on the Houston Ship Channel, and Humble Oil a new plant in Baytown. Continental Oil opened a refinery at Wichita Falls and Magnolia Oil a cracking plant in Beaumont. Champion Paper and Fibre Company opened a plant at Pasadena near Houston, Southern Paper Mills one near Lufkin. And there were the new pulp and paper mills at Orange on the Gulf Coast. For the first time, there was a steel mill in the southwest, on the Houston Ship Channel. There was frantic activity at the shipyards in Beaumont, Orange, and along the Houston Ship Channel. Women were helping to staff those plants or had followed their husbands and were making shift to live in cramped quarters.

The result of the growth of industry was an influx of men, some with families, to these places. But where were they to live? There were only a million new dwellings built during the entire war in the United States, and 4 million workers migrated to war-production centers.

A few job-seekers took advantage of the moving of wives who, like Mary Nell, went to live with their parents. But that accommodated only a small percent. Some enterprising and penurious homeowners converted their houses into small apartments and moved in with a relative or friend, but the scarcity of lumber, plumbing supplies, etc., made this also an impossibility for all but a few. Some rented out rooms in private homes.

"It was really a sleepy little town that nobody ever heard of till they built the shipyard there. Then class 2-A men just poured in. Even if they didn't know anything, that was okay. They trained them, and they got good money, though it was hard to find a place to live. We moved in with my sister and rented out our house."
—*a woman from Corpus Christi*

One woman from Kansas, Lucy, followed her husband to Corpus Christi, bringing her one-year-old daughter with her. He was provided a room, along with some of his fellow-workers, in a newly converted rooming house, but there was no place for Lucy and the baby there, or anywhere else. Finally she prevailed on the owners of the rooming house to make a place for her, and in return she would look after their children. They boarded up a part of the porch for a bedroom. It was cold or hot in the room. There was no window. There was no fresh milk for her baby. But there she stayed for the duration.

"I remember one time waiting two and a half hours in line trying to get into the service station. I was two cars from the pump, when two men got into a fight, and they closed the station down for the day. I barely had enough gas to get home."
—*a woman from El Paso*

These hairstyles were designed to be "streamlined" in view of the chemicals and metals "being sucked into the defense maw." (Institute of Texan Cultures, *The San Antonio Light* Collection)

CALIFORNIA OR BUST

In August 1944, the month I turned eight, my mother, who refused to drive a car, put my 15-year-old brother behind the wheel of a 1941 Chevrolet and we set out for California to meet my Marine Corps father. As the family of a marine officer, we had a C gas ration sticker, but acquiring tires was a far greater problem. We solved it when the father of a teenage girl we were taking with us provided them. He owned a filling station and must have had some tires left over from before the war. He came up with the tires we needed—but they were the wrong size!

We spent the first night in Sonora, Texas, the second night in Las Cruces, New Mexico, and the third night in Yuma, Arizona. My mother, always bothered by Texas heat, was miserable in the desert, so we actually traveled most of that trip in darkness. We would leave at 3:00 A.M. and stop around 1:00 or 2:00 in the afternoon and find a cool spot in the shade to hole up and sleep and start off again the next morning. Most of my sightseeing must have been done between sunup and whenever we stopped the car.

I remember arriving at Laguna Beach, California, during a blackout. The whole coast was dark as a precaution against Japanese attack. The fear of bombing was a real threat to the grown-ups, but for me it was just more excitement and another peculiarity on the part of the adults. As we were driving down the darkened main street of Laguna Beach, hoping we could find either my father or the address of the temporary quarters he had rented us, we spied him walking down the street accompanied by another Trinity County resident who was also in the marines. All these misplaced East Texans fell upon one another out there in the dark of the night with the ocean crashing close by and no other familiar faces around even if we could have seen them.

—Frances Brannen Vick

Capt. Carl Andrew Brannen also served as a private in World War I and fought at Belleau Wood, Soissons, St. Mihiel, Blanc Mont, and Meuse-Argonne.

Despite the fact that their wives were living on boarded-up porches or 500 miles away, factory workers, because they were making more money than most people thought possible, were sometimes the object of envy. In the larger cities they were usually accepted, but in the rural areas of Texas and in small towns, occupational deferments—although everyone knew that crops had to be planted and reaped, hogs had to be butchered—aroused the ire and sometimes hatred of neighbors. Remarks were made: "How come you aren't in uniform, doing your part. You look healthy enough to me." White chicken feathers were tied to rural mail boxes. Wives and children of these deferred men felt a sense of shame. Despite wartime posters presenting factory workers as heroes, everyone knew who the real heroes were—the men in uniform.

The need for workers and the subsequent rise in wages affected lower-income families the most. In fact, between 1935 and 1944, the income for poorer families jumped 52 percent. And with more money to spend, despite rationing, which was begun in 1942, people ate better, were healthier. Indeed, people had more money and rationing stamps for meat than there was meat in the stores.

It was these shortages, deprivations, this extra work, this worry and concern, that made 90 percent of the people in 1944 respond to a poll that, despite the rise in their income, their families were worse off than they had been before the war.

> "My mother planted a Victory garden and canned a lot of vegetables. But later we threw most of them out. They were really terrible. My mother felt bad about that."
> —a woman from Brownsville

Schoolchildren enjoyed helping in paper drives, tin-can drives, even string drives. They enjoyed being a part of the war effort. They enjoyed buying a 25-cent stamp at school once a week to paste in their books so that when they got enough—it took 75 stamps—they could convert the book to a bond that supported the war.

"The sewing students at St. Gerard's school work on garments for beleaguered Britain under Red Cross auspices."
(Institute of Texan Cultures, *The San Antonio Light* Collection)

Some children were frightened. They heard the news broadcasts their parents listened to—the mellifluous tones of Kaltenborn, the educated, elite accent of Roosevelt, the gruff, clipped messages of Churchill—and were awed by the language, by the gravity of the situation. They saw bombs in newsreels. They cheered at the movies when the stars and stripes was shown—in a parade, being planted on a beachhead. They huddled close to one another during blackouts, imagining bombers flying overhead dropping missiles of destruction.

Many were without their fathers, who were in the service or in distant cities working in factories. Mothers worried about a child being raised without a father. Grandfathers tried to fill the gap. What would be the fate of children without a man in the house? Especially what would that absence mean to boys? Nothing good, all were convinced.

CHILDHOOD

My father volunteered for the Army Air Corps shortly after Pearl Harbor and was inducted in the spring. My brother, mother, and I moved from Palmer to Port Arthur to live with my grandparents for the duration of the war. Mom went to work as a nurses' aide, my grandmother looked after my infant brother, and I was quickly accepted as one of the gang by the other kids in the lower-middle class neighborhood where we lived.

The urgency of peace and the violence of the war missed those of us who were pre-teens. In that older and more gentle time, when violence was seen as an overseas phenomenon, the neighborhood kids wandered through the streets, playing children's games, or gathered to listen to the "Lone Ranger" on the radio, and were checked on rather casually by neighborhood mothers who were not working. I wished my father were home, of course. But swaggering service men returning on leave captured my imagination and envy.

The casualties of war were not apparent to me until after it ended. Those who worried about death belonged to that strange adult world, which also worried about such things as rationing, and like my grandfather, marked the campaigns on big wall maps and followed the news day-by-day. Somehow adults, unlike kids, failed to realize that all life would turn out fine.

The one time that the horror of war did sink into my childhood consciousness—never to really leave—was the dropping of the bombs on Hiroshima and Nagasaki. Not that I minded the devastation to Japan, but because even children recognized that the photographs and newsreels of the mushroom clouds and the accounts of the bombs' deadly radiation meant an end to the world as we knew it. I still mark the report of the bomb as the end of my childhood.

As with many families separated by war, mine never re-formed. My Mom and Dad divorced in 1946. The memories of war faded with adolescence and an interest in young women. The old neighborhood fell into decay as the postwar industrial boom that swept through Texas propelled the young families to the suburbs. But for those of us who were children in World War II, it was the "last good war"—and maybe the best time to have been a child.

—Robert Calvert

For every soldier, sailor, and marine who is fighting for my country. For you there can be no rest, for me there should be no vacation from the part I can play to help you win the war. I therefore solemnly promise to continue to buy United States War Savings Stamps and Bonds to the limit of my ability throughout my summer vacation and until our victory is won.

—Pledge in the stamp book.

Growing up in the face of war
(Texas State Archives)

190 LOVE, MARRIAGE, & THE FAMILY

Books were published with such dramatic titles as *You . . . Your Children . . . and War*, books that told parents how to cope with their children's fear and anger and hate, how to improve their schools, how to deal with teenagers. Such books advised mothers, among other things, to keep the home clean and orderly.

"Juvenile delinquency" became a common term, referring to the rebelliousness and mischievous behavior of teen-age boys. Gangs made their appearance. It was the absence of fathers. Everyone knew that. And the neglect of mothers. Churches were quite concerned that mothers spend their time with their children, not with volunteer work, not on any paying job. What are we fighting for anyway? Our children. The sacredness of the family.

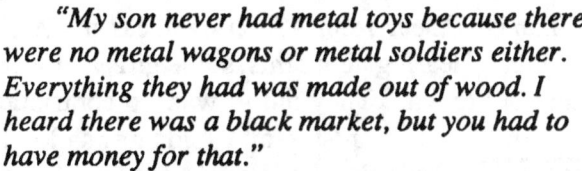

"My son never had metal toys because there were no metal wagons or metal soldiers either. Everything they had was made out of wood. I heard there was a black market, but you had to have money for that."

—*a woman from Dalhart*

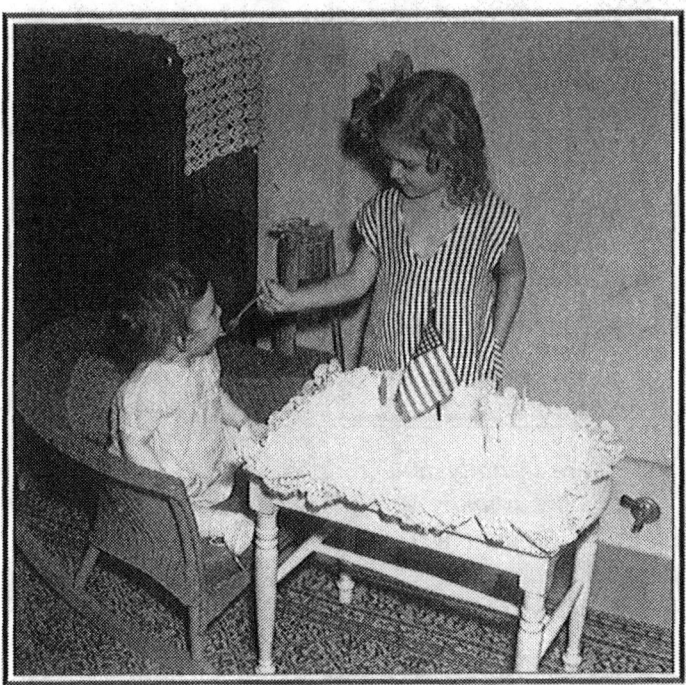

Sisters celebrate the same birthday—and the flag.
(Institute of Texan Cultures,
The San Antonio Light Collection)

Herman and Helen Pennington with their daughter Sue

Everyone was afraid of what the war was doing to love, to marriage, and to the family. Everyone felt such ties more strongly than ever, but the very strength of the emotions, the unmet needs, the danger to relationships, seemed to put a terrible strain on them. What they wanted and needed most seemed as elusive as the face one tried to remember when one awoke alone in the middle of the night. The face was unclear, and the more it was evoked, the hazier it got.

Twenty-nine percent of servicemen did not go overseas during the war but had jobs stateside, running installations, attending to troop movements, transporting war materials, running hospitals. Some of these men, separated from their wives, found other female companionship. Wives of absent soldiers and factory workers found other male companionship. Engaged girls met new soldiers, met boys in the ASTP, met officers.

The letters these women wrote, breaking off their engagement or their marriage, became so common as to have a name—"Dear John." Men overseas made bitter jokes about Dear John Letters. Hearing about this, some girls and women decided not to write them but to wait. They didn't want to contribute to the hardship of a soldier or sailor. Stories circulated of airplane crashes after pilots received Dear John Letters, of soldiers not taking proper precautions after receiving such letters.

"When he came back, he wouldn't even see his wife. I don't know why. He had some wounds, but they had pretty near all healed. But he wouldn't see her and he wouldn't tell anybody why. I heard later they got a divorce."
—*a man from Big Spring*

There are no records of the number of engagements broken during or after the war, but certainly there were more of these than divorces—and the divorce rate increased dramatically. In the late 1930s, 85 marriages in 10,000 ended in divorce. From 1941 to 1945 that rate had increased to 114 in 10,000. In 1946 and 1947, at the end of the war, there were 158 divorces for every 10,000 marriages.

"There sure were some changes in our town. There were sexually deprived women and some wild scenes. Young wives, with their husbands gone, took out high school boys and introduced them to sex. So there were quite a few divorces after the war, when the husbands came home."
—*a man from Greenville*

192   LOVE, MARRIAGE, & THE FAMILY

We come to God's altar today—a group of friends, loved ones, neighbors—in memory of a loved one who has given his life for freedom. We come to honor AAF Pilot Lt. Cecil Willard Biggs who, on September 23, 1944, gave his life over Arnheim, Holland, in order that his father and mother and wife and son and sister—and other men's loved ones might live in a free world.

And, of course, there was the inevitable toll of the destruction of war itself. Of the 16 million men in the service, 27 percent were in combat, 300,000 died, and 500,000 were seriously disabled. Many Texans returned to Brooke Army Hospital in San Antonio, which became the largest military hospital in the world.

So the Texas servicemen came home: a few to broken marriages, many more to sweethearts who had been waiting for them patiently. Few of them came back to houses or apartments to call their own. Few of them came back to the jobs they had left. The industries that grew up in Texas were largely manned by workers from elsewhere. Everything was scarce if not impossible to procure. With nothing to lose, many of them took advantage of the law that gave them tuition-free education at universities, colleges, and training schools. So it was that men who had never even thought of attending college found themselves on college campuses, often becoming the first person in their families to attend an institution of higher learning.

"In my town they hired an older man who had some sensitivity to deliver the telegrams telling about some soldier dying. They couldn't just call you over the phone, because a lot of people just fell apart when they did that."
—a woman from Mexia

Texas went to war as a more or less non-industrial, culturally isolated place, where men were men and women were women. It came out of the war changed economically but not as culturally different as some hoped it would be. Women, who worked during the war for their fighting men, now found themselves working to put their husbands through school. Women who did not have to work started having babies, lots of babies. Many "Texas girls" were glad the war was over so they could get back once more to a normal life.

ENTERTAINMENT AT HOME & ABROAD

by
DAWN DUNCAN

The biggest entertainment in the Dallas-Fort Worth area on December 6, 1941, was the spectacular Texas Air Fair, which re-created the Battle of Britain. Amazed spectators watched the aerial destruction of a ten-acre mock village at Arlington Downs as dive bombers, booming anti-aircraft guns, and the stab of searchlights imparted a sense of reality. Lt. Comdr. Ralph Goodwin, manager of aviation for Shell Oil and a member of the United States Naval Reserve, orchestrated the staging to resemble the German *blitzkrieg* of England. Goodwin had traveled to England as an unofficial observer, returning with what was considered valuable information for the army and navy. Ironically, the spectacular air fair foreshadowed an event less than 24 hours away—the Japanese attack on Pearl Harbor.

In a second ironic twist involving battle of another kind, Texas high school football fans witnessed two surprising upsets on December 6 as underdog Austin High beat Corpus Christi, the highest scoring Texas team of the season; and Highland Park's "silk-stocking boys from Snob Hill" whipped the Paris Wildcats' "country boys" to advance to the state quarter finals.

After the air spectacle and the football surprises of December 6, the following day in Dallas promised to be classically refined. The Dallas Symphony featured Irma Gonzalez, guest soloist from Mexico City, singing selections from Handel and Mozart. King Vidor, famed Hollywood director and native of Galveston, added to the afternoon's musical artistry with his guitar performance. Local actor Louis V. Quince narrated Prokofiev's *Peter and the Wolf*, and the concert was rounded out with Mark Phillips's arrangement of "The Star Spangled Banner."

While society swells attended a classical concert in Dallas, the Japanese wolf was ripping at the star-spangled banner in Pearl Harbor. Thousands around the state heard the initial reports over the radio. Bill and Lela Mae Sullivan, a farming couple in Muleshoe, listened in silent shock as their toddlers, three-year-old Loretta and one-year-old Charles, made mud pies and had "tea" in the back yard. Jim Turner, a jeweler in El Paso, and his wife Harriet called their ten-year-old daughter Sarah in from skipping rope with a friend on the front porch. They felt that she was old enough to join her parents as they huddled in horror near the radio for the latest reports. Families across the state gathered close to one another and to their sets, waiting, fearing, and finally becoming infuriated.

Capt. Edward Charles McGuire and his Texas buddies enjoy a night on the town in New York. Leon & Eddie's was a popular stopover for troops before shipping out.

The attack on Pearl Harbor changed America forever, and entertainment reflected the changes. Sergei Rachmaninov opened as planned at SMU's McFarlin Auditorium on December 11. By that date thousands of war tunes had poured into music publishers. Although the war in Europe had been going on for over two years, the United States' involvement upped the number of war lyrics submitted to publishers by a third. A few of the war-inspired songs Texans were soon tuning in on the radio were "You're A Sap Mister Jap," "The Jap Won't Have a Chinaman's Chance," and "Good-by, Mama, We'll See You in Yokohama."

According to the 1940 census, Texas boasted 56 radio stations, and 65 percent of all homes had at least one radio set. Throughout the war years, radio continued to be for many the major source of news and entertainment. During the day, housewives worked while listening to the news and to such favorite soaps as "Guiding Light," "Young Widder Brown," "Young Dr. Malone," and "Our Gal Sunday." In the evening, the whole family would gather to laugh along with "Bergen and McCarthy" or stifle screams as the sound of a squeaking door announced another half-hour of the chilling "Inner Sanctum Mystery." Other popular non-musical shows on Texas radio were "Dick Tracy," "Red River Dave," "Ma Perkins," and "Stella Dallas."

WAC representative, Lt. Van Acken, accompanied by Perrin Field Band at an outdoor concert
(Texas Woman's University Library, *Daedalian*, 1944)

There was also an abundance of musical variety shows. Texans turned up the volume on "Guy Lombardo," "Fred Waring," "Western Serenade," and "Alexander's Variety Hour." Later in the war, Sgt. Gene Autry broadcast his "Melody Ranch" across the nation. The sounds of Oscar Levant playing George Gershwin tunes on "Music From America" or Percy Faith conducting his own arrangements on "American Melody Hour" could be heard both at home and abroad. The shows were re-broadcast for the American armed forces. Other special radio programs broadcast for the troops included "Command Performance," "Jubilee," and "G.I. Jive."

Some radio shows originated from military bases. Fort Sam Houston broadcast "Army Matinee," which included the "Soldiers' Singing Sweetheart Selection," in which Texas servicemen would ask their favorite songstress to sing on the show. NBC singer Kay Carlisle, who in five months had performed for over half a million soldiers, sailors, and marines, was selected for the first week's performance. Some military radio shows were broadcast from overseas to the folks back home: a group of Texas soldiers got together at Christmas and broadcast a show from North Africa for friends and relatives back in the Lone Star State.

Sometimes popular performers serving in the military would take part in broadcasts from their home bases. Virginia O'Neal, a civilian working in the Chaplain's Office at the Corpus Christi Naval Base while her husband served in the Philippines, recalled watching Tyrone Power rehearse a radio broadcast while he was stationed in Texas. O'Neal thought the movie idol was a "dreamboat, just the cutest guy." In fact, she said, "He reminded me of my husband."

Sophomore Soldier Dance,
Texas State College for Women
(Texas Woman's University Library)

HIT PARADE

December 6, 1941
Tonight We Love
Elmer's Tune
Chattanooga Choo Choo
Shepherd Serenade
I Don't Want to Set the World on Fire
This Love of Mine
You and I
Jim
A Sinner Kissed an Angel
Everything I Love

August 11, 1945
Dream
There, I've Said It Again
If I Loved You
The More I see You
Sentimental Journey
I Don't Care Who Knows It
You Belong to My Heart
Bell Bottom Trousers
Gotta Be This or That
I Wish I Knew

One of the most popular radio variety shows was "The Music Hall." A typical episode featured music by the Sons of Pioneers, a comedy routine known as the Physical Culture Club with gags to get listeners going in the morning, and musical comedy numbers by couples like George Murphy and Marilyn Maxwell. Wartime romances provided the subject matter for many a duet: Murphy and Maxwell sang a duet, "Count Me In," which told of a cute conflict between a wartime couple.

The music of the war years was fired with romance and patriotism, sometimes mellow and moody ballads, other times humorous harmonies with laughable lyrics.

One patriotic song which surged to the top of the charts in 1941 was "Deep In the Heart of Texas." In 1942, Texas soldiers wrote home to their sweethearts to remind them "don't sit under the apple tree with anyone else but me." Pop-music love ballads and novelty songs like "Praise the Lord, and Pass the Ammunition" were not the only tunes rising on the charts.

The war years caused an upsurge in the popularity of home-bred hillbilly music. As Texas soldiers relocated throughout the States and were shipped across the world to fields of combat, they took with them a love of country music. Barracks resounded with the music of guitars and twangy voices. Juke-

Parade of stars through downtown San Antonio: Harpo Marx and Lucille Ball
(Institute of Texan Cultures, *The San Antonio Light* Collection)

box operators and record-retailing firms discovered that the popularity of country tunes endured long past the time it took for pop tunes to decline. Bob Wills, born and bred in the Panhandle town of Turkey, Ernest Tubb from Crisp (in Ellis County), Gene Autry from Tioga, and Tex Ritter, once a law student at the University of Texas, were the kings of country during the war years.

Autry's "Be Honest with Me," and "Tears on My Pillow" were hits at the beginning of the war, and his "Mail Call Today" sold over a million records after Autry enlisted in the U.S. Air Corps. Ernest Tubb's "Blue Eyed Elaine" and "I'll Get Along Somehow," both recorded in San Antonio in 1940, joined his country standard "Walking the Floor Over You," recorded in Dallas in 1941, as wartime favorites. During the war, Tubb made four westerns in Hollywood, but was best known among the troops for such hits as "Seaman's Blues," "Rainbow at Midnight," and "Filipino Baby."

ARMY SPECIALISTS—THE BALL BEARING WACS

Gen. George C. Marshall, Commanding General of U.S. Armed Forces during World War II, was determined that U.S. soldiers under his command would have outstanding special services—recreation, education, athletics, music, etc. To that end, General Marshall organized the Army Specialists Corps. This corps was made up of outstanding nationally known leaders in music, theater, and education.

I received orders to report to Fort George G. Meade on October 17, 1942, where I was to become a member of the first class to enter the Army's Specialists Corps. I told my students at Baylor University goodbye—said a sad farewell to my wife, Kitty, and two babies—made a mental picture of my barn-red house on a hill and took off for Fort Meade.

Ten specialists from music, ten from education, and ten from theater were to be taught "the army way" in a short two-week course. All 30 had the rank of captain. The 30 specialists were housed in one long barrack, and as I walked timidly to my bunk that first night of army life, popular faces showed up in the gloom of the poorly lighted barrack—Glenn Miller, the great band director; Dean Linton, noted educator from Columbia University; Maurice Evans, famous Shakespearean actor; Eddie Dowling; Sid Pierpont; John Shubert, of the Shubert theatrical family in New York, and many others—all stars in their own right.

The next day we bought our army officers' uniforms at the PX. There was only one difference between our uniforms and the standard officer's uniform—our buttons were not shiny brass, but were dark gray plastic buttons.

Not long after our graduation, we were assigned in groups of three—a musician, an educator, a theater specialist—to selected Army Headquarters. There began to be sly looks of puzzlement regarding who we were. Were we army or not? Whoever heard of the army having specialists in education, music, theater? There were snickers and laughs behind our backs. Finally some smart-ass GI or shave-tail lieutenant came up with a new name for our Specialist Corps—THE BALL BEARING WACs.

We moved about among suppressed snickers and distant gales of laughter. We gave orders but very few listened, saying "That's a BALL BEARING WAC!" Someone must have told General Marshall because three months later, we were inducted into the Army Special Services Corps and given Brass Buttons.

—Paul Baker

Fraternizing with the troops at a military social
(University of North Texas Archives)

Bob Wills, remembered best for his 1940-41 hit "San Antonio Rose," disbanded his Texas Playboys in 1942 and joined the army—at age 38. He remained in the service only a short time before moving to Hollywood to make westerns and re-form his "Western Swing" band. Tex Ritter, the other "king" of Texas music in the '40s, made many of his 80 westerns during the war and had several country hits—"There's a Gold Star in Her Window," "There's a New Moon Over My Shoulder," and "Rye Whiskey."

Aiding the spread of country music's popularity were two labor disputes within the music industry which turned out favorably for downhome performers. Until December 31, 1940, ASCAP was the only American licensing firm for protecting the material of musicians. With a virtual monopoly, ASCAP made the mistake of doubling their permission fees for broadcasters. Consequently, the National Association of Broadcasters put a ban on ASCAP-protected materials and started a new licensing firm called Broadcast Music, Inc. (BMI). ASCAP had usually shunned hillbilly musicians, so most country music was up for grabs. BMI attracted country/folk musicians and new composers.

Then on August 1, 1942, the American Federation of Musicians went on strike as a protest against recorded music, which they claimed took jobs away from musicians. The continued struggle between broadcasters and recording companies on one side and traditionally legitimate musicians on the other enhanced the status of the country performers. Small, independent recording firms began to emerge and sign local talent. Nashville became the new hub for the burgeoning country music industry, but the stars came from all over the South and West.

The sounds of Texas in country music were being heard world-wide. Despite the music industry strikes (which lasted until November 1944) and a government freeze on shellac, an important ingredient in the manufacture of records, an average of three country records a week were recorded, indicating the new priority placed on this style of music. Even the editors of the pop music weekly newspaper, *Billboard*, sat up and took notice. In January 1942, the magazine began running a column devoted to country music. At first it was titled "Western and Race," but by February the name had been changed to "American Folk Records." In 1944, *Billboard* began to list the most popular hillbilly tunes.

Because there was a recording ban which, with the exception of new composers or country performers, involved a great many musicians, radio stations and record companies were limited in what they could give the public. However, musicians were as patriotic as most Americans and wanted to do their best to encourage our boys abroad. The result was a military program for recording free musical entertainment for the troops. The greatest musicians of the time volunteered their talents in the service of their country to make V-discs ("V" for victory). The troops listened and danced to the likes of Hoagy Carmichael, Bing Crosby, Benny Goodman, Count Basie, Louis Armstrong, the Dorsey brothers, Gene Krupa, Ella Fitzgerald, Les Brown, Marian Anderson, and Glenn Miller.

> **AMERICA'S TRUMPETER**
>
> Harry James and Louise Tobin met while they were both with Benny Goodman and His Band. James was the thrilling trumpeter and Tobin was the sensational singer. Married for eight years, they made some beautiful music together. However, they ended the partnership when Mrs. James agreed to give her handsome husband an amicable Mexican divorce so that he could marry actress Betty Grable in 1943. Miss Grable, famous for her legs, was chosen by American soldiers as the number one pin-up girl of World War II.

Pretty Texas talent goes Hollywood as proved by these three Lone Star starlets signed by a major studio.

One Texan who took the country by storm during the war years was Harry James. James, a native of Beaumont, and his lovely singing wife, Louise Tobin of Denton, with their big band backing them made the joint jump in many an officers' or enlisted men's lounge. James was also making the teens back home tremble when he triple-tongued his trumpet. At one engagement, police had to be called out to control screaming fans. Hoping to help clear the hall, James announced that he would give out autographed pictures at the stage door. The house cleared but then the mob had to be handled at the door.

Not all the greatest music of the time was heard on records. The soothing live sounds of bands and blues could be heard in many a small, dark club or large, aristocratic hotel throughout the state. If you wanted to dance until dawn, you could find a place like the Century Log Cabin on Metropolitan in Dallas which hosted Leroy Tolbert and his ten-piece orchestra "from 4 P.M. until ?" for a cover charge of a quarter. Rain or shine, the jitterbuggers and slow-dancers could dance to Pinetop Smith's "Boogie Woogie" or Glenn Miller's "String of Pearls." Or if you preferred to sit back and be entertained, you could slide into a hotel lounge and listen to the likes of the Herman Waldman Orchestra at the Adolphus while feasting your eyes on the band's beauties or laughing at the loonies who made up the floor show. Whether recorded or live, country, big band, or blues, music made the tough times of the war years a bit more bearable.

1940 ACADEMY AWARDS	
Actor:	James Stewart *The Philadelphia Story*
Actress:	Ginger Rogers *Kitty Foyle*
Supporting Actor:	Walter Brennan *The Westerner*
Supporting Actress:	Jane Darnell *The Grapes of Wrath*
Director:	John Ford *The Grapes of Wrath*
Picture:	*Rebecca* Selznick International

Another on-going source of rich entertainment full of Texas talent was the movies. Some of the finest films ever made came to the screen in the '40s.

Fort Worth proudly claimed Academy Award-winning actress Ginger Rogers while San Antonio hailed hometown girl Joan Crawford, and Texas was later to be the home of another wartime Academy Award-winner, Greer Garson, who settled in Dallas after the war as the wife of local oilman Buddy Fogelson. Other notable Texans in the film industry were Mary Martin of Weatherford, Linda Darnell of Oak Cliff, Joan Blondell and Ann Sheridan of Denton, King Vidor of Galveston, Ann Miller of Cherino, and millionaire producer/director Howard Hughes of Houston.

The week which began with the attack on Pearl Harbor featured some of these Texas notables in its headlines. Hughes was experiencing his own siege of sorts as Faith Dorn, 17-year-old New Orleans actress, announced that she and the oil-rich airplane manufacturer-gone-Hollywood were engaged. Hughes would not comment on the claim but did admit to buying out the starlet's contract from Warner's.

Rise and Shine, starring Linda Darnell, George Murphy (later a U.S. Senator from California), and Walter Brennan, was opening in theaters across the state. And King Vidor donated scripts, costume designs, model sets, and other movie materials to the University of Texas as part of its new study of film as an art form. Ann Sheridan, beautiful pin-up pal, sent four signed posters, one for each mess, to the British corvette *Nigella*. The British sailors had selected the striking Texas star as the woman they would most like to adopt.

1941 ACADEMY AWARDS

Actor:	Gary Cooper *Sergeant York*
Actress:	Joan Fontaine *Suspicion*
Supporting Actor:	Donald Crisp *How Green Was My Valley*
Supporting Actress:	Mary Astor *The Great Life*
Director:	John Ford *How Green Was My Valley*
Picture:	*How Green Was My Valley* 20th Century Fox

On December 7, Texas theaters were showing some of the following films: *Eternally Yours, Two-Faced Woman, International Squadron, Dive Bombers, Lone Star Ranger, Men at Large, Northwest Passage, Ridin' the Wind,* and *The Iron Claw.*

John T. Smith of Dallas recalled sitting in the Tower Theater with his father, laughing at the antics of Abbot and Costello as a pair of inept air corps soldiers in the hilariously patriotic *Keep 'Em Flying.* When they came out of the matinee, 11-year-old John could tell by the strained mood and behavior of the people on the street that something was wrong, but it was not until he and his father got home to Oak Cliff that he heard the news about Pearl Harbor.

Even before the attack on Pearl Harbor, Texas audiences were clearly concerned with war and patriotism. Showing in every major Texas city and many small towns, the most popular film at the time was *Sergeant York.* It featured Gary Cooper's performance as the World War I hero who was a model for American soldiers during the early days of the World War II. American sympathies were clearly already on the side of the British as the top Academy Award winner of 1940, *Mrs. Miniver*, a movie about resiliency and bravery in a small English town, continued to pack houses. The closing speech of the film, spoken by a preacher in the bombed-out shell of a church, proclaimed that World War II was a war of "all the people." Texans soon found themselves in agreement with the prophetic film.

WE'VE NEVER BEEN LICKED

To be a Texas Aggie means to endure satire or enjoy sainthood, depending on the parties doing the discussing. The film *We've Never Been Licked,* produced in 1943, does a lot to fuel the fires of wise-cracking and hero-worship. Still shown at A&M as a campy favorite, the movie extols the wonders of Aggiedom. The central plot involves an uppity freshman who gets taken down a tack by upperclassman Robert Mitchum. Seeing the light, of course, means appreciating the glory of A&M. Set in the war years, a secondary plot revolves around a Japanese spy. Of course, the heroes win the day and prove all cynics wrong. Perhaps not a great film, the movie is still great fun—at least for Aggies.

Throughout the war years, movies remained a favorite and affordable form of entertainment. Adults could see a matinee for 40¢ or an evening show for half-a-dollar. Children got in for a mere 11¢. And several towns, like Houston, instituted a junior rate to enable teenagers to afford some fun for only 20¢.

The film industry rallied to produce quality entertainment, whether of a patriotic nature or for sheer escapism, and Texas stars continued to shine. Joan Blondell stayed in the starlight with MGM's *Cry Havoc* and was a Broadway stage sensation in *Naked Genius*. King Vidor capitalized on the love of homeland with his film *America* about an immigrant who makes good. Mary Martin's stage show *One Touch of Venus* became the biggest hit on Broadway in 1943, tying that other state-glorifying musical, *Oklahoma*. And Joan Crawford paid tribute to the industry that entertained the world even while at war in 1944's *Hollywood Canteen*.

1942 ACADEMY AWARDS	
Actor:	James Cagney *Yankee Doodle Dandy*
Actress:	Greer Garson *Mrs. Miniver*
Supporting Actor:	Van Heflin *Johnny Eager*
Supporting Actress:	Teresa Wright *Mrs. Miniver*
Director:	William Wyler *Mrs. Miniver*
Picture:	*Mrs. Miniver* MGM

Nancy Gates
(Texas Woman's University Library)

At Christmas 1942, Texas sent another gift to Hollywood. Nancy Gates, a talented young singer from Denton, had caught the eye of Orson Welles after being featured in several newspapers and magazines. The 16-year-old made a good screen test and found herself courted by studios. She lost several starring roles because of her age. California Board of Education rules forbade her working past 6 P.M. However, she won a role as one of the Tuttles in *The Tuttles of Tahiti* with Charles Laughton and played the female lead in *The Great Gildersleeve*. As second-love interest in another Charles Laughton film, *This Land Is Mine*, Nancy Gates established her stardom. The film become popular stateside and on military bases.

Aside from the escapist musicals and expected romances, war films captured the audiences. In 1944, when young reviewers aged 8 to 18 were asked to pick the ten best films of the

1943 ACADEMY AWARDS

Actor:	Paul Lukas *Watch on the Rhine*
Actress:	Jennifer Jones *The Song of Bernadette*
Supporting Actor:	Charles Coburn *The More the Merrier*
Supporting Actress:	Katina Paxinou *For Whom the Bell Tolls*
Director:	Michael Curtiz *Casablanca*
Picture:	*Casablanca* Warner

With the war effort uppermost in everyone's mind, the live USO shows given at military posts provided some of the best entertainment of the time. Texans among the troops had the opportunity to see stars performing in the flesh, an opportunity many would have missed in peaceful times. Individual performers volunteered their talents, private groups mounted roadshows, and the United Service Organizations (USO) coordinated all types of entertainment for our servicemen and women. Six national welfare agencies—YMCA, YWCA, Jewish Welfare Board, Salvation Army, National Travelers Association, and National Catholic Community Service—had united to form the USO with the purpose of raising $10 million to go toward providing amusement and relaxation for the troops.

year, only two were not war related. The top three were *This Is the Army*, *So Proudly We Hail*, and *Stage Door Canteen*. The two non-war films selected were sentimental animal movies: *Lassie Come Home* and *My Friend Flicka*.

Films were also shipped to military bases around the world. The air force magazine *Brief* printed a weekly list of coming movies. On the average, four new films a week made the rounds. A typical slate might include: Jean Arthur and Joel McCrea in *The More the Merrier*, Red Skelton and Eleanor Powell in *I Dood It*, Barbara Stanwyck and Edward G. Robinson in *Flesh and Fantasy*, and Dorothy McGuire and Robert Young in *Claudia*.

Ann Sheridan learns the history of the *Bolivar*. "Damndest mission I was ever on," she said after climbing through the plane. (*Brief*)

Red Skelton entertains servicewomen. (*Brief*)

TEXAS GOES TO WAR   205

The "Grand Ole Opry" responded by sending out a group of 20 entertainers called the "Camel Caravan" to tour the bases. The shows were free to all military personnel and any civilians serving on the bases. Some of the stars seen by Texas soldiers included Bob Hope, Frances Langford, Jerry Colona, Minnie Pearl, Ann Sheridan, Frank Sinatra, and Edgar Bergen and Charlie McCarthy. Golden Apple Awards were presented by the Hollywood Women's Press Club to Bob Hope and Texas's own Ann Sheridan for being the most cooperative actor and actress.

Though many of the shows were variety-oriented and had a musical comedy bent, the troops also were treated to Broadway dramas and straight comedies. Occasionally, stars would drop in on troops for reasons other than live performances. Personnel at Randolph Field were pleased by a personal appear-

1944 ACADEMY AWARDS

Actor:	Bing Crosby *Going My Way*
Actress:	Ingrid Bergman *Gaslight*
Supporting Actor:	Barry Fitzgerald *Going My Way*
Supporting Actress:	Ethel Barrymore *None But the Lonely Heart*
Director:	Leo McCarey *Going My Way*
Picture:	*Going My Way* Paramount

Entertainment for servicemen at Fort Wolters
(Texas Woman's University Library)

Veronica Lake visits Randolph Field for the premiere showing of *I Wanted Wings*
(Institute of Texan Cultures, *The San Antonio Light* Collection)

ance from Veronica Lake for the premiere of her film *I Wanted Wings*, which was playing on the base. Sharp-sighted soldiers in San Antonio might have caught a glimpse of Jeanette MacDonald when she arrived to visit her husband, Capt. Gene Raymond. San Antonio residents would not have had to look so hard to see Harpo Marx riding in a parade through their streets.

1945 ACADEMY AWARDS

Actor:	Ray Milland *The Lost Weekend*
Actress:	Joan Crawford *Mildred Pierce*
Supporting Actor:	James Dunn *A Tree Grows in Brooklyn*
Supporting Actress:	Anne Revere *National Velvet*
Director:	Billy Wilder *The Lost Weekend*
Picture:	*The Lost Weekend* Paramount

When not being entertained by stars, drilling, or fighting battles, Texas soldiers hungry for a little female companionship might have been lucky enough to find themselves entertained by volunteers who made up the USO Victory Belles. With over 500 USO clubs throughout the world, women of "good character" with talent and personality were needed to run the lounges and game rooms and to act as partners for the servicemen. The girls might be called upon to jitterbug or waltz, play bridge or pack a picnic lunch, act as guide or secretary, cheer at a ball game or help with a theater production. Dallas boasted one of the most active Victory Belle groups with over 1,500 girls participating. Among other things, the girls arranged for the men to have access to free showers and ironing prior to a night of jitterbugging at the Baker Hotel. Service clubs abroad also catered to Texas tastes. At Ala Moana Park in Honolulu, all officers, enlisted men, and civilians from the Lone Star State were invited to "dig those spurs and saddles out" of their B-bags and feed their hunger at a hoedown which would include "a shipload of beef from the mainland to be barbecued in good old Texas style, and plenty to drink." Each Texan was allowed to bring one non-Texan guest. A number of marriages evolved from such evenings of pleasant companionship.

Though Texas civilians may not have enjoyed all the privileges extended to military men in time of war, there was still a thriving theater community which staged good live shows for local audiences. When the U.S. declared war on Japan, live theater was an important part of the artistic scene in Dallas. Early 1942 productions included *Old Acquaintance* at the Dallas Little Theater and *King Lear* at McFarlin Auditorium. The Melba Theater season produced *Life with Father*, *Arsenic and Old Lace*, *My Sister Eileen*, and *Macbeth*. As the war progressed, some theaters cut back or failed while others turned to producing lighter fare. The summer season of 1945 in Dallas provided the operetta *Maytime* at the Fair Park Casino as its ninth offering. The Madcap Players in Grand Prairie staged the mystery/comedy *Spooks*. And the Wade hosted Jackie Russell's *Adorables* and *Woman in the Window*.

Local San Antonio teams play first all-star game to benefit the USO
(Institute of Texan Cultures, *The San Antonio Light* Collection)

Sergeant McGinnis of the 9th Cavalry and Headquarters Troop team prior to 1943 2nd Cavalry Division championship game at Fort Clark
(Mountain Empire Historical Society, Col. Morris H. Marcus Collection)

Not all entertainment of the time was limited to the arts. As always Texans enjoyed an active involvement in athletic events, but wartime called for some changes. Gas rationing created a need to re-district UIL games, forcing teams to play one another several times in a season. Military teams came to the forefront of sports as a result of the enlistment of many fine athletes. And civilians in hometown communities took to the fields and courts for good, cheap fun.

When the war broke out, football held a favored spot in many a Texas heart as can be seen from the fat sports sections in the newspapers. In 1941 the UT Longhorns trampled all over Oregon, 71-7. But it was Texas A&M which reigned as Southwest Conference champs, earning a trip to the Cotton Bowl. In the high school quarter-final games, the line-up included Wichita Falls Coyotes vs. Ysleta, Sunset (Dallas) vs. Highland Park, Lamar (Houston) vs. Austin, and Temple vs. Tyler.

In 1943 the University of Texas won its way to the Cotton Bowl, losing one game that season, only to be tied by another one-game loser, Randolph Field of San Antonio. The Texas soldiers could not only fight, they were formidable in football. Texas A&M, beaten by UT and tied by the North Texas Aggies (now the University of Texas at Arlington) in the same season, played Louisiana State in the Orange Bowl. A&M had already beaten LSU once in the regular season, but would lose to them in the bowl game, 19-14. When the sports writers made their selections for the top 20 teams of '43, no Texas teams appeared in the top 10, but UT was ranked number 14, and one of their players, Joe Parker, made the Associated Press All-American Team.

But no matter how the Texas teams fared in the final scores, the football fans were always full of the fighting spirit. When the Abilene Military Police Training Center played Southwestern, soldiers almost killed themselves cheering. After a Southwestern touchdown, one GI got so rowdy that he fell out of the stands and broke his collarbone. Despite the enthusiasm of such die-hard fans, the military lost the day to Southwestern 45-6.

Texans also kept themselves actively entertained with basketball, baseball, and track. In basketball for 1943, Southwestern upset Texas, 50-41. Baylor took a court victory over the soldiers from Waco Army Field, 36-29, in the first month of 1944. And at the high school level in 1944, Dallas's Sunset became state champs, outscoring Childress 29-20.

That same year, Charlie Parker, 17-year-old San Antonio high school student, was billed as the "schoolboy dash sensation." He had stopped the clock at 9.5 in the 100 and 20.6 in the 220. The running world watched the young man in amazement, considering that Jesse Owens held both world records at the time with a 9.4 in the 100 and 20.3 in the 220.

Baseball, the all-American pastime, became a favorite way for military personnel to have fun. At Ellington Field, softball was reported as the major sport the men chose for a little active recreation. Texas athletes who did not get the chance to fight it out in stadiums because they were busy fighting on the fields of Europe, Africa, and Asia, followed games via the radio and military magazines. In 1944, the American League decided on a way to help the servicemen see the World Series. The league sent 125 copies of the World Series pictures, including shots of every scoring play, to our men overseas. After the copies made the rounds abroad, they were sent to home bases. Civilians saw the pictures only after all military personnel had the opportunity.

Boxing, especially on Texas bases, gave many an individual athlete the chance to show his prowess while pounding his opponent. Since many boxers were drafted to fight a bigger enemy, the sport became almost entirely the realm of the military. World titles were set aside until after the war. (World Heavyweight Champion Sgt. Joe Louis did not defend his title for six years but gave boxing exhibitions during the war.) The sport was so popular on bases that prior to Pearl Harbor an amateur military tournament was scheduled for Houston City Auditorium on December 11, 1941. At press time 84 entries from a dozen bases were included to go the distance in the ring, and more were expected to enter before the actual event. Unfortunately, Pearl Harbor made another sort of fight the priority for the week and the tournament was forgotten. But boxing remained a regular part of military post activities.

Houstonite Al Garcia, welterweight winner Hawaiian Grand Championships, is presented with trophy by Brig. Gen. Robert W. Douglass, Jr.
(*Brief*)

Rodeos and livestock shows drew crowds each year. Local luminaries would put in appearances. Gene Autry, the singing Texas cowboy and Hollywood star, put his rope to work in the ring at the Houston Fat Stock Show and Livestock Exposition, February 4-18, 1944.

At the same time that some Texans enjoyed watching cowboys getting bounced around on broncos and bulls, other Texans got involved in the midget auto racing craze before gas rationing curtailed that sport. In 1941, the *Houston Chronicle* reported that the best attended sport in town was midget auto racing. On the same day that the Japanese were bombing Pearl Harbor, 100 laps were being run at the Speed Bowl in Houston for the Third Annual Southern Grand Prix in midget auto racing.

Roy Rogers and Trigger
(Institute of Texan Cultures,
The San Antonio Light Collection)

(Institute of Texan Cultures,
The San Antonio Light Collection)

Texans entertained themselves in a less active but equally engrossing manner through reading. From comic strips to Pulitzer Prizes, romance to non-fiction war accounts, the presses continued to produce, and Texans continued to read. Comic strips, not merely a source of laughter but also a chance for political satire, underwent drastic changes after the United States' entrance into the war. Prior to the bombing of Pearl Harbor, only about a fifth of the strips in Texas newspapers referred to the war. After December 7, 1941, over half of all the comics were definitely war-related. Favorite strips of the time for Texans included: "Joe Palooka," "Donald Duck," "Alley Oop," "Wash Tubbs," "Our Boarding House," "Red Ryder," "Thimble Theater Starring Popeye," "Little Orphan Annie," "Terry and the Pirates," "Li'l Abner," "Barney Google and Snuffy Smith," "Mutt and Jeff," and "Gasoline Alley."

On Pearl Harbor Day the best-selling novel in Texas was Louis Bromfield's *Wild is the River*, set during the Civil War in New Orleans. The best selling nonfiction was John Gunther's *Inside Latin America*.

During World War II reading gained in popularity and importance. Magazine sales improved to such an extent that editors felt themselves free from money worries for the first time in years and were able to concentrate on content. Many publishers, such as Curtis, with its popular *Saturday Evening Post*, were able to increase the number of writers they hired as the circulation of the magazine steadily rose.

Texans were not only consuming short pieces of journalism, books too grew in popularity. Membership in the Book-of-the-Month Club doubled. The Pocket Book company had introduced paperbacks in 1939. These editions broke sales records as soldiers and civilians began carrying the books to work and to war. Mysteries alone sold 150,000 copies a week. Fiction tended to be escapist, usually in one of three veins: sexy romance, such as Kathleen Winsor's *Forever Amber*; historical romances like Adria Locke Langley's *A Lion Is in the Streets* based loosely on Louisiana politician Huey Long's career; or popular religious stories such as Lloyd C. Douglas's *The Robe*.

By 1945 readers longed for books on the light side. Humorous books like Bennett Cerf's *Try and Stop Me*, Betty MacDonald's *The Egg and I*, and James Thurber's *The Thurber Carnival* sold especially well. And humorous books about soldiers' lives in wartime were popular: Marion Hargrove's *See Here, Private Hargrove* ran to ten printings between May and October 1942.

However, not all books of the time were about laughter and love—far from it. In trade books, nonfiction outsold fiction, with a great deal of interest in history and technical subjects. Readers wanted information on current affairs, and they were especially interested in eyewitness war accounts. By April 1943, more than 100 eyewitness books had been published. The favorites were Ernie Pyle's *Here Is Your War*, selling nearly 2 million copies, and his

Pulitzer Prizes for Literature

Fiction	Drama
1940: John Steinbeck, *The Grapes of Wrath*	1940: William Saroyan, *The Time of Your Life*
1941: not awarded	1941: Robert E. Sherwood, *There Shall Be No Night*
1942: Ellen Glasgow, *In This Our Life*	1942: not awarded
1943: Upton Sinclair, *Dragon's Teeth*	1943: Thornton Wilder, *The Skin of Our Teeth*
1944: Martin Flavin, *Journey in the Dark*	1944: not awarded
1945: John Hersey, *A Bell for Adano*	1945: Mary Chase, *Harvey*

Library at Camp Maxey. The book displayed in the background is entitled *Victory Through Air Power*.

Brave Men, reaching second place on the best-seller list for 1944; Bill Mauldin's *Up Front*, combining prose and GI cartoons; and Bob Hope's *I Never Left Home*, his account of entertaining troops, selling over a million copies.

While the folks back home kept track of the war with their reading material, Texas troops, once again, did not have to do without. The military saw to it that the soldiers and sailors had access to a wide selection of reading materials. Under the Armed Service Edition program, cheap paperbacks made to fit the military pocket were printed. Titles included current best sellers, classics, and long-standing popular selections. At its peak, the program printed 40 titles per month. A total of 100 million copies of 2,000 titles were issued free to servicemen.

The genres servicemen requested most often were westerns, mysteries, and humor. The author in top demand, with eight Westerns under his pen, was Ernest Haycox. Max Brand came in second, followed by Thorne Smith (author of the Topper series) and C. S. Forester, whose sea stories about Horatio Hornblower had attracted a wide audience when serialized in the popular magazines. Because the government okayed all selections, some censoring occurred. The army permitted the issuing of *A Bell for Adano* despite the presence of a crude general who reminded some readers of Patton, but the navy vetoed the book for sailors.

Victory Book Campaign sponsored by a local library to obtain books for soldiers (Institute of Texan Cultures, *The San Antonio Light* Collection)

Texans who enjoyed reading had ample opportunity to read books by Texans about Texas. In one of its ads, Cokesbury listed 49 Texas works and claimed that in their stores a reader could choose from among 1,343 other Texas titles, most for about $2.00.

Cokesbury featured books by Texas folklorist J. Frank Dobie, whose story about Texas's signature cattle, *The Longhorns*, came out in 1941, and his *A Texan in England* in 1944. Books by George

Volunteer worker helps servicemen with reading selections.
(Brief)

Sessions Perry included *Texas—A World in Itself* and *Walls Rise Up*, a novel that came out in 1939, as well as *Hold Autumn in Your Hand* published in 1941, the only Texas novel ever to win a National Book Award. Indian Springs native Katherine Ann Porter's *Pale Horse, Pale Rider* had come out in 1939, and her collection *The Leaning Tower* in 1944.

Other Lone Star writers making a splash in 1941 were former marine colonel John W. Thomason with *Lone Star Preacher*; Mary King, whose *Quincie Bollivar* told of the oil strike at Spindletop; and Elizabeth Lee Wheaton's *Mr. George's Joint*, about life among Texas City blacks. Humorist Boyce House boasted *Texas—Proud and Loud* and *Tall Talk from Texas*. In juvenile literature, Siddie Joe Johnson stood out with *Cathy* and a history for juveniles, *Texas—the Land of the Tejas*. Sam Acheson's work reached the shelves in two forms: a biographical history, *35,000 Days in Texas*, and a play, *We Are Besieged*, which was included in the collection *Three Southwest Plays*.

For many Texans most entertainment was homespun. Sue Watson lived out in West Texas in a little town called Spur. She recalls, "We couldn't get gasoline to go anywhere in the car, so the family would get together and play. We played bridge. There wasn't any other game; as a family, we were addicted."

Games other Texans enjoyed during days of gas rationing included dominoes, checkers, and rummy. Sometimes families and friends would hold dances at home, get up parties, or go on picnics. Square dancing was extremely popular. Harriet and Jim Turner square-danced in El Paso at least once every week with a group of people who had organized a

"Pass through and promenade!" Texas folk kept their feet busy with the downhome fun of a square dance.
(Texas A&M University Archives)

A parade on "Theatre Row" (University of North Texas Archives)

local club. Jim not only danced, he did the calling as he do-si-doed. Local musicians made most of the music—with the fiddle always prominently featured.

Occasionally, carnivals and traveling tent shows would appear in the rural areas. Country folk would flock to see a screening of *The Sinking of the Titanic* under the canvas for a quarter or ride the Tilt-a-Whirl for a nickel. Kids would beg their parents to buy Cracker Jacks so they could get the prizes hidden inside. Churches held socials and schools hosted plays, musical evenings, and carnivals.

And as always, children played with dolls, wagons, and whatever else came handy. "Cowboys and Indians" was still a favorite activity for the youngsters, but playing "War" now became daily fun. Though adults took the times more seriously, with the war far away most children went on with life as before, playing happily.

Texans have always shown great resilience in times of trouble. The Texas spirit is lively and fun-loving. The war did not change the Texan's love of laughter or need for release of high spirits. Texans continued to entertain themselves, making the most with what they had. So the music played on, the dancers danced, and children of all ages found time to make merry in the midst of the war.

COMING HOME

by
MICHAEL HOBBS

May 8, 1945   *V-E Day, Germany Surrenders*
August 6, 1945   *First Atomic Bomb dropped on Hiroshima*
August 9, 1945   *Atomic bomb dropped on Nagasaki*
August 14, 1945   *V-J Day, Japan Surrenders*
September 2, 1945   *Japan signs surrender on USS* Missouri

On August 9, 1945, Houston native Kermit Beahan, bombardier on the B-29 superfortress "Bock's Car," pressed the button that ended World War II. People were stunned by the suddenness of the victory, but when the nuclear dust cleared, life in the United States and especially in Texas began a scientific, cultural, and economic boom.

After the initial jubilation on V-J Day, a period of readjustment began for Texas civilians as well as returning GIs. The veterans returned to a Texas that welcomed its heroes into strange arms.

Homecoming happiness was tainted by the bureaucratic headaches of service discharges, GI-Bill blues, and a sense of letdown and disillusionment over the difficulties of returning to peacetime life. Veterans had to begin anew the life they had left behind almost four years earlier, and home-fronters had to adjust their wartime ways to accommodate the heavy numbers of men flooding the job, housing, and education markets.

> Somehow the news got out that the Japs had surrendered. Such noise — The OD had to come to the scene.

Courage in danger is half the battle.
—*Plautus*

from the diary of Sgt. Harve King

Sgt. Harve King

Resentments, tensions, and clashes were inevitable, but out of the turmoil of victorious return and reconversion burst the prosperity of postwar Texas. The process of shifting the nation from wartime to peace was complicated. One problem was that World War II was fought on a double front and in a sense had two endings. Just as V-J Day was ushered in by the tremendous holocaust of the atomic bomb, V-E Day was preceded by the death of President Franklin Roosevelt on April 12, less than a month before the end of the war against Germany. The loss hurt Americans emotionally, but the spirit to persevere in the fight against fascism never waned. Roosevelt died before the surrender of Germany, but he knew victory was at hand.

When Victory in Europe was announced on May 8, 1945, the celebration in Texas was subdued. Civil defense sirens sounded in cities across the state, and churches planned special afternoon services, but from Amarillo to Midland to Corpus Christi hurrahs were restrained. With the prospect of a stepped-up war against stubborn Japanese resistance in the Pacific, President Truman requested that everybody continue the home-front effort. Texas civilians and GIs knew that the invasion of Japan loomed on the horizon. Celebrations had to wait!

> We were going to the Phillipines, but now things have changed V-J day is very near

The fight is over when the enemy is down.—*Ovid*

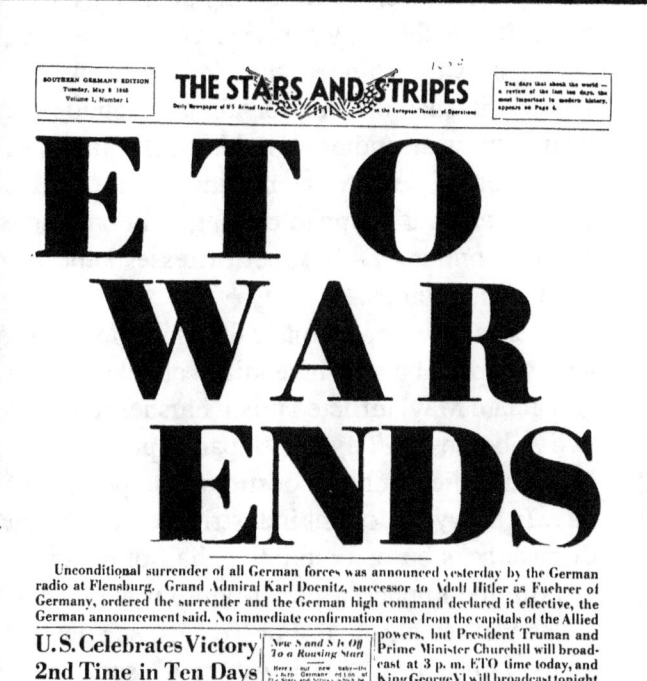

Still, some soldiers had done their share and more and were ready for discharge. After Germany's surrender, the military began a partial demobilization and redeployment of European Theater of Operation (ETO) forces. The process of determining who could go home was based on a complicated point system that puzzled almost everyone during the disbanding of the citizen army between the end of the war and 1947. In a press release on May 10, 1945, the Secretary of War, Henry L. Stimson, explained the point system:

Each month of service .... 1 Point
Each month overseas .... 1 Point
Each medal earned .... 5 Points
Each child waiting at home .... 12 Points

After Germany's surrender, the minimum requirement for a trip home was 85 points. Those soldiers in the European Theater who had fewer than 85 points were either shipped directly to the Pacific or brought home for a 30-day furlough before being shipped out to prepare for the coming invasion of Japan. No matter how many points they had, officers and specialty personnel had to be designated as nonessential to the needs of the army before they were discharged. For radio operators, diesel mechanics, teletype operators, and the like, the war continued on a different front.

Everyone is tense — we are waiting nervously for Japan's answer to the Allied surrender terms.

Who hath not served can not command.—*John Florio*

The army planned to reduce its numbers from 8,300,000 to 6,968,000 prior to the final assault against the Japanese. But all plans for redeployment were thrown into chaos when Japan suddenly surrendered under the threat of atomic annihilation. Texans breathed a sigh of relief as the necessity of a Japanese invasion disappeared.

On August 14, 1945, Japan announced the acceptance of the Allies' unconditional terms of surrender. Beginning on August 14 and continuing for several days, Texans indulged in a long-awaited celebration of victory. They had waited impatiently for Japan to surrender following the August 6 devastation of Hiroshima by America's new secret weapon.

Japan was whipped and Texans knew it. "The Bomb" finished off a nation already pounded to ash by merciless incendiary bombings. But Japan's final admission of defeat was not immediate. A second atom bomb was dropped on Nagasaki on August 9, and firebombing B-29 superfortresses kept peppering Japanese cities.

Texas newspapers made the most of the nation's new weapon, but the incendiary attacks, which began in late May, inflicted much harsher ruin than the two A-bombs. In Toyama, Japan, a place the size of Lubbock, firebombings destroyed 96 percent of the city. In every important industrial center, the incendiary attacks burned more than half of the city.

But the impact of the A-bomb was psychological as well as physical. For Texans, science fiction seemed to become real as America's secret weapon generated much sensational press. According to the papers, what made the A-bomb so terrifying was that one plane carrying one bomb packed the same

Sweating it out

If a house be divided against itself, that house cannot stand.—*Mark III: 25*

punch that 2,000 superfortresses could deliver with conventional bombs. Headlines about America's new power leaped off Texas newspapers in bold, black type. Stories told how the tremendous sight of the atomic explosion inspired frightened awe even in battle-hardened fliers. The A-bombs served notice that a different age of weaponry and energy had arrived.

Like everyone else in the world, Texans immediately sensed that such weapons could lead to unforseen consequences. On the one hand, Japan had been brought to her knees without an invasion. A Japanese D-Day with its heavy casualties had been averted. Top brass in the army claimed that if the bomb had been available in Europe, the invasion on Normandy and Omaha Beaches would have been unnecessary. But the power of the weapon frightened and oftentimes outraged people. From the beginning, some Texans on the home front wondered if the bomb should have been dropped. Why had it been dropped on a city instead of in some empty field? Why, wondered Texans like Lela Mae Sullivan, was the bomb not dropped where it might demonstrate its potential without the cruel destruction to civilian life and property?

The terrible surprise of the atomic explosion was at once both its absolute effectiveness and its absolute cruelty. Normally, attacks meant a sky full of roaring superfortresses, sirens, exploding flak. No one expected a single plane to attack with only one bomb as its payload. Death and destruction came without much notice.

The Waiting Is at an End!

THE GUNS ARE STILLED AT LONG LAST . . . AND IT IS WITH DEEP AND REVERENT JOY THAT WE RECEIVE THIS NEWS.

Ring & Brown
Military and Sportswear
1803 ELM

> *The news that I have waited 3 years for was announced today "V-J day"*

Leave not a stain in thine honor.
—*Ecclesiasticus XXXIII: 22*

Articles in Texas newspapers compared the power of the A-bomb to other weapons. One headline announced, "Cupful of Atom-Bomb Material Enough to Destroy All of Dallas." The same article then went on to claim that a three-foot cube of uranium could power a car at 60 miles per hour around the globe 30 million times. Editorials began to appear suggesting the dark consequences of the new weapon that America had unleashed. One editorial cartoon depicted Uncle Sam standing in the bow of a skiff sailing forth into a dark sea labeled "Atomic Age." The caption read, "We were the first that ever burst into that silent sea."

"We thought it was a terrible thing," said Lela Sullivan, who lived in Muleshoe at the time. But she also remembers feeling immense relief when victory over Japan was finally announced. The Sullivans owned a farm, and because farmers were exempt from the draft, Mr. Sullivan had remained a civilian. They sold the farm in the summer of 1945, and the government was in the process of altering Mr. Sullivan's draft status when the war ended. The draft was canceled and Mr. Sullivan was able to stay in Muleshoe and run the new service station he had purchased with the money from the sale of his farm. V-J Day in Muleshoe, Mrs. Sullivan remembers, was about like any other day, except that people went to church in the evening. In fact, FDR's death seemed to have more impact on the Muleshoe townspeople than the return of peace.

People in the larger Texas cities released joys that had been pent-up since Pearl Harbor. In Austin a deliriously thankful GI danced on top of a mailbox. Mrs. Harriet Turner, who lived in El Paso at the time, remembers that she was at the Singer Sewing Co. taking a sewing lesson when the news came. "We heard a commotion in the streets below and knew immediately that the war was over." She remembers how everybody rushed into the streets, "crying and laughing at the same time and hugging and kissing friends and strangers too."

The announcement that Japan had accepted unconditional terms of surrender was made at six o'clock on a Tuesday evening and the celebrations lasted into the morning hours in cities across the state. The actual signing of the surrender and the official proclamation of V-J Day did not occur until September 2, but this did not prevent a nationwide

REMEMBER PEARL HARBOR?

Don't mention Pearl Harbor to me. I don't mean Pearl Harbor when the Japs hit it on December 7.

I mean Pearl Harbor when I hit it early in 1945.

I was new on the Harkness, and I guess I was nervous. Anyhow, when we came sailing into Pearl that morning, I was on the bow with the heaving line. We were tying up alongside another minesweeper, so I let go and flung the monkey's paw as hard as I could. I missed the bow by twenty feet and that hunk of lead sailed right through the radioman's wires and two clothes lines of clean skivvies. They were all screaming and yelling on the sweep, and our bosun was hollering bad words, and I was dragging the line back, tearing up as much coming out as I did going in.

I finally got it back to throw to the right place, but by the time they got hawsers secured we had overshot the sweep. We warped around and scraped and made an awful mess on both bows. And I could tell that the skipper was aggravated, although he had brought the Harkness in too fast. I didn't mention that, though.

I went on the gangway watch at noon and got to feeling pretty tough when I strapped on the guard belt with that big .45 automatic and cartridge cases and all the ship's keys hung on it. In the middle of my watch the cook's helper came dragging in a big box of bread for the galley. Doing my duty, I leaned across to the inboard ship to take the box. The only thing is, I leaned against the rail and unsnapped my guard-belt buckle. I heard this thud and looked down in time to see belt, .45 pistol, and all the ship's keys bounce off the deck and make like the Arizona to the bottom of Pearl Harbor.

I knew that this was one of those things that regularly happened in the line of duty, but I did have a hard time making myself go tell the skipper about it. He acted like he could hardly believe it. And he brought it up that I was handling the bow line that morning! I could tell he was still upset about his poor show at tying up. Scratching up his ship didn't help either.

I got off guard duty at 1600, and the gunner sent me to the fantail to clean up the mess that everybody else had made unpacking stores and cleaning the .50 caliber stern guns. I had to carry all that crap across three inboard ships and throw it in the gondola car, which was our dock's garbage dump. That job took me an hour, and I barely made it for chow time.

A bunch of us were sitting on the quarterdeck after chow when the gunner hollered up to me to secure the 3-inch gun forward and the 20 mms amidships. He sent the other striker to secure the .50 calibers on the fantail. There was some discussion and I could tell there was a problem below, but I didn't pay much attention till I heard my name called.

"What did you do with the canvas gun covers on the fantail?"

"What did they look like?"

"Like canvas gun covers!"

I dug for an hour before I finally got down through all that garbage to those gun covers. It took another hour to scrub the smell off so the gunner would let me bring them aboard. And it took another hour to get the smell off me so I could go to the crew's quarters and hit the sack.

I don't know why everybody made such a big fuss. It was no big deal, and anyhow, we won the war. But I'd just as soon not be reminded of that first day at Pearl Harbor.

—Francis Edward Abernethy

> The whole island is in an uproar — The news is almost too good to be true. The whole company got drunk.

Glory is the true and honorable recompense of gallant actions.—*Le Sage*

(Brief)

party on August 14. As on V-E Day, churches held special services that evening, and the next day Texas businesses ran special ads giving thanks and announcing memorial closings.

Virginia O'Neal, who lived in Corpus Christi at the time, remembers being at home and hearing the announcement over the radio. "We sat stunned just as we had done on the day Pearl Harbor was bombed." The same sensation of disbelief washed over her at the end of the war as at its terrible beginning. But on V-J Day the disbelief was accompanied by elation instead of fear and anger. This announcement meant that her husband, John, would be coming home.

For Texans overseas and for those about to be redeployed to the Pacific, the surrender meant the realization of what had a few weeks earlier been a distant dream. No longer would the return trip home to family, friends, and a civilian job be for the lucky few. Soon everyone could go home.

Ruben Moreno of Dallas was awaiting battle orders on the minesweeper USS *Chandler*, docked at Honolulu Harbor, when Japan's surrender was broadcast. Moreno recalls that the whole of Honolulu seemed to be glowing from the many lights that had been blacked out for four years. Moreno knew then that the war was over and thought to himself, "There is nobody that stands as tall as you right now."

According to Bill Burden, who was discharged and arrived home only a few days before V-J Day, there was no viciousness or meanness during the celebrating. People only wanted to have fun. To help keep the lid on the victory festivities, most Texas beer and liquor vendors had voluntarily suspended

Parade to celebrate the end of World War II, on the campus of Texas State College for Women
Texas Woman's University Library

224 COMING HOME

> The last few days have passed pretty quietly. Everyone has that "when are we going home look" on their face.

Memorial Service Set
HILLSBORO, Texas, Aug. 18.—A memorial service will be held at the First Baptist Church at 10:50 a.m. Sunday for members of the armed services reported dead or missing during the war.

plants have been furnished by the greenhouses of A. & M. College.

The fight is over when the enemy is down.—*Ovid*

V-J DAY HOUSTON

On Tuesday evening, August 14, 1945, my father, who worked the second shift at the Houston shipyard building Liberty Ships, came home early, bringing the news that Japan had surrendered. The shipyard he worked in closed down, and everyone was sent home. Daddy wanted to go downtown to celebrate, but we went on the bus instead of taking the car because he was afraid the traffic would be heavy.

I was only 12 years old but I still remember Main Street in Houston that night. The noise was tremendous: people screaming and laughing, car horns honking, sirens blaring on fire trucks and ambulances, church bells ringing. And, of course, there was a lot of dancing, kissing, hugging, and drinking. One liquor store owner passed out free bottles of liquor as fast as he could. It was after 2 A.M. before we were able to catch a bus and get home.

—Margie Burns Noneman

sales for two days after the announcement of the war's end. Many Texas GIs were home on furlough expecting to return to the Pacific for a tough invasion of Japan, so the announcement of peace was doubly welcomed by them.

For too many Texans, however, the news of the end came late. The celebration of Japan's defeat tasted bittersweet to those who had lost fathers or sons or husbands. The chaotic shuffle of demobilization soon began to shift into high gear. After Japan's surrender, the government began to lower the point requirement for discharge, and before long a torrent of GIs was pouring back into Texas.

By the fall of 1945, the peacetime invasion of Texas by returnees rivaled a military advance. Between August and December, the army discharged more than 4 million soldiers. The freshly returned Texans spent the first Christmas after the war with their loved ones, and by the beginning of the year, they were stalking

(Brief)

> The whole month has passed quietly. All activities are drawing to a close and all eyes are looking toward the States.

Take fast hold of instruction; let her not go: keep her; for she is thy life.—*Proverbs IV: 13*

Reunited: Virginia and Hugh O'Neal a few minutes after Sgt. O'Neal's homecoming.

new jobs, new homes, and the American dream instead of Nazis and the Nipponese.

There were problems, not only for the returnees but for Texas home-fronters. Veteran Clyde Childress of Fort Worth captures the emotion many must have felt: "After 23 miserable days on an overcrowded troop ship I was back in San Francisco walking down Market Street like nothing had happened. What a let-down!" The intensity of combat and the exotic places seen by Texas troops overseas caused many of them to balk at the placidness of the states. According to Willie Benton, "When I first got home I was restless. I drank a lot, which I don't do anymore."

The very harshness of life during the war far from home and then the nearness of home while the war was still such a fresh memory kept veterans like Benton from relaxing. "I was high-tempered. I had a

A big coming-home smile: Albert Kennedy of Edna, Texas—a survivor of the sinking of the USS *Houston*.

> Things are moving very slow — ships are coming in one a month, but it looks as though I will be home for Xmas.

I speak the password primeval, I give the sign of democracy.
—*Walt Whitman*

chip on my shoulder. I didn't want anybody telling me anything to do. I'd been taking orders so long unwillingly that I just didn't want nobody giving me no more."

At the peak of the citizen army's return to civilian life, approximately a million GIs a month poured back into the States. Six million soldiers had returned home and been discharged by the end of summer 1946. Once released, a soldier could look forward to a long voyage home—a month was not unusual—since the seas were still considered unsafe and ships navigated tortuously to avoid danger zones.

Back in the states, GIs were moved from central disposition stations by train to separation centers like Fort Sam Houston in San Antonio. Here they were issued new clothes, given physical examinations, counseled about the GI Bill and life as civilians, and then, after receiving $100 of their $300 mustering-out pay, sent on their way, ready to be reunited with family and friends. All this was supposed to take 48 hours. But the two-day layovers usually stretched into longer stints.

Bill Burden of the 112th Cavalry remembers that his mustering out lasted for two weeks. During his first week, Burden thought he was simply on leave and would soon be returning to help with the invasion of Japan.

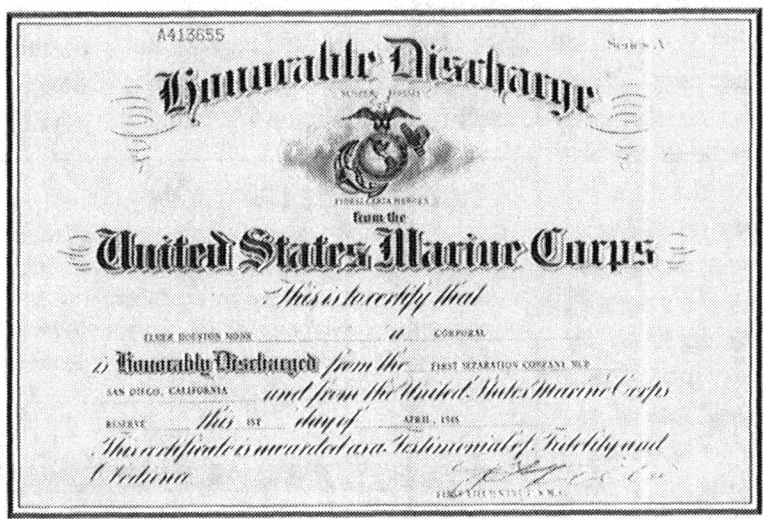

(*Brief*)

This is it. 4:30 AM we started loading on trucks that took us to the ship.

Courage in danger is half the battle.
—*Plautus*

(Brief)

Only during his second week at Fort Sam, after the first A-bomb attack on Japan, did he learn of his discharge. Burden became a civilian again between the bombings of Hiroshima and Nagasaki, when it became apparent that the invasion of Japan was no longer necessary. Aside from all the physicals and "lots of paperwork," Burden's two weeks at Fort Sam were pleasant and relaxing—"you could get a cold beer and go to the show"—and his jubilation when he realized that he had been discharged made the second week pass quickly.

Burden still feels great pride that the 112th Cavalry of Texas—nicknamed the Little Giant of the Pacific—had received excellent training and performed its task with valor and success. The fact that he and his Texas buddies had accomplished what had been asked of them made his homecoming especially grand. Since none of his family knew exactly when he was to arrive home, Burden, like many other Texas GIs, planned to surprise his family. He rode the Greyhound bus home and remembers, "When I saw the red horse on the Mobil building, I thought to myself that I was just about home."

There was much reminiscing when the family finally gathered together, and Mrs. Burden promptly informed her son that she knew all along he would return. It was Bill's older brother, who had a cushy assignment in Paris, that she had been most worried about. Such light-hearted exchanges helped ease the dark fears that had haunted Texas home-fronters like Mrs. Burden before their loved ones returned safely.

A CHILLY RECEPTION

"I was on Guam when the war ended, and of course we didn't need heavy clothes there. When the marines decided to ship us home, they sent us to China in the dead of winter and put us on a train that had no windows or heat. We had nothing to protect us from the cold: no coats, no hats, no gloves. Many of us promptly caught pneumonia; luckily, I recovered after several weeks. Our homecoming was definitely not what we had expected!"

—*Jim Montgomery*

Burden arrived home in time to help celebrate V-J Day and remembers that "everybody was happy and proud and relieved so they celebrated a couple of days, then got down to the business of returning to peacetime and civilian life."

At times, that return was wrenching. Texas rode an emotional roller-coaster in the first year after the war. Front page headlines such as "40,000 Texas War Workers Laid Off" in the August 16 edition of the *Austin Statesman* bespoke the frightening difficulties of reconversion. As the war ground to a close, Texas civilians and soldiers alike waited to see which way the economy would turn.

228   COMING HOME

> 10:20 A.M. I was aboard ship. 10:45 am we pulled away from the dock and headed toward Frisco.

Learn to obey before you command.
—Solon

(Brief)

One of Texas's largest layoffs took place at North American Aviation, which presented pink slips to almost all of its 15,000 employees in Garland and Dallas. On Wednesday, August 15, the government canceled all its contracts with the large plant, and the aircraft manufacturer simply shut its doors. An ad in the August 19 *Dallas Morning News* told NAA workers where to go to pick up their final checks. The ad began: "To the men and women of the Texas Division who have all worked diligently to build the aircraft that helped to bring peace once again to the world." It went on to thank the dedicated workers for their meritorious efforts, then listed times for different groups to assemble and pick up their pay.

NAA employees, along with many other war-born industry workers, received their own version of postwar mustering-out pay. Their jubilation at the war's end brought the realization that they must now look for new work in a swelling flood of job seekers. Still, the outlook was not entirely gloomy. Rural towns were encouraged by the prospect of returning workers who had been lured away to big-city companies such as Consolidated Vultee and North American Aviation. People in dusty towns like Kaufman and Rockwell and McKinney hoped that the temporary urbanites who had headed for the big city at the outbreak of war would come home and reawaken the rural economies that had been faltering since the birth of the war industry.

Ruth Benton, who had been a door riveter on NAA's production line, returned to Waxahachie and her old job at Haggar Manufacturing for a time before landing a job as a clerk in a shoe store. Many years after, while visiting a Boeing plant in Seattle, Mrs. Benton would recall the nauseating odor of machine oil and metal that had sickened her in the Dallas war plant.

After the intensity and larger-than-life effort of the war, some GIs experienced a letdown of sorts, but for Bill Burden there was none. He simply felt overjoyed that America had a job to do and did it well. Finding a job and readjusting to civilian life

> "16" We are well on our way, and no parts New Guinea can be seen. The fact that I am on my way home doesn't seem real.

In a democracy only will the freeman of nature deign to dwell.—*Plato*

(*Brief*)

was not that difficult for Burden. With the help of the GI Bill and the money he made selling printing, he attended Rutherford Business School at nights where he took math, English, and business courses. Later, he ran into a former officer of the 112th Cavalry who offered him work as clerk at the Dallas County Courthouse. On January 1, 1947, Bill Burden began the job that became his lifetime career.

Others found the adjustment more difficult. In a series of articles in the 1945 *Dallas Morning News*, Don MacIver interviewed veterans freshly returned to civilian life. Their outlooks ranged from bleak to highly optimistic. He told of two veterans who were having difficulty making ends meet, either because the jobs they obtained paid too little or because there were no satisfactory jobs to be had. Even though he had passed his civil service exam, Eddie Vaughn's attempt to land a job at the VA hospital in Waco was unsuccessful. He felt angry that a civilian held a position similar to the one he was seeking. And Carl McIntosh simply refused to take positions in jobs that were less than what he felt a Texas veteran deserved. According to MacIver, the men seemed poorly informed about their rights under the GI Bill.

Many Texas vets believed that it would be tough to rejoin the civilian work force, and some even made job choices based on what industries they felt would be less affected by the influx of discharged GIs. Homer Partlow claimed that he went to work in Longview as a pipeline worker because he thought there would be too many layoffs in the metal industry. In Palestine, Jack Vedre began a fish market with the money he had saved during his time in the army. After his discharge, R.C. Ammons of Stephenville returned to his former job as manager of the parts department at Stephenville Motor Co. And John O'Neal returned without difficulty to his former job with a Texas oil company, working his way up from tank gauger to a spot in the front office.

In September 1945, the War Manpower Commission predicted that Texas unemployment would be lower than before the U.S. entered the war. Even United States Employment Service figures took some of the bite out of ugly predictions about Texas's loss of war industry. The USES stats indicated that about a third of the war-industry layoff victims had acquired new jobs in less than a month. The unemployment scare seemed worse than it was.

Living space, on the other hand, became a very real vexation. By November 1945 it was painfully

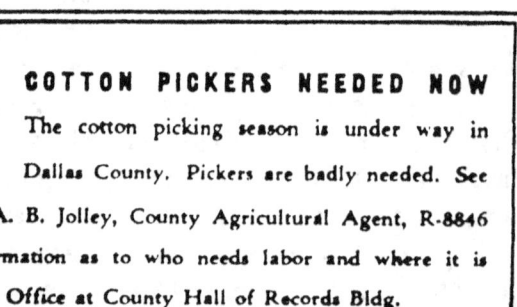

COTTON PICKERS NEEDED NOW
The cotton picking season is under way in Dallas County. Pickers are badly needed. See or call A. B. Jolley, County Agricultural Agent, R-8846 for information as to who needs labor and where it is needed. Office at County Hall of Records Bldg.

GLOSSARY

ash can: a depth charge

(to go) Asiatic (or ape): to lose one's mind; or "go bamboo" from too much service in the Far East

battery acid: coffee; also Joe, java

bogie: a radar man's term for an enemy contact

Box 13: address for prisoners in the guardhouse; also called "Company Q"

to buy the farm: pilots' term for being killed, usually in a crash

Dear John: the letter a girl back home wrote to break up with a serviceman

Dugout Doug: unflattering term for General MacArthur following his departure for Australia after the fall of Corregidor

flat-top: an aircraft carrier

fruit salad: ribbons denoting medals, battles, and theatres of operation that servicemen wore on their chests

geedunks: cokes, candy bars, snacks

(to) GI: to clean up; "GI the barracks"

GI: government issue

GI Jesus: Chaplain

GI Joe: a soldier

gizmo: anything hard to name

goldbrick: a slacker; "to goldbrick" or goof off

Gorgeous Georgie — unflattering name for General George S. Patton, who was given to flashy uniforms and ivory-handled pistols

gremlins: unseen spirits that cause machines to malfunction

gung ho: full of spirit; probably from the Chinese phrase meaning "work together"

Mae West: a life jacket named in honor of the bosom of the famous actress

milk run: an easy bombing mission

R & R: (behind the lines) rest and relaxation (sometimes I & I: intercourse and inebriation)

ruptured duck: the uniform insignia given to discharged men and women

sad sack: a lazy, lethargic soldier; from Sargeant George Barker's cartoon character

Section 8: discharge based on insanity

sky pilot: Chaplain

SNAFU: acronym for "situation normal, all fouled (?) up"

snow job: an excuse designed to confuse a superior

SOP: acronym for "standard operating procedure"

T.S. card: the Chaplain's advice; when you visited the "padre," he punched your "tough shit" card

Returning troops often brought an unfamiliar lingo with them.

A POW'S STORY

Volunteered in April 1943 and asked for infantry or paratroops, but was made an aviation cadet and turned into a B-24 navigator. After a bombing raid on Vienna, my crew parachuted (to avoid incineration) over Dobre Voda, Slovakia. Was kept briefly in a dungeon of the castle at Tristin and in Bratislava jail before interrogation at Uberursel near Frankfurt and imprisonment for the duration at Barth on the Baltic.

In March 1991 went back to Dobre Voda. The "Mayor" read me the town archives account of our 1944 arrival, bowling me over with emotions I had somehow suppressed 47 years before. Two 71-year-old ex-militiamen told me they had driven me in Tristin (Don't you remember me? I had big mustaches), and a man who as a child turned me in to the Germans appeared. Saw the school building (in 1944 the German komandantura) where I was interrogated, and was walked to my airplane's crash site by the militiamen. Hundreds, maybe thousands, of bits and pieces of airplane were still scattered up the forested mountainside. Collected several. Another emotional experience.

At Tristin Castle, the Director of the Girls Reformatory now housed there showed me the dungeon where I had been warm and well fed for the last time as a prisoner.

—John Howison

Tristin Castle

John Howison in Dobre Voda with T. Lukasovic, who as a child in 1944 turned Howison in to the Germans. (Photos courtesy John Howison)

apparent that housing was becoming the major problem of reconversion. There was simply no place to put the approximately 100,000 men per month who were returning to Texas. Some of the housing shortage was blamed on bureaucratic red tape. Temporary housing that had been used for war workers stood vacant while returning soldiers moved in with relatives and lived in overcrowded conditions.

The Texan's belief that a man's home was his castle was crumbling into disillusionment for many battle-weary returnees. Red tape was not the sole reason for the housing shortage. The building industry had been crippled by the loss of workers to

> The time seems to be passing very slowly, but each hour I am closer to home. 3° from the equator Weather hot.

Freedom exists only where the people take care of the government.—*Woodrow Wilson*

the war overseas, and simply stated, it took longer for the housing industry to get on its feet than for the GIs to return home. The dilemma was unavoidable. Texas soldiers who could provide manpower for the building of houses had to return home before they could construct the housing needed to provide them with homes.

The federal government had foreseen the possibility of the housing shortage at the war's end and tried to head off the problem. The Lanham Act, which had provided for the construction of temporary housing for war workers, was modified early in 1945 and authorized "the National Housing Administration to convert previously built . . . housing into facilities for the families of servicemen and veterans who could not find housing; new, temporary facilities for the same groups could also be constructed."

But application for war housing units available through the Lanham Act meant time-consuming paperwork and numbing encounters with the federal bureaucracy. Texas veterans blamed the shortage on striking workers and entanglement in red tape, labor blamed management and legislative inaction, and the federal government shrugged its shoulders and ploddingly crept toward improvement.

In the meantime, many Texans suffered. After James H. Lindley's return from the war, he and his wife, along with two other families, lived with Mrs. Lindley's mother. Mrs. Lindley's father had been killed in the fighting in Italy in 1944, so the pain of their loss compounded the stress of crowded conditions. Even more tragic was that Mrs. Lindley had recently given birth to a child who died at birth. The ordeal had left Mrs. Lindley near death as well. The doctor's advice for Mrs. Lindley was "rest and quiet in a place by yourself," but the Lindleys had no home of their own. Lindley was a highly decorated veteran, but his most difficult struggle seemed to begin when he returned home.

For some the crowding was not intolerable. As late as the summer of 1946 Elias Benavidez and his brother Cruz, both discharged veterans, were living at home with parents and brothers and sisters. In fact, the two brothers still shared the same bed they had slept in while growing up. Benavidez remembers that his older brother had been wounded in the wrist by a German machine gunner and for some time after his return wore a brace on his arm. "In the mornings before Cruz put his brace on, I would roughhouse with him to give myself an advantage, you see. I remember that my mother would come in with the broom and shoo us apart, two grown men and veterans of a war."

Returnees without children and with enough money simply rented for two or three years until the construction industry got back to normal. But renting was a problem, too. Texans with children had difficulty renting because many landlords did not allow children. Although rentals were regulated by the Office of Price Administration, by the end of the war the controls were rarely enforced, causing tension between tenants and property owners.

Still, things did improve, even if too slowly. Once the housing boom started in the late '40s and early '50s, Texas builders began erecting houses "by the ton" according to Delbert Bailey. Whole cities of

> Arrived at Seattle Washington. A fine reception— all the things to make us feel at home.

In a democracy only will the freeman of nature deign to dwell.—*Plato*

houses seemed to grow up overnight, and with the easy money available through the GI Bill, Texans began to acquire some of the hoped-for security and happiness for which they had sacrificed so much.

The GI Bill of Rights, officially known as the Servicemen's Readjustment Act of 1944, came into being on June 22, 1944. The GI Bill, along with the Veteran's Preference Act, which gave returnees preferred status in Civil Service jobs, and the Mustering-Out Pay Act went a long way toward smoothing the transition of Texas and the U.S. from war to peace. The GI Bill provided special job placement services, up to four years of college or vocational education, 52 weeks of unemployment insurance (known as the 52-20 Club), and VA-guaranteed loans for the purchase of homes, farms, and businesses.

Soldiers going through the discharge process were briefed about the rights and benefits given them by the GI Bill, but many Texas returnees had other things besides life insurance or home loans on their minds during orientation lectures at separation centers. Some Texans took advantage of their rights upon returning to civilian life, but many spent months unaware of their hard-earned benefits. Of course, low-interest home loans were hardly useful when there were no houses to be had.

For many GIs, the financial aid allotted for education simply was not enough. One Texas veteran said that his ambition had always been to become a doctor, but upon his return he found that, since his father had died, his family was dependent upon him as its major source of income. The aid allowed by the GI Bill, he thought, would be plenty for a single person pursuing a career as a physician, but it could never support a large family during four years of undergraduate work and three years of medical school.

Since veterans were awarded, under the Veterans Preference Act, an extra 10 points on their Civil Service exam scores, many Texans opted for jobs as firemen or police officers or postmen. Texas veterans who chose to go to college faced large problems. The GI Bill provided for up to $500 a year for tuition, books, and other education-related costs. But if school costs were under $500, the surplus was not awarded to the veteran. Living allowances were separate from tuition aid. Single men were given $50 a month and married men $75 to pay the rent and bills and buy the groceries—bills which often ran $95 or $100 a month. In order to pursue a degree in engineering at a school like Texas Tech, a veteran had to have a part-time job to make ends meet.

In addition to money problems for the veteran-turned-student, there was the problem of simply finding a place to live. As with housing in general, on-campus living quarters were scarce, and as more and more veterans returned, the shortages became more acute. Texas colleges and universities searched frantically for dormitory space, but demand far exceeded supply.

The GI Bill of Rights provided opportunities for Texans who might otherwise never have gone to college, but many veterans found it impossible to take advantage of the privileges they had earned, especially those who returned to married life and the immediate need to make a living. Therefore, ap-

Waiting for train to Fort Sam Houston, should leave tomorrow.

A faithful friend is the medicine of life.
—Ecclesiasticus VI: 16

proximately two-thirds of Texas returnees chose instead of college either to attend vocational school or to participate in on-the-job vocational training.

Ruben Moreno learned how to rewind electric motors and upholster furniture. With his double trade, he made sure that he could land a job in a scarce job market. Elias Benavidez learned to operate a printing press and worked for the same firm for forty years.

For Texas minorities the problem was compounded by the harshly ironic fact that society was still segregated and "facilities for Negro education" as well as for the education of Hispanics were hard to find.

The reconversion process itself seemed to encourage freshly discharged Texans to enter immediately into the work force rather than spend four years pursuing a degree. Ads in all the papers proclaimed the debt of gratitude owed to the men who had preserved democracy for America and went on to emphasize the need to move from wartime manufacturing to peaceful production. Phrases such as "the time has now come when we can all pick up the tools for the job of peace once more" seemed to invite Texas returnees to jump into the fray of peacetime capitalism.

Symbolizing the huge economic and social shift that was underway, the War Production Board was deactivated in 1945 and the Civilian Production Administration was established. Manufacturing firms such as Humble Oil and Refining of Ingleside or Sinclair Rubber of Houston, both seized by the government "for the duration," were returned to private ownership.

The automobile industry began to rumble back into civilian production. Ads announcing the new 1946 models began appearing in the papers as early as September 1945, long before any new cars had been made. All auto production had been geared to building military vehicles since the outbreak of war, so every Texan not only desired but honestly needed a new car at the war's end. Playing on V-J Day sentiments, ads announced the approach of "V-8 Day" when new Fords would appear on the lot for purchase. New models, however, were not available for purchase until 1946, and even by October of that year, Texas dealerships still could not match demand.

Overall there was a bit of gear grinding as Texas industry shifted from war to peace, but by 1947 almost all of the troops had been discharged and were back at work. Industries like construction, which

> **THE PEACE ROSE**
>
> During World War II a new variety of rose was tested in France. The seeds were smuggled out to France, Italy, Germany, and the United States, countries which all bred the rose and submitted names for the new variety. At the end of the war, the name submitted by the United States was selected, and the PEACE ROSE has since stood as an emblem for the international hope that World War II would be the war to end all wars.
>
> — Carol Mackenzie Jones

"4" Washington, Idaho, Montana—
The train ride so far has been
very boring.

In a democracy only will the freeman of nature deign to dwell.—*Plato*

FIFTY YEARS LATER...
Pearl Harbor survivor, Houston F. James, president of North Central Texas Chapter 4 of the Pearl Harbor Survivors Association, spearheaded the movement to finance, design, and ship to Honolulu a commemorative monument—a granite pedestal with bronze tablet—paying homage to those who lost their lives during the December 7, 1941, attack on the island of Oahu. The memorial is to be dedicated at sunrise services, December 7, 1991, at the National Memorial Cemetery of the Pacific ("the Punchbowl") in Honolulu, Hawaii.

had been stymied early on, began to race toward the boom experienced in the second half of the 20th century. Like North American Aviation, much of the war-born manufacturing in Texas simply shut down after the summer of 1945. But firms such as Consolidated Vultee (which later became General Dynamics) and the Pantex weapons plant in Amarillo remained in operation to supply the military's postwar needs. (Eventually, the North American Aviation plant in Dallas became the branch headquarters for the regional Veterans Administration offices that served Texas, Louisiana, and Mississippi.)

The war placed America in the pole-position in the race for postwar power industrially, militarily, and culturally. And Texans played a vital role in the assumption and wielding of the nation's new power. The continued development of the state's oil resources made Texas an important supplier of petroleum to an energy-hungry nation. Cotton growing and cattle raising were affected by the technological sophistication learned during the war. Water co-ops, funded by the federal government, began appearing across the state and dramatically increased the value of Texas soil.

New marketing techniques learned from the war effort were put into practice. Sears Roebuck introduced a time-payment plan so that townspeople from Lubbock to Leander could take home a new washer and dryer without handing over a large chunk of

"5" Wyoming New Mexico
"6" Texas

Harold D. King

Liberty means responsibility.
—G. B. Shaw

After the war, Frank Ficklin of Wichita Falls returned to Burma where he had worked as a POW on the infamous "Death Railway." He helped build a bridge over the River Kwae-Noy (below), the "River Kwai" of the book and movie.

their postwar savings. Things were changing radically in America and Texas. Washing machines looked oddly like jukeboxes at the end of the war. One newspaper ad proudly announced, "Only 30 days after V-J Day, and the Bendix automatic home laundry is here." The ad claimed that "This Bendix is a genuine postwar product," using language that thousands of other publicity blitzes adopted after the war as Texas was thrust into high-gear consumerism.

Texans had gone without for so long that the end of the war seemed to signal an end to sacrifice, scrimping, and rationing. With America's victory came the desire for bigger and better and more, especially in Texas. Although unemployment claims had risen sharply between V-J Day and the first week of October—from 305,000 to 1,700,000 nationwide—production of new consumer products seemed already in full swing.

TEXAS GOES TO WAR   237

"They used to fly in the same squadron."

(Brief)

When a Houston department store put an early version of a 1946 Ford on display, store clerks had to refer many customers to the local dealerships to be put on waiting lists. According to Mrs. Harriet Turner, the reappearance of women's hosiery—between 40 and 80 pair—caused a near riot in a downtown El Paso department store. People were not, according to Mrs. Turner, suffering for things under the rationing system, but things were missed. And when they reappeared, people did not fail to take advantage.

When the OPA announced the end of gasoline rationing, motorists spent the next few days exulting over the fact that gas-rationing coupons were no longer needed. Warnings about traffic fatalities appeared as "motorists with a 'so what' attitude trotted out the old car to use up all the family gas in one spree." And things got worse a few days later when the government did away with the 35-mph speed limit, which had been instituted in order to conserve tires.

Bizarre notions were in the air, indications of the near-ludicrous gaiety of the time and the approach of the light-hearted '50s. When a hurricane blew through the Florida Keys in September, a newspaper headline promptly announced the proposed "Atomic Bombing of Hurricanes." People were switching off the radio and the "Inner Sanctum Mystery Hour" and tuning in TV and "Your Show of Shows." Cars were faster, planes were replacing trains, medicines were being developed that would prevent diseases like polio and tuberculosis.

The world was shrinking, but the United States and Texas seemed to gain prominence in the new age. The war shook Texas out of its adolescent doldrums, awakened the state to its own potential in a world simultaneously teetering on the brink of destruction and standing on the pinnacle of scientific and cultural achievement.

Index of Names

Abernethy, Francis Edward 223
Acheson, Sam 214
Acken, Van 197
Adams, Austin 101
Adams, Carmen 101
Adams, Lucian 131
Akata, Ruth 141
Alexander, Marvin 19
Allen, Larry 107-08
Allred, James V. 2
Alsmeyer, Marie Bennett 164
Ammons, R. C. 230
Anderson, Marian 201
Andrews, Dana 104
Armstrong, Louis 201
Arnold, Henry H. 30, 164
Arthur, Jean 205
Astor, Mary 203
Autry, Gene 197, 199, 210

Bacall, Lauren 106
Bailey, Delbert 233
Baillie, Hugh 108
Baker, Kitty 199
Baker, Paul 199
Ball, Lucille 198
Barrow, Clyde 2
Barrymore, Ethel 206
Basie, Count 201
Baskin, Mona 139
Beahan, Kermit 217
Belcher, William F. 35, 68
Benavides, Joe S. 129
Benavidez, Cruz 130-31, 233
Benavidez, Elias 233, 235
Benny, Jack 100
Benton, Ruth 229
Benton, Willie 57, 68, 226
Bergen, Edgar 206
Bergman, Ingrid 106, 181, 206
Berry, Margaret 153
Biggs, Cathy 66
Biggs, Cecil Willard 66, 193
Block, Bill 28, 155
Blondell, Joan 105, 202, 204
Bly, Albert 120
Board, Woodrow 19
Bogart, Humphrey 105, 106
Booth, Maude 24
Bourke-White, Margaret 109-10
Boyd, Sylvia 149
Brackett, Edna 162

Brand, Max 213
Brannen, Carl Andrew 188
Brant, G. C. 30
Brennan, Walter 202
Bromfield, Louis 211
Brown, Andy 70
Brown, Jack 19
Brown, Les 201
Bruce, Andrew 11
Bruce, Nigel 100
Burden, Bill 52, 224, 227-30
Burden, Mrs. 228
Burge, J. O. 48

Cagney, James 204
Calvert, Robert 104, 190
Campbell, Herb 52
Campbell, S. W. 53
Capa, Robert [Endre Friedmann] 109-10
Capra, Frank 101-02
Carlisle, Kay 197
Carmichael, Hoagy 201
Carroll, Naunita Harmon 124
Carver, George Washington 118
Casteñada, Jesusta 133, 154
Cerf, Bennett 211
Chandler, Tom 49
Chase, Mary 211
Chennault, Claire iii, 12, 56-57
Childress, Clyde 226
Churchill, Winston 47, 102, 109, 189
Clark, Mark 65, 66
Coburn, Charles 205
Cochran, Jacqueline 167
Colbert, Claudette 105
Cole, Robert 67
Colona, Jerry 206
Connally, Tom 3, 8, 16, 78
Cook, Robert Gould 48, 50
Cooper, Gary 16, 203
Crawford, Joan 202, 204, 207
Crisp, Donald 203
Cronkite, Walter 107
Crosby, Bing 201, 206
Cruz, Dave 139
Curtiz, Michael 106, 205

Daniels, Sam 125
Darnell, Jane 202
Darnell, Linda 202

Davidson, Bill 118
Davidson, James 32, 73
Davis, Bette 103
Davis, Mrs. Coy 160
Davis, Elmer 97
Dealey, Sam ii, 43, 45
Dempsey, Jack 120
Dial, Jr., Preston 143
Dies, Martin 5
DiMaggio, Joe 13, 24
Disney, Walt 103
Dobie, J. Frank 213
Donlevy, Brian 105
Donnell, Earl 45
Dorn, Faith 202
Dorsey Brothers 201
Douglas, Lloyd C. 211
Douglass, Jr., Robert W. 209
Dowling, Eddie 199
Doyle, Lois 84
Doyle, Madge 84
DuBois, W. E. B. 117
Duke, Ernest 160
Dunn, James 207

Edwards, Sterling 68
Eisenhower, Dwight D. ii, vi, 21, 43, 52, 62, 66, 115
Eisenstaedt, Alfred 109
Espinosa, Jesse 130
Evans, Maurice 199

Faith, Percy 197
Ferguson, Ma 2
Ferguson, Pa 2
Ferguson, Warren 53
Ficklin, Frank 49, 237
Fink, Bob 64
Fitzgerald, Barry 206
Fitzgerald, Ella 201
Flavin, Marvin 211
Flynn, Errol 105
Flynn, Robert 77
Fogelson, Buddy 202
Fontaine, Joan 203
Ford, John 101-03, 202, 203
Ford, RIP 29
Forester, C. S. 213
Fowler, Wick 108-09
Friedmann, Endre (see Robert Capa) 109-10

Fujita, Frank 142

Gable, Clark 103
Garcia, Al 209
Garcia, Hector 134
Garcia, José 134
Garcia, Marcario 128, 134
Garfield, John 105
Garner, John Nance 1, 3, 5
Garson, Greer 104-05, 202, 204
Gates, Nancy 204
Gehrig, Lou 13
Gershwin, George 197
Glasgow, Ellen 211
Goddard, Paulette 105
Goering, Hermann 65, 70
Gonzalez, Irma 196
Goodman, Benny 201
Goodwin, Ralph 195
Grable, Betty 201
Graham, Don 69
Graham, Samuel 64
Grant, Cary 105
Greene, A. C. 11
Greene, Sarah 157
Greenstreet, Sydney 106
Groves, Leslie 166
Gunther, John 211

Harada 14
Hargrove, Marion 211
Harmon, Hubert R. 29
Harmon, Leonard 117, 124
Harrell, William 45
Haycox, Ernest 213
Heflin, Van 204
Henreid, Paul 106
Hepburn, Katharine 103
Herrera, Silvestre S. 134
Hersey, John 211
Hidalgo 128
Hirohito 107
Hitler, Adolf 5, 8, 12, 28, 85, 98, 106, 107, 109, 117
Hobby, Oveta Culp iii, 165-66
Holly, Bernard 111
Hope, Bob 206, 212
Hosaka, Ayako 141
House, Boyce 214
Howison, John McCoul 232
Howze, Hamilton 65
Howze, Robert Lee 65
Hughes, Howard 202
Hull, Cordell 13
Huston, John 101-02

Ikeminya, Thomas 141
Imai, Shigeru 137

Jacobi, Manfred 141
Jacoby, Edmund 19
James, Harry 201
James, Houston F. 236
Jingu, Helen Eiko 143
Jingu, Jimmy 143
Jingu, Kimi E. 142-43
Jingu, Lillian 143
Jingu, Mary 142
Jingu, Mrs. 142
Johnson, Lyndon 1, 2, 4, 134
Johnson, Siddie Joe 214
Johnston, Stanley 108
Jones, Carol Mackenzie 235
Jones, James 56-57
Jones, Jennifer 205
Jopling, Dan 157
Jopling, Lucy Wilson 156, 157
Jordan, Willie 50

Kalahani, Beni 14
Kaleolano, Hawila 14
Kaltenborn 189
Kanogawa, Shoji 141
Kawaguchi, Harry 141
Kawahira, Doris 141
Kawamura, Mutsuo 135
Kelton, Elmer 5, 25
Kennedy, Albert 47, 48, 226
Kennedy, John F. 69
Keppler, Victor 98
Kimbro, Truman 67
King, Harve 218, 237
King, Mary 214
Kirkpatrick, Hugh 33
Kitamura, George R. 136
Koller, Leonard 40
Kostelanetz, Andre 71
Krueger, Walter 52, 56
Krupa, Gene 201

Lake, Veronica 105, 206
Langford, Frances 206
Langley, Adria Locke 211
LaRoche, Clarence 128
Laughton, Charles 204
Lea, Tom 111-12
Lee, Robert E. 29
Levant, Oscar 197
Lewis, James 131
Lindley, James H. 233
Lindley, Mrs. 233
Linton, Dean 199
Livingston, Mary 100
Logan, James 63
Long, Huey 211
Longoria, Felix 128
Lopez, José M. 117, 128, 132
Lord, Elton P. 98

Lorre, Peter 106
Louis, Joe 118, 209
Love, Nancy 167
Lovett, R. A. 30
Lukas, Paul 205
Lukasovic, T. 232
Lummus, Jack 45

MacArthur, Douglas 53, 54, 56, 57
MacDonald, Betty 211
MacDonald, Jeanette 206
MacIver, Don 230
MacLeish, Archibald 98
Mahoney, James 64
Maizumi, Fred 4
Marcus, Morris H. 118, 119, 120, 121, 122, 208
Marcus, Sally Craighead 156-58, 171
Marcus, Stanley 81
Marshall, George C. 10, 120, 199
Martin, Mary 202, 204
Martínez, E. 132
Marx, Harpo 198, 206
Massey, Raymond 105
Matano, Albert 141
Mathis, Jack 67
Matthews, Martin 17-18
Mauldin, Bill 114-15, 212
Maxwell, Marilyn 198
Mayborn, Frank W. 11
McCarey, Leo 206
McCarthy, Charlie 206
McCrea, Joel 205
McGinnis, Sergeant 208
McGuire, Edward Charles 57, 196
McGuire (Froendhoff), Mary Nell 185, 187
McGuire, Dorothy 205
McIntosh, Carl 230
McKnight, Felix 120
Mercer, Bill 55
Milland, Ray 207
Miller, Ann 202
Miller, Doris ii, 19, 122-24
Miller, Glenn 199, 201, 202
Miller, Henrietta 123
Mitchum, Robert 203
Monk, Elmer Houston 60-61
Monk, Lucy 61
Montgomery, Jim 228
Montgomery, R. E. 70
Moore, Ben 61
Moreno, Leon 131
Moreno, Ruben 128-29, 224, 235
Morgan, Francis 170
Murphy, Audie ii, 43, 69
Murphy, George 198, 202
Murrow, Edward R. 98, 107
Mussolini, Benito 5, 65, 107

Nimitz, Charles 44
Nimitz, Chester 11, 43-45, 52, 53, 62
Nolan, Lloyd 104
Noneman, Margie Burns 182, 225

O'Daniel, W. Lee "Pappy" 2, 6
O'Neal, Hugh 226
O'Neal, John 230
O'Neal, Virginia 197, 224, 226
Odom, Dale E. 86, 197
Ortego y Gasca, Felipe de 130
Owen, Bobbie 181
Owen, J. B. 181
Owens, Jesse 209

Parker, Charlie 209
Parker, Joe 208
Parker, Sophie 2
Partlow, Homer 230
Patterson, Paul 5
Patton, George S. 66, 109, 115, 120, 213
Paxinou, Katina 205
Pearl, Minnie 206
Pennington, Helen Stafford 151, 192
Pennington, Herman 192
Pennington, Sue 192
Perez, Jose 19
Perry, George Sessions 213-14
Pershing, John J. "Blackjack" 29, 120
Peterson, Pete 108
Phillips, Mark 196
Pierpont, Sid 199
Pollard, Clarice 148
Pons, Lily 71
Porter, Katherine Anne 214
Powell, Beverly 6
Powell, Eleanor 205
Power, James 19
Power, Tyrone 197
Pyle, Ernie 61, 107, 129, 211

Quin, C. K. 139
Quince, Louis V. 196

Rachmaninov, Sergei 196
Rains, Claude 106
Rankin, Jeannette 21
Rayburn, Sam 4
Raymond, Gene 206
Revere, Anne 207
Ritter, Tex 199, 200
Roach, Curtis (Mr. & Mrs.) 78
Roach, Joyce Gibson 186

Robinson, Alymer 14
Robinson, Edward G. 205
Rodriguez, Cleto 133
Rogers, Ginger 202
Rogers, Roy 210
Rooke, Allen Driscoll 28
Roosevelt, Elliott 29
Roosevelt, Franklin D. 1, 3, 5, 7-9, 15, 17, 20-21, 23, 29, 45, 46, 62, 66, 90, 97, 99, 132, 139, 179, 189, 218
Roosevelt, Theodore 29
Rosenthal, Joe 111
Rubio 128
Russell, Jackie 207
Rutledge, Orbin 71

Saroyan, William 211
Schama, Simon iii
Scharff, Hanns 65
Schmelling, Max 118
Scott, Randolph 104
Segura 128
Shelton, Clyde 48-49
Sheppard, Morris 3
Sheridan, Ann 202, 205, 206
Sherman, William Tecumseh 29
Sherwood, Robert E. 211
Shubert, John 199
Sikes, Melvin 119
Sinatra, Frank 206
Sinclair, Upton 211
Singletary, Ed 57
Skelton, Red 205
Smith, John T. 203
Smith, Maceo 120
Smith, Pinetop 202
Smith, Thorne 213
Smith, W. Eugene 109-11
Sothern, Ann 105
Stalin, Joseph 102
Stanwyck, Barbara 205
Steichen, Edward J. 108, 109-110
Steinbeck, John 211
Stevens, Bob 84
Stevens, George 101
Stevenson, Coke 63, 78
Stewart, Jimmy 103, 202
Stimson, Henry L. 219
Strock, George 109-10
Sullavan, Margaret 105
Sullivan, Bill 196
Sullivan, Charles 196
Sullivan, Gene 179
Sullivan, Lela Mae 221-22
Sullivan, Loretta 196

Tanamachi, Saburo 117
Tate, R. C. 140

Taylor, Robert 104
Thomason, John W. 214
Thornton, Bob 120
Thurber, James 211
Tiscornia, Ed 61
Tobin, Louise 201
Togo, Admiral 45
Tokyo Rose 53
Toland, Gregg 101-03
Tolbert, Leroy 202
Toliver, Raymond F. 65
Tracy, Spencer 105
Trigger 210
Truman, Harry 55, 218
Tubb, Ernest 199
Turner, Harriet 196, 214, 222, 238
Turner, Jim 196, 214-15
Turner, Sarah 196

Uno, Bob 141
Uyehara, Emi 141
Uyeshima, Kyoko 141

Vasquez 128
Vaughan, Fred 71
Vaughn, Eddie 230
Vedre, Jack 230
Veidt, Conrad 106
Vick, Frances Brannen 188
Vidor, King 196, 202, 204
Villa, Pancho 29
Villarreal 128

Wadel, Mrs. Ernest 155
Waldman, Herman 202
Walker, Fred 63
Walker, James 121
Walker, Wiley 179
Wallace, Henry A. 3
Wallace, Herman 67
Washington, George 219
Watson, Sue 214
Wayne, John 104
Weinberg, William 69
Welles, Orson 204
Wells, Keith 111
Wheaton, Elizabeth Lee 214
White, Frederick 123
Whitson, Bill 70-71
Whitson, John 70-71
Whitson, Warren 70-71
Wilder, Billy 207
Wilder, Thornton 211
Williams, Ted 13, 24
Wills, Bob 20, 199, 200
Wilson, Dooley 106

Wilson, Lucy Iris (see Jopling, Lucy Wilson) 156, 157
Wilson, William D. 65
Wilson, Woodrow 21, 28
Winsor, Kathleen 211
Woodchick, Chuck 125
Wright, Teresa 204
Wyler, William 101, 204

Yeager, Chuck 70
Young, Evelyn 158
Young, Robert 105, 205
Yung-Chang, Hsu 57

Zanuck, Darryl F. 101, 103

www.ingramcontent.com/pod-product-compliance
Lightning Source LLC
Chambersburg PA
CBHW051209290426
44109CB00021B/2389